MEDIA AND POWER IN MODERN IRAN

To Mike, Jacoby, and William - the three loves of my life.

MEDIA AND POWER IN MODERN IRAN

Mass Communication, Ideology, and the State

Emily L. Blout

I.B. TAURIS
LONDON • NEW YORK • OXFORD • NEW DELHI • SYDNEY

I.B. TAURIS
Bloomsbury Publishing Plc
50 Bedford Square, London, WC1B 3DP, UK
1385 Broadway, New York, NY 10018, USA
29 Earlsfort Terrace, Dublin 2, Ireland

BLOOMSBURY, I.B. TAURIS and the I.B. Tauris logo are trademarks of
Bloomsbury Publishing Plc

First published in Great Britain 2023
This paperback edition published 2024

Copyright © Emily L. Blout, 2023

Emily L. Blout has asserted her right under the Copyright, Designs and
Patents Act, 1988, to be identified as Author of this work.

For legal purposes the Acknowledgments on p. ix constitute an
extension of this copyright page.

Series design by Adriana Brioso
Cover image © هلا نيع يف/Unsplash

All rights reserved. No part of this publication may be reproduced or
transmitted in any form or by any means, electronic or mechanical, including
photocopying, recording, or any information storage or retrieval system,
without prior permission in writing from the publishers.

Bloomsbury Publishing Plc does not have any control over, or responsibility for,
any third-party websites referred to or in this book. All internet addresses given
in this book were correct at the time of going to press. The author and publisher
regret any inconvenience caused if addresses have changed or sites have
ceased to exist, but can accept no responsibility for any such changes.

A catalogue record for this book is available from the British Library.

A catalog record for this book is available from the Library of Congress.

ISBN:	HB:	978-0-7556-3903-8
	PB:	978-0-7556-3907-6
	ePDF:	978-0-7556-3904-5
	eBook:	978-0-7556-3905-2

Typeset by Integra Software Services Pvt. Ltd.

To find out more about our authors and books visit www.bloomsbury.com
and sign up for our newsletters.

CONTENTS

Figures   vii
Foreword   viii
Acknowledgments   ix

INTRODUCTION   1

Part I
PAHLAVI AND THE MAKING OF THE MASS COMMUNICATION SYSTEM

Chapter 1
THE BIRTH OF THE MASS COMMUNICATION MONOPOLY   21

Chapter 2
MASS COMMUNICATION IN REVOLUTION AND REGIME BUILDING   41

Part II
A DIFFERENT SORT OF WAR: THE CRISIS OF SATELLITE TV

Chapter 3
PRELUDE TO A CRISIS   59

Chapter 4
THE CRISIS OF SATELLITE TV   69

Chapter 5
THE BIG DISH: DIRECT BROADCAST SATELLITE, SYMBOLISM, AND THE POLITICS OF CULTURE   83

Part III
SOFT WAR: THE POLITICS OF THE INTERNET

Chapter 6
ENTER THE INTERNET   95

Chapter 7
THE 2009 ELECTION CRISIS   107

Chapter 8
AFTER THE CRISIS: SOFT WAR AND THE '88 FETNEH 125

Chapter 9
THE NATIONAL INTERNET 133

CONCLUSION 149

Notes 157
Bibliography 193
Index 216

FIGURES

1. Capture of National Iranian Radio and Television by Iranian revolutionaries — 50
2. Piles of shredded classified documents left behind by US embassy staff in their rush to evacuate — 54
3. Ratified Islamic Republic of Iran Broadcasting Budget in Millions of Rials, 1357–69 (1978–91) — 64
4. Digital poster from Green Movement website calling on Iranians to shout, "God is great" and "death to the dictator" from their rooftops — 121
5. Digital poster from a Green Movement website featuring the artistic appropriation of the Hand of Fatima — 122
6. Infographic of the "Internet-Intranet Cohesion Model" 2012 — 134
7. Changes to domestic bandwidth relative to bandwidth for international traffic 2010–18 — 136
8. "The Big Migration from Telegram" — 144

FOREWORD

Ideology has always occupied an essential place in the Islamic Republic of Iran.

Indeed, the Islamic Republic of Iran was founded on a kind of ideology that was both new and an artifact of the past. It was an ideology of revolution—in which the material and social circumstances that people found themselves bound to could be shed and built anew from the authentic culture and values of Iran's Islamic past. The Islamic Republic was founded on an ideology in which religion—Twelver Shi'ite Islam—would serve as a comprehensive, all-encompassing *lifeworld* and provide the moral, cultural, social, and legalistic building blocks of a utopian nation in the heart of the Middle East.

Just as John Winthrop envisioned Plymouth Rock as a place of promise for the persecuted, pious Puritans, the Islamic Republic was to be a city on a hill for the Muslim world to emulate.

Perhaps it was my own particular heritage, steeped in the lore and battlefield reenactments of childhood in Lexington, Massachusetts—where in 1776 the descendants of John Winthrop waged a revolutionary war to shed the tyranny of colonial rule and replace it with a system of their choosing—that inspired my interest in the revolutionary project of Iran's Islamic Republic.

Or perhaps it was my appreciation of the revolutionary power of communication. Colonial historians point to the central role of the print media in the American revolution of 1776. John Paine and his contemporaries used his pamphlet *Common Sense* to spread revolutionary fervor among the colonies and introduce the ideas that would become the keystones of American ideology.

Iran scholars similarly point to the important role of the cassette tape in the revolution of 1979. Followers of the future founder of the Islamic Republic, Ayatollah Ruhollah Khomeini, used recordings his lectures to mobilize the opposition and spread his vision for an alternative system of government built on Islam. Khomeini remained keenly aware of the power and danger of mass communication media as Supreme Leader of the Islamic Republic.

This book is the product of more than three years of research. It is based on thousands of primary documents and digital artifacts in Persian and English. It is both a labor of love and a love of labor. It is my hope that you, the reader, will enjoy the fruits of my labor as I have enjoyed them and that this study will serve you like it has served me—as a window into the politics of media in Iran.

Emily Blout, Georgetown University, 2023

ACKNOWLEDGMENTS

The first book is always the most difficult (I am told). I would be remiss not to acknowledge all the friends, colleagues, and loved ones who were essential to completing this journey. This includes my mother, whose shining example taught me that I could pursue both a family and a doctorate, and my husband, Michael Signer, for reading countless drafts, following me to Scotland, and never doubting my dreams. Second only to my family are my dissertation supervisors, Ali Ansari and Stephen Tyre at University of St. Andrews, who opened my eyes to the importance of history and rigorous sourcing. I extend my appreciation to Shane Drennan, Heather Robinson, Pardis Minuchehr, Mike Gubser, Farzaneh Milani, and Jay Parker and to my colleagues in my writing group: Ira Bashkow, Caitlin Wylie, and Feyza Burak Adli, without whom I would still be writing this book today. I would also like to thank Laura Denardis and David Karpf for their help with the proposal, as well as Hector Amaya, Andrea Press, and Len Shoppa at the University of Virginia, who graciously offered me a home for my research and a captive audience of students to test out my ideas. Finally, my deepest thanks to my publisher and editors at Bloomsbury, Rory Gormley, Giles Herman, Viswasirasini Govindarajaniswas, Balaji Kasirajan and Yasmin Garcha, whose patience and persistence got this project across the finish line despite the exceptional challenges of the COVID-19 pandemic.

INTRODUCTION

In its contemporary, complex forms, information technology represents one of the highest achievements of modern culture, which uses its control over information to solidify its domination of the world.
—Former President Mohammad Khatami, 1994[1]

The war in the world today is within the media. The progress of international policies and actions of various establishments and fronts is through propaganda, news creation, meaning creation, and the formulation of right and wrong, truth and lies.
—Supreme Leader Ali Khamenei, 2004[2]

Information communication technology has become the great equalizer in global politics. It has empowered armed non-state actors, allowing them to compete with nation-states in the battle over public opinion in peace, war, and protracted conflict.[3] It has allowed minor military and economic powers to project force in a way that influences the policies and strategies of major world powers. Digital media has also transformed domestic politics. It has empowered publics, allowing individuals to exchange information and ideas, express dissent, and mobilize masses toward a political outcome.[4] It has empowered politicians, parties, and regimes, providing the means to shape public opinion and mobilize supporters at home, and project strength and curry influence abroad. Nowhere is the power of media more apparent than in the politics of the Middle East. Nowhere is it more appreciated than within the ruling establishment of the Islamic Republic of Iran.

The story goes back decades. In the days before his death, the Supreme Leader and founder of the Islamic Republic, Ayatollah Ruhollah Khomeini, ordered the Constitution amended to place the state-monopoly television and radio broadcasting service, Voice and Vision of the Islamic Republic (*Seda va Sima-ye Jomhuri- ye Eslami-ye Iran*), under the singular control of the office of the Supreme Leader. Previously, it functioned as an independent agency supervised by a board of representatives from three branches of government. The amendment was one of a handful of provisions aimed at consolidating power and creating a more unified, dynamic state. The change was indicative of the importance Iran's leadership assigned to mass communication media for maintaining control of the nascent

Islamic Republic after the death of its charismatic founder. It also anticipated the emergence of public opinion as a critical battlespace in the regime's struggle for internal security and regional leadership.

But Khomeini demonstrated appreciation for the power of media well before the constitutional changes of 1989. In the years before the ouster of Shah Mohammad Reza Pahlavi, Khomeini cultivated support from exile in Iraq through the reproduction and dissemination of cassette tape recordings of his sermons by his followers. He continued this activity in France, where he used his exposure to foreign press and exile status to bolster his reputation inside Iran as a leading opponent of the monarchy. He rallied popular support through a religious nationalist discourse that rejected the Shah's slavish propagation of Western cultural products through television and film. These activities sowed the field for Khomeini's celebrated homecoming and ascendance to power in 1979. They foreshadowed the importance that mass communication media was to have in the contemporary state.

Media was a critical battleground in the struggle to chart the direction of the young Islamic Republic. Newspaper headlines of *"shah raft"* rapidly gave way to an internal struggle over the composition of the new state. Khomeini's swift consolidation of control over the institutions of mass communication helped enshrine his religious nationalist faction in power and install his Islamic model of government, *velayat-e faqih*, as the law of the land. The many ideological groups that had united in opposition to the Shah Mohammad Reza Pahlavi[5] and his authoritarian constitutional monarchy, soon found themselves out maneuvered and purged from the political process, their members executed or forced to flee the country.

Mass communication media was an important, though underappreciated, aspect of Khomeini's post-Revolution power consolidation. Paradoxically, the same men who had been vocal critics of the media system under the Shah as revolutionaries, now coveted and defended the state broadcasting monopoly as essential for safeguarding the revolution.

Today, more than three decades after Khomeini's death, the information battleground he anticipated has come to fruition. Iran, like the rest of the Middle East, has undergone an "information revolution." Thanks in part to the import of cheap satellite dishes and cell phones from Asia and significant advances in communication technology, the near instantaneous transfer of information is now the norm. In Iran, as with elsewhere in the Global South, these advances have served individuals as a means of education, communication, and economic advancement. It has also served leaders and states as an instrument for hegemonic power, extraterritorial influence, and domestic repression.

++++

Successive Iranian leaders have struggled to navigate the fraught political-cultural space of media in the Islamic Republic— skirting the lines between embracing the Western communications technologies and ethos and rejecting them, between condemning social networking sites as foreign treachery and promoting themselves on Facebook. How does a political regime that derived its hegemony from the ability to mass communicate its ideology, protect its ideological dominance in an environment characterized by "disruptive power" and "mass self-communication"?[6] What is the role of mass communication in the construction of power? This book investigates these questions by examining the media institutions, policies, and discourses of two Iranian regimes over nearly eight decades. Beginning in the late twentieth century in the flagging days of the monarchy, it takes us through the revolution of 1979 to the present, where we see a regime struggling to manage the divergent impulses of the nativist, populist, revolutionary movement that brought it to power and the challenges of maintaining that power today.

Both a study of political communication and media history, this book is organized around a number of *media inflection points*—periods of crisis and public debate in which the popularization of a new mass communication technology challenged the dominant media system and the real or aspirational mass communication monopoly of the state. Of primary interest are the strategies and actions taken to manage the challenges associated with technical-communicational change. Of equal interest is the ways in which media systems and discourses serve as a tool for power construction and legitimation. In this introductory chapter, I discuss concepts and themes central to this inquiry.

Consent, Consensus, and the Legitimation of Power

The overarching problem at the heart of this book is the surprisingly durability of the contemporary Iranian regime. One characteristic problematized by democracy scholars is factionalism and intra-regime conflict. These scholars hold that consensus among the ruling establishment is requisite for regime stability.[7] Still others have extended that logic to argue that lack of elite consensus leads to regime decay and ultimately to regime failure.[8] Democracy scholars similarly point to elite fragmentation as a harbinger of authoritarian breakdown and democratization.[9] But this notion opens up an important question in its own right. If elite fragmentation leads to regime failure, why, then, has the current regime remained in power? Or, if we accept the premise that elite fragmentation leads to authoritarian breakdown, why hasn't Iran democratized?

Clearly, the aforementioned theories, while valuable, are individually and collectively unable to account for the confounding question of regime longevity in Iran. Such a case requires a different set of questions and a different lens of focus for describing the contemporary situation. Instead of asking why the regime has not collapsed, it may be more productive to ask, why, and how, has the regime endured?

For Arang Keshavarzian and other structuralists, the answer to these questions has to do with the political system. Iran's constitution and political trajectory institutionalizes both the notion of popular sovereignty through parliament and the president and the notion of divine sovereignty through the position of the Guardian Jurist (the Supreme Leader) and the Assembly of Experts, thus reflecting principles of republicanism and mass participation characteristic of democracy while also presenting structures characteristic of authoritarian and theocratic states. Given even this elementary description, the logical question becomes: what type of system is the Islamic Republic of Iran? Answering this question has been the remit of Iran experts for decades. Some of the more compelling descriptors of the Islamic Republic are "factionalized authoritarianism," "fragmented autocracy" and "hybrid regime."[10]

Just as scholars have sought to give a name to the political system of the Islamic Republic, they have sought to identify the sources of the regime's authority. The power of the Supreme Leader is great (some would say absolute), but who or what gives him his power? In other words, where does his sovereignty reside? According to Article 2 of the Constitution, sovereignty belongs exclusively to God; Chapter 5 (Art. 65–61) is titled "The Rights of National Sovereignty and the Powers Deriving from Them." Article 56 says sovereignty belongs to God but is delegated to all humans and that God made humans "master over their social destiny."[11]

Roozbeh Safshekan and Farzan Sabet investigate the question of sovereignty in Iran as manifested in the public debate leading up to the elections for the Assembly of Experts in 2016. The discourse reflected a major divide within the ruling establishment regarding the source of authority of the Supreme Leader, and by extension, who, or what, is empowered to choose his successor. One side said the power of the Leader is given to him by the people. It is popular will, delegated through the parliament, that is the source of his sovereignty. The other side asserted that sovereignty belongs to God and is delegated to the Supreme Leader through his clerical representatives via the Council of Guardians.[12]

Here, as in other cases, we see the question of sovereignty bound up with the question of legitimacy. Yet the question of legitimacy, what it is and why it is important, deserves greater examination in its own right. A similar concern can be offered regarding studies of political communication. Though the term "legitimacy" in Iran has been raised in the context of governmentality of action and revolutionary mobilization,[13] the precise relationship between legitimacy, media, and political power construction has yet to be sufficiently investigated in the literature. This book ventures such an investigation. To begin, we must clarify what we mean by legitimacy and the legitimation of power.

Popular Legitimacy

Throughout history, the power of a ruler over his subjects has resided first and foremost in his ability to command obedience through force or the threat of violence. The inverse has also been true. Without control over the means of violence, for instance, a ruler could not command universal obedience. Indeed, in many cases in history, the loss of the allegiance of the armed services was often the death knell of a dying regime. Today, the monopoly on force is necessary, but rarely sufficient, for hegemonic power.[14] Instead, hegemonic power requires a compilation of the numerous sources of power within the modern state. This amalgam of power is what scholars often refer to as "legitimacy."[15]

In this book I adopt a neo-Weberian conception of legitimacy influenced by the work of social theorist David Beetham. Beetham says a government or regime can be said to be legitimate to the extent that it conforms to established rules, the rules can be justified by reference to shared beliefs, and there is evidence of the consent of the subject population.[16] Hegemonic power that is justified by consensus of the ruling establishment and conferred by the demonstration of consent by the subject population is what I term "popular legitimacy." A major argument of this book is that in the Islamic Republic, mass communication is coveted because of its potential to serve as a means of popular legitimacy.

Similar to Beetham's conception of popular legitimacy, the term, as used throughout, describes a type of power validation that is uniquely symbolic and performative. Often, it operates where other sources of legitimation are deficient. Beetham refers to this type of legitimation as the "mobilization mode" of consent. In his words:

> In mobilization mode, consent is expressed through continuous mass participation in political activity supportive of the regime and contributive to the realization of its political goals. Regimes originated this way typically take their origin from a revolution and the continuing popular mobilization can be seen as a perpetuation of the revolutionary process in the post-revolutionary era.[17]

The relevance to the case of contemporary Iran is clear. The Islamic Republic was born from a revolution, and it is on the basis of this foundation myth that the ruling establishment makes it claim to power. Beetham continues:

> Although the majority of the population may in fact be politically inactive, the commitment of the substantial minority makes up in degree for what it lacks in universality. Moreover, because the "vanguard" movement or party is in principle open to all, and those participating in it are distinguished simply by their greater commitment rather than by privilege of birth or property, they can be seen as representative of the people as a whole, and their activity in the regimes cause as demonstrative of the continuing support of the society at large.

In post-revolutionary Iran, the *Basij-e Mostaz'afin* (Basij hereafter) serves this vanguard function. The "people's militia," was established on April 30, 1980 and operates as a branch of the Islamic Revolutionary Guard Corps (*Sepah-e Pasdaran-e Enghelab-e Eslami,* Sepah or IRGC hereafter), a military police and intelligence force founded as an ideological custodian of Iran's 1979 revolution and charged with defending the Islamic Republic against internal and external threats. Members of the Basij are often distinguished not by class or merit, but by the zeal of their commitment to the regime. The Basij, along with the IRGC and the Ministry of Culture and Islamic Guidance (*Vezarat-e Farhang-e Ershad-e Eslami*), (Ershad hereafter) is at forefront of the project to "protect" Iranian culture from foreign influence and corruption through media. This is what various members of the establishment call "soft war" (*jang-e narm*) and it is addressed in detail later in the book.

The Basij plays an important activating role also (the word, after all, means "mobilization"). With reports of Basij membership anywhere from 400,000 to 10 million and with chapters in every city in Iran, the volunteer paramilitary force is often tasked with bringing large numbers of people to the streets for made-for-TV displays of fealty to the Supreme Leader and consent to the system he represents.

Such populist expressions were an integral part of regime power construction in both the late Imperial Iran and the early Islamic Republic. It is perhaps even more important for regime power today. In as much as it is a historical commentary on populist aspect of the Islamic revolution, this book joins the work of scholars such as Fred Halliday, Ervand Abrahamian, and Mohsen Milani.[18] It also compliments more contemporary works on nationalism and Islamist discourse by scholars such as Shabnam Holliday and Mohammad Ayatollahi Tabaar.[19] Holliday, for instance, argues that Islamist populism is a staple of elite discourse today. She points to a speech by Iran's Supreme Leader, Ali Khamenei, as illustrative of the explicit link the Leader makes between populism and Islam in regime ideology:

> Populism of the Islamic Revolution is an important characteristic which is revealed in the term 'republic'. Populism of the Islamic Revolution differs from other revolutions in two ways. First is that populism is part of the essence of Islam, not something apart from it… Second, Islam in its true form and in a real manner safeguards the people. Deceit, lies, and forging statements in the presence of the people does not have a role in the spheres of the revolution. The true presence of people in the Islamic Republic, their role in electing officials, and safeguarding the outcomes of the Islamic Revolution are themselves symbols of the truthfulness of the Islamic regime and its populism.[20]

In these remarks, we see that the Supreme Leader uses political participation, and in particular voting, as proof of public support for the system and the righteousness of the ideology that undergirds it. It is such symbolically mediated signaling of consent that is of interest in the study. This book makes the media-specific argument that the nationalist, populist aspect of political culture is an essential – but by no means the only – means for understanding regime longevity.

In political science especially, there is a tendency to focus on the sectarian and liturgical sources of authority in the Islamic Republic. This is understandable, as the theocratic republican model of government birthed from the Iranian Revolution of 1979 was for all purposes a stunning outlier to the global standard. This book does not discount the religious-doctrinal aspects of regime power. On the contrary, it considers such modes of popular legitimacy as complementary, and at times overlapping, elements of regime hegemony. After all, popular legitimacy is just one of a number of sources of legitimation from which both Pahlavi and Khomeini drew to justify their power. In the last decade of the regime, the Shah leveraged the monarchical tradition to support and obscure his increasingly despotic rule. The Pahlavi state circulated powerful stories, images, and narratives about the Shah as the heroic savior of Iran and the embodiment of the Iranian people. The Shah summoned the legacy of Cyrus the Great, positing his rule as a natural extension of a long tradition of imperial rule.[21] He also drew on Islam as a source of legitimation, albeit superficially. Amid a rising tide of criticism from the ulema and Islamist intellectuals in the years leading up to the revolution, Pahlavi increasingly appropriated the language and framing of Shia Islam in his public remarks. It can be argued that the power of the Shah was legitimated by law also, with the sovereignty of the monarch enshrined in Iran's original constitution of 1906.

While tradition and law may be important for legitimation, consent of the subject population is essential. The public airing of this deficit punctuated the last years of the Pahlavi monarchy, culminating in what Habermas terms a "legitimacy crisis." The story of Pahlavi and the crisis of legitimacy that presaged his downfall is told in this book.

In 1979, in what Amir Arjomand has described as the "turban for the crown," the mullah replaced the monarch as sovereign in the newly minted Islamic Republic of Iran.[22] In the founding constitution, elements of republicanism were subsumed by a theocratic system premised on *velayat-e faqih*, or guardianship of the Islamic jurist. A radical re-interpretation of Shia Islam, the system established a clerical class with a dual spiritual and political injunction to serve as guardians of Iranian society along the lines of Socrates's philosopher king.

When Ayatollah Ruhollah Khomeini originally proffered the idea of *velayat-e faqih* in a series of sermons in Najaf, he used rational and traditional proofs to buttress the case that the clergy must rule society until the return of the Mahdi (Hidden Imam), whom believers hold went into occultation. It was the obligation of the Islamic Jurist (or jurisconsult, the former being the Supreme Leader) to implement Islamic rulings, not only in matters of devotion and personal affairs, as had long been the case, but also in the realm of politics and society writ large. A qualified Islamic jurist (one man or a group of men) was to serve as guardian(s) of society to ensure that Islamic rulings were adhered to and implemented within the broad outlines and general principles of *Sharia*. The authority of the Supreme Leader under the new constitution thus became a corporeal manifestation of the authority enjoyed by the divine guides, also known as "the infallible Imams".[23]

Another key measure melded legalistic and religious authority. In January 1988, soon before his death, Khomeini issued a proclamation that dramatically expanded the scope of the Supreme Leader's religious and legal authority. It said that the Supreme Leader could overrule a dictate of of Sharia in cases of "imperative necessity," where religious law conflicted with the national interest and general welfare. What constituted the "general welfare" and "imperative necessity," was left undefined. The change elevated the preservation of the Islamic Republic regime (*nezam*) to a primary injunction and downgraded rituals (e.g., the obligatory prayers and fasting) to secondary injunctions. The effect was to render all state ordinances religiously and legally binding. Non-performance was not only illegal, but a sin.

It is not coincidental that the Constitutional amendments of 1989 that sought to legitimate the hegemony of Supreme Leader, also shifted the control over the state broadcast radio and television monopoly, the Islamic Republic of Iran Broadcasting (IRIB), to the Leader's singular remit. While the efficacy of the state mass communication media monopoly was a matter of debate even in the first decade of the Islamic Republic, its potential as a means of power and legitimation of the Supreme Leader appears to have never been in dispute.[24]

Mass Communication and Ideology

Through the course of this book, we see the continuance of a particular conception of mass communication that came to Iran during the Second World War and its Cold War aftermath. It is a general understanding of the applied theory that originated in the United States in the 1930s and reached its heyday in the 1950s. The theory, put simply, says that mediated communication like television and radio is unidirectional, from message sender to message receiver, and that such messages are sent to a mass public by a small, powerful group of producers cum broadcasters.

Today's scholarship has largely moved on from this understanding. Social scientists such as Steven Chafee and Miriam Metzger have gone so far as to argue that advancements in communication technology have rendered the study of mass communication obsolete. They correctly contend that the present communications environment no longer reflects the defining features of mass communication, which is mass production, lack of individual control and finite available channels, and production is no longer "en masse" thanks to the fragmentation of media institutions and the democratization of mediums of communication.[25] The information environment today, Chafee and Metzger argue, is no longer characterized by lack of individual control. Quite the opposite. Individuals have control over the media they use and the information they consume. Finally, whereas the mass communication paradigm was characterized by a limited number of communication outlets, today there are more readily accessible "channels" of information than ever before. Chaffee and Metzger point to the implications of this "de-massifying" of mass communication. "The trend towards redistribution of power over the media from elites to users makes obsolete the idea of a small handful of willful individuals attempting to impart a dominant ideology to maintain the status quo."[26]

Yet other scholars hold that mass communication continues to be relevant in the context of power and ideology. According to Joseph Turow, "mass media are part of the process of creating meanings *about* society *for* the members of society."[27] Sociologist John Thompson similarly contends that mass communication should be studied as a site of ideology. In an environment characterized by media fragmentation and "self-mass communication," it is my position that the study of the history of mass communication and the politics around it remains valuable as a window into power and ideology in the modern and contemporary Iranian state.

The importance of mass communication is indicated in its place in the founding documents of the Islamic Republic of Iran. The preamble to the Constitution reads: "The mass communication media, radio, and television must serve the diffusion of Islamic culture in pursuit of the evolutionary course of the Islamic Revolution."[28] Through the constitution and other laws, the state retains a legal monopoly on television and radio production and broadcasting, and through law and religious edict, the state exercises control over other means of communication en masse. This limits the producers and arguably enlarges the audience.

Yet Raymond Williams's maxim also remains true— there are no masses, only ways of seeing people as masses.[29] The evidence suggests that key players in the state-sponsored media industry do, in fact, see audiences as passive receivers with little differentiation. In her ethnographic study of state sponsored media production, Narges Bajoghli observed that the film producers she interviewed saw the audience of their work as the masses, and specifically, the faceless, homogeneous masses of young men.[30]

Just as the subjects of mass communication are relegated to the role of receivers and audience of the masses, the products, processes, and institutions that speak to them fall under the umbrella of mass communication and mass media so far at the nezam is concerned. This way of seeing and communicating has not changed from the Pahlavi era. Indeed, as this book will show, the regime's treatment of media continues to be colored by the same, homogenizing, monopolistic impulse that sought to enshrine the state's dominion over mass communication in the Islamic Republic's founding documents.

This book is interested in the process and politics of mass communication as well as the technology that makes mass communication possible. In the following pages, I use the term "mass communication" to indicate the scale, scope, and unidirectionality of the transmission of meanings and symbolic forms.[31] What qualifies as mass communication is not as important as what the ruling establishment considers it to be. This is an important distinction, as each of the inflection points examined are situations in which a particular communication technology is recognized, tacitly or otherwise, as a medium for mass communication. This book looks at the words and actions of the ruling establishment regarding these technologies with an eye to what these discourses and government actions might tell us about the nature of power and the role of media in its construction, preservation, and legitimation.

To be clear, this is not a technological determinist argument. The inflection points chronicled here were not caused by mass communication media. But media it was a feature of each crisis, and a crucial one. Similarly, the political crisis that punctuated periods of transition and development did not come out of thin air. Quite the opposite. The media was already the subject of debate and concern among the ruling establishment, and there was a recognition and appreciation of the power and continued popularization and socialization of the technology.[32]

I have made an effort to select sources and use language that is contemporaneous with the time period in which these developments occur. At the same time, I try to avoid the somewhat artificial binaries of "small media" versus "big media" and "new media" versus "old media" that dominate much of Iran media scholarship at the end of the century. The focus of this investigation is instead the point at which these modes and logics collide. Such *media inflection points* are political manifestations of sociological communicative transformation; they reflect the transformation of a previously limited medium of communication to one that can communicate *en masse*, thus upending the existent media system characterized by the market dominance, if not monopoly, of the state.

The book employs a conception of ideology guided by neo-Marxist thought as articulated by Antonio Gramsci in *The Prison Notebooks,* where a force relation achieves hegemonic power through the dominance of its ideology. Ideology, as taken here, largely tracks with Thompson's definition as discourse and symbolic forms that sustain relations of domination.[33] We can see this neo-Marxist conception of ideology at work in both revolutionary and post-revolutionary Iran. Analyzing events, actions, and discourses through this prism, where ideological dominance is a central requisite for hegemonic power, we begin to understand the ruling establishment's thinking about media and the fragility of its own power.

Myth and Spectacle

The term "spectacle," as taken here, refers to images and symbolic forms constructed to attract attention, evoke emotion, and entertain. This book is interested in *political spectacle*. What Murray Edelman calls a "meaning machine," political spectacle is defined as news accounts, images, and discussion about political events that create the illusion of political action and objective fact.[34] As a communicative process, the transmission is linear and one-sided. The audience of the spectacle is the spectator—an uncritical and unobtrusive "mass" that consumes but does not give feedback. The process echoes that of mass communication in this way. As a legion of examples from modern Iran demonstrate, a key function of political spectacle is to reinforce and justify unequal power relationships and obscure the ideology that underpins them.

We find numerous examples in Iran. Perhaps the most well-known in the Pahlavi era is the Shah's lavish celebrations marking the 2,500[th] anniversary of the founding of the Persian Empire in 1971. Mass mediated parades of wealth and power offered a history of Iran that was largely imaginary. And yet, one can argue that such pageantry and the highly embellished story of Iran that it presented to the masses served to legitimize Pahlavi's claim to power. Later, in revolutionary and post-revolutionary Iran, spectacle was used again to great effect. We see Khamenei's militant revolutionaries use spectacle in the embassy seizure of 1979, for example, and in regime rejoinders to the Green Movement protests of 2009.

These instances of political spectacle, expressed through mass communication media, depend on a broader underlying foundation essential to the fusion of legitimacy and populism: myth. What Carl Friedrich and Zbigniew Brzezinski describe as a "chain of logical reasoning," myth serves as an encompassing frame of reference in society, providing people with a practical understanding of the world they view around them.³⁵ An essential function of myth, according to George Sorel, is its capacity to generalize many events into a singular experience of one nation or group, thus rendering "the mass of sentiments" an "undivided whole."³⁶ Roland Barthes builds on this conception, adding that myth works to "naturalize" a singular story in society and thought. Myth, therefore, can be understood as an experience of a particular person or persons in history that is generalized to apply to many people regardless of time and space and naturalized in society through institutions and language. Myth helps to explain problems and create a shared worldview. As such, myth functions to enforce and extend the existing relations of domination.³⁷

As we follow the progress of communication technology in Iranian society from Pahlavi to Supreme Leader Ali Khamenei, one myth stands out: the nationalist narrative in which Iran is in a constant struggle against the ideological tentacles of the West, and foreign adversaries are constantly on the attack, using covert means to undermine Iranian identity and culture. This political myth has been nurtured by the contemporary establishment and wielded as a crudely cut cudgel against those who would hold it accountable for poor economic conditions and other government failures. In the course of the book we see how such political myth, in turn informing powerful spectacles, becomes an essential communication technique in the maintenance of hegemonic power.

Just as this investigation is concerned with the strategies and actions taken to manage the change associated with the sociological and technological challenge of media, of equal interest is the ways in which media systems and discourses serve as a tool for power construction and legitimation. In the contemporary period, "soft war" is one such discourse and tool. In the political lexicon of the ruling establishment, "soft war" has been a euphemism for Western cultural products that pose an ontological, spiritual, and economic threat to the nation. Iran's highest authority, Supreme Leader Khamenei, first used the term in a speech in November 2009:

> The priority today is what is called soft war; that is, war using cultural tools through infiltration, through lies, through spreading rumors, through the advanced instruments that exist today. Communication tools that did not exist 10, 15, and 30 years ago have become widespread.³⁸

Such "deviant" cultural values and practices are bound up, rhetorically and symbolically, with the medium through which they are transmitted and consumed in society—that is, information-communication technology (ICT), and particularly media that can communicate to the masses. It is here, at the crossroads of mass communication and culture, that the dominant ideology is propagated and maintained. Such an understanding and appreciation of the potency of media is born out of historical experience and canonized in the Islamic Republic's founding documents.

The term "soft war" appeared in the remarks of public officials as early as 2004 and gained prominence during the events surrounding the presidential election of 2009. While the narrative frame of soft war finds purchase across the factional spectrum within the ruling establishment, the terminology began and remains a favorite discourse of the conservative and hardline factions. The prevalence of the term ebbed and flowed over the years. Usage peaked in June 2010, and then reemerged (though with less intensity) with the reelection of Hassan Rouhani in 2016.[39]

Yet the significance of soft war should not be determined by its prevalence in newspapers and online discourse alone. While the terminology has changed over the years, the underlying logic and system that it describes remains remarkably consistent. Thus, soft war and its previous iterations is useful as a window into relationships of force in Iranian society—be it between the public and the state, the state and security services, or among the various factions within the ruling establishment.

The term finds its epistemic roots in two interrelated concepts: cultural imperialism and "westoxification." Cultural imperialism theory gained currency in the 1960s as a way of understanding the new dynamic of international relations during the Cold War. The view holds that rather than seeking to occupy and colonize lands, as had been the practice of empire during and before WWII, Western powers pursued domination of foreign nations and peoples through economic and cultural means. While there are multiple variations of the theory, most place the United States as the major perpetrator of cultural imperialism. Media scholar Colin Sparks names two propositions at the core of most concepts of cultural imperialism: (1) "the media and cultural apparatuses of the USA, aided by the government, dominate the international trade in media," and (2) "the result of the continual consumption of this US-made material is effective propaganda for the ideas and values of the USA." The spin-off theory of media imperialism makes the role of mass communication even more explicit. According to the theory, the unidirectional flow of cultural products from sender (the West, the US) to receiver (nations like Iran) creates dependency and undermines a nation's cultural autonomy. Both concepts denote a deliberate attempt to dominate, invade, or subvert the cultural space of others.[40]

Soft war can be understood as an extension of cultural imperialism theory. It places mass communication media as part of a US strategy to undermine national identity and culture and to corrupt the minds of the Iranian public, particularly those of Iran's impressionable youth. The unspoken premise of soft war is that such Western originated messages and symbolic forms, when communicated en masse, pose a threat to the ruling regime which, along with its monopoly on violence and religion, maintains hegemony through the dominance of its ideology.

Jamal Al-e Ahmad was a popular public intellectual cum (quasi) academic of the 1960s. His speeches offered an anti-imperialist philosophy and positivist rejoinder to Western cultural imperialism and informed the nascent but growing political opposition to the Shah that would later coalesce around Khomeini and his religious nationalist faction. Indeed, we see Al-e Ahmad's ideas, if not his specific terminology, in the sermons of the future founder of the Islamic Republic in Najaf and carried over by his successor, Khamenei.

In a speech that was later published as a book in 1962 titled *Gharbzadegi* (Westoxification), Al-e Ahmad laid out a powerful critique of Western hegemony centered around the concept of "westoxification" which he used to describe the unequal power relationship between the Iranian people and America and the amorphous West. The metaphoric narrative frame cast the West, and America in particular, as purveyors of a disease that, through a potent payload of cultural products, ideas, and norms, infected the Iranian people and made them enamored with the West at the expense of their own national identity.[41]

At a time when the Shah's top-down push toward industrialization and Western "modernity" was in full swing and the US military presence in Iran was nearing its pinnacle, Al-e Ahmad's *Garbzadegi* both explained the felt and observed effects of American hegemony and offered an alternative paradigm rooted in the idea of Iran as a proud and independent civilization. It called upon Iranians to reject Western culture and return to an "authentic" self. The power of the argument was not so much the coherence or depth of the theory, or even its solutions. It was instead the identification of the problem. Westoxification gave name to a feeling percolating within society and its intellectuals—one of alienation, victimization, and trauma connected to the large-scale changes handed down by decree and imposed seemingly overnight by the Shah's White Revolution, as well as the flood of Western technology and industry into cities and villages the country over.[42]

In other words, where cultural imperialism described the West's strategy of oppression, westoxification described the Iranian condition under the heel of Western hegemony. So too with "soft war" which, nearly six decades later, was used by the Shah's Islamist usurpers to explain the continued pull and popularity of Western ideas, lifestyle, and cultural products among the Iranian people. This despite three decades of life in the Islamic Republic under the sway of the regime's Islamic revolutionary ideology and state-sponsored cultural productions disseminated by national radio and television and in madrassas and mosques nationwide.

In the most superficial sense, soft war is an adaptation of the concept of "soft power" coined by Harvard University professor Joseph Nye in a *Foreign Affairs* article in 1990 and reinvigorated and expanded upon in a book of that name in 2004. Nye defined soft power as "the ability to get what you want through attraction rather than coercion or payments." The attractiveness of a country's culture and political ideals constitute the "currency" of soft power.[43] This argument and theory of international relations again takes its cues from the experience of the Cold War and the post-Cold War "American century" where the US was the singular global power and benevolent hegemon. While the term is relatively new, the basic premise is that that the American empire is not primarily (or at least singularly) based on colonialization of foreign lands. It is instead, to borrow from Michael Axworthy, an "empire of the mind."[44]

Such appropriation of Western concepts and terminology is not unprecedented. Indeed, Iranian politicians have a track record of drawing upon U.S. foreign policy and international relations concepts. Reformist leader and former Iranian President Mohammad Khatami called his policy of engagement with the West a "dialogue of civilizations." The term was likely intended as both a play on the title of the famous treatise on international relations by Samuel Huntington, *Clash of Civilizations*, and as a rejoinder to it.[45] Similarly, following US President George W. Bush's designation of Iran as a member of the "axis of evil" in his State of the Union address in 2002, Iranian officials and state media began using the phrase "axis of resistance" to highlight Iran's leading role among Muslim countries in the Middle East.

But while soft power described the application of US power in its most benign sense, soft war, in the Iranian lexicon, was far from benign. It signified a cultural imperialist strategy of aggression by the United States against the Iranian people. Similar to westoxification, soft war positions the Iranian people as unwitting victims of this particularly potent brand of information and psychological warfare.

Which leads us to another ideation of soft war, one of praxis. This book joins a small but growing body of research on the subject. Media scholar Monroe Price has argued that soft war is a strategic narrative of the state, an analysis that has drawn criticism from Annabelle Sreberny, an Iranian media scholar and co-author of the seminal book on the events of 1979, "Small Media, Big Revolution." Sreberny has called Monroe's strategic communication frame "too soft," arguing that such an interpretation overlooks the atrocities and repression justified and empowered by the rhetoric.[46] Others have looked at soft war as manifest in defensive and offensive military operations.[47] Still other scholars have examined the term as it reflects a narrative of anti-imperialism.[48] Soft war has been used as a catch-all for malign cyber operations, encompassing activities such as surveillance and criminal exploits.

It is my contention that soft war should be understood as *all* of these; it manifests in strategic communication, media policy, state violence, and cybernetic operations. It also must be understood in terms of history. As I argue later in the book, *jang-e narm* is a form of political myth—the latest iteration of a long running nationalist narrative about Iran's relationship with foreign powers; it is simultaneously a strategy of legitimation.

The Prussian military strategist Carl Van Clausewitz famously wrote that politics is war by other means.[49] In Iran, the concept of "soft war" can be understood as a contemporary iteration of that classical maxim. In other words, in the political ideology of Iran's Supreme Leader, media is war. As Khamenei has said himself, the survival of the system will be determined by "war within the media."

Sources

This book is born from more than three years of research and over 3000 primary source documents and digital artifacts in English and Persian, the majority of which have never been used. My sources include collections of Iranian government documents and diplomatic and foreign correspondence in Persian made available through the Iranian Studies Collection at the University of St. Andrews.[50] The book also incorporates eyewitness accounts in English and Persian made available to me via the Foundation for Iranian Studies Oral History Project. An invaluable resource for historians of modern Iran, it is an archive of audio recordings and transcriptions of interviews with government officials, diplomats, newspaper editors, artists, scholars, literary figures, and other decision-makers as well as witnesses to the events that have shaped recent Iranian history.[51]

This book is enriched by information gleaned from interviews with Iranian human rights activists, bloggers, journalists, analysts, and technologists. Many names have been withheld due to security concerns. Discussion of contemporary internet practices and structures has been informed, in part, by records from the International Broadcasting Union (IBU) and the Internet Corporation for Assigned Names and Numbers (ICANN) as well as reports by Small Media, the Center for Human Rights in Iran, and other research and monitoring groups.

The history in the second half of the book is based on Iranian media content such as newspaper articles, blog entries, television clips, and other artifacts collected online and via the secure communications platform Telegram. Several chapters draw from transcriptions of foreign and domestic broadcast media provided through the UK British Broadcasting Corporation (BBC) and the US Foreign Information Broadcasting Service (FBIS). Many transcripts were not digitized, thus requiring I spend numerous (delightful) weeks retrieving the records stored on microfiche at the University of Virginia and other government repositories.

BBC Monitoring and the Open Source Center (OSC, formerly FBIS) are open source intelligence services of the United Kingdom and United States, respectively. They put their more recent coverage in digital collections that are invaluable to historians of the contemporary period. Unfortunately, the barriers to access have become increasingly high. A decade or so ago the material was available to anyone through their local public library. Later, access required an application from a government or university email account. In 2015, the US government cut off public access to OSC completely. It is now only open to select government employees. I believe this is a mistake as it precludes scholarly research that might provide new insight into the culture, politics, and media environment of countries the world over. It is a tremendous loss for would-be Iranian media scholars and historians. So, in the spirit of transparency and collaboration essential for the creation of new knowledge and the writing of rich histories, I have made BBC and FBIS/OSC material collected in the course of my research, as well as photocopies of non-digitized archival documents, available to the public as a supplement to the print and online addition of this book via my website, www.emilyblout.com. A complete, annotated bibliography of all primary material is also available upon request. A note on annotations and citations: I indicate the source of US and UK transcriptions of radio and television broadcasts using the acronyms just referenced in parenthesis.

For internet sources, I use brackets to indicate the date accessed. On Persian language sources, I have made an effort to translate the titles into English using a phonetic approach and spelling consistent with popular usage on the internet. The same applies to Iranian names. Regarding dates of Persian sources and data, I include the Iranian, Jalali dates and their Western, Gregorian equivalents with as much accuracy as possible using the Iran Chamber Society's "Iranian Calendar Converter."[52]

The practice of censorship and historical revisionism on the internet by the Iranian state and its sponsored groups has been commonplace since at least 2003. The deleterious effect is particularly obtrusive in recent years, forcing me to deploy (and dream up) creative research strategies. The Internet Archive was paramount to the forensic research in this book. The non-profit, non-governmental initiative uses web crawlers to record digital images of websites over time. It is an invaluable tool to test, verify, or invalidate claims regarding the origination of a particular website or narrative. The history told in these pages incorporates digital artifacts from the Internet Archive as well as screenshots of social media accounts that Iranian government censors sought to erase. It is my hope that this book will aid future research by providing a road map for uncovering and using such digital material.[53]

Plan of the Book

A basic premise of Gramsci's work is that to be fully assessed and appreciated, ideologies and hegemonies must be studied from the point of view of history. Only in retrospect—outside the temporal demands and limitations posed by action—can one begin to form a comprehensive understanding of a subject. At the same time as an idea or phenomenon must be investigated in its singularity, that is, as a self-contained historical bloc. It should also be examined contextually as an idea or phenomenon that exists within, and in relation to, its larger intellectual, economic, and social circumstances.

The structure of the book reflects this historical and analytic logic. It is organized chronologically into three parts. Each part features a political crisis. Each crisis is examined not as sui generis or a one-off event, but as part of a continuum. The story of each crisis, or media inflection point, is preceded by a discussion of the historical context and precursors, and followed by close analysis of the event and overview of development in the years after. These chapters offer a deeper level of analysis from a historical perspective as well as in relation to the major questions and themes of the book.

Our historical investigation commences in imperial Iran under the increasingly despotic rule of Mohammad Reza Pahlavi. Chapter 1 begins with radio in the late 1940s and 1950s, charting its progress from a limited communication medium to one with the potential to reach large audiences across the country. I argue that the Shah's decision to develop and expand the reach of the state radio service was partly a reaction to the influx of anti-regime radio propaganda and political developments in neighboring states. The chapter goes on to chronicle the birth of commercial television and the founding of the national television and radio monopoly.

The Islamic Revolution brought the Shah's reign to an end in 1979 and mass communication media became an important battleground in the struggle to decide the nature and composition of new state. Chapter 2 looks at the role of the state media monopoly in the fall of the monarchy and the legitimation of the religious nationalist faction that took its place. It describes a seminal conflict between factions within the religious opposition and discusses changes and consistencies in the enterprise and institutions of mass communication in the first critical years of the Islamic Republic.

This leads us to Part II and the crisis of satellite TV. The entry and proliferation of cheap satellite receptor technology into the Iranian marketplace between 1991 and 1994 challenged the monopoly on mass communication that the government had enjoyed since coming to power in 1979. Satellite television, the technical name is Direct Broadcast Satellite (DBS), gave Iranian consumers choice in what television channels to watch for the first time. Conversely, it challenged the state's dominion over television as part of its apparatus of hegemonic power. For some within the ruling establishment, the proliferation of dishes in urban and rural areas was proof of public preference for non-state sources of information and entertainment. For others, it exposed the impossibility of realizing IRIB's original charge, that is, to safeguard and perpetuate regime ideology.

Direct Broadcast Satellite was a significant deviation from the existent system of Fixed Satellite Service (FSS), which had both limited bandwidth and limited available channels. Indeed, up to 1994, IRIB offered just two: Network 1 and Network 2. DBS created new channels of diffusion which bypassed the traditional, land-based broadcasting networks. It expanded the universe of news and information, education, and entertainment Iranians could access through their TVs, easily winning audiences once held captive to the national broadcaster. Now, rather than Iranian regime, commercial multinational conglomerates dominated Iranian airwaves. Thompson calls DBS a "new modality of cultural transmission," and for good reason. DBS, as this book will show, helped bring about a new technological-communicative paradigm. But for the Iranian government, the new technology was not an improvement but a threat.

I begin Chapter 3 by examining a key historical precursor to the public debate over satellite dish ownership. I chronicle the public investigation of IRIB by the *Majles-e Showra-ye Eslami* (Islamic Consultative Assembly, parliament or Majles hereafter) in 1993 and 1994 and argue that the discourse concerning the state broadcaster was an early indicator of the mounting ideological and logistical challenges confronting the state-controlled media system. This episode offers insight into the politics of media in Iran the early 1990s. It also gives us a sense of the technical and ideological landmines lying beneath the seemingly esoteric policy debate. From this analysis, a picture emerges of a national media organization struggling to navigate the divergent requirements of the nezam and the Majles on the one hand, and on the other, the imperatives of market globalization and the changing demographics of post-war Iran. It is equally instructive as a historical prelude to the year-long debate over the appropriate government response to the popularity of Western-origin satellite television, which I examine in depth in the chapter that follows. Chapter 4 looks at the rise of DBS as a mass communication medium and challenge to the extant broadcast television system. I reconstruct the debate within parliament about how to respond to DBS using detailed minutes of the multiple Majles sessions published in a government newspaper. Chapter 5 offers a deeper analysis of the narratives and socio-political currents that colored the satellite television crisis. The discourse was both a continuation of the nationalist myth about Iran and its relationship with the West and emblematic of a deeper struggle of the founding generation of the Islamic Republic to manage cultural, technological, and generational change. The crisis of satellite TV was a media inflection point–a time of political pressure and debate where a particular communication platform becomes so popular it is seen as a threat to the status quo. Iran weathered a second inflection point less than two decades later, with the rise of the internet.

Part III looks at the politics of the internet and its rise to a medium for mass communication. It also tracks the concomitant rise of soft war as a rhetorical strategy for nationalism and consensus building. We begin in Chapter 6 with the entry and early development of the internet between 1993 and 2008, with a particular focus on narratives surrounding the rise of the Persian blogosphere. We follow the progress of the internet from a limited medium for communication to a potential means of mass communication in Chapter 7. This chapter historicizes the 2009 election crisis that saw the incumbent president, Mahmood Ahmadinejad, return for a second term despite clear indications of fraud. In the protests which emerged in response, we see the internet become a key site of contestation between the state and Iranian activists. For the latter, it was used for the expression and mobilization of dissent. For the former, it was a tool for projecting popular legitimacy and surveilling and silencing demonstrators.

As the crisis progressed, so too did the establishment's proficiency in using the internet to pacify the opposition and re-affirm official political and ideological legitimacy. In Chapter 8, I examine the evolution of government media policy in the wake of the election crisis. I chart the rise of the "soft war" frame articulated by a number of Iranian intellectuals and as operationalized by the Iranian government through its far-reaching media and security complex.

Finally, in Chapter 9, I look at developments in the technology and politics of the internet under Ahmadinejad's successor, Ayatollah Hassan Rouhani. The chapter draws on secondary sources and forensic research to tell the story of Iran's national internet project, now called the National Information Network, beginning with its earliest conception and network architecture. It goes on to look at the government's decision to ban the hugely popular communication platform, Telegram, as part of the state's drive to complete the national internet—a digital network that could be completely cut off from the world while functioning as normal at home.

Part I

PAHLAVI AND THE MAKING OF THE MASS COMMUNICATION SYSTEM

1

THE BIRTH OF THE MASS COMMUNICATION MONOPOLY

Political parties and gatherings are forbidden ... the mosques and the pulpit are almost obsolete ... taking the place of all these things are the cinemas and televisions, and the press, which everyday expose thousands of our honorable urban population to the antics of some movie star.
—Jamal Al-e Ahmad, 1968[1]

In Iran, it seems to be unnecessary (and perhaps even dangerous) to defend the status quo, the legitimacy of an absolute monarchy ... Iran being Iran, of course, one does not expect a public breath of questioning of the political legitimacy of the Shah's absolute rule.
—Telegram from the US Consulate in Tabriz, 1973[2]

Today, in the eyes of the ruling regime, mass communication and power are closely bound. To understand this relationship, we must begin at the beginning of the mass communication age with the birth of radio. In this genesis story, we start to uncover a pattern of development which links the practice and industry of mass communication to the security of the regime (*nezam*) and the power of the state (*dowlat*). This chapter begins with the introduction of radio in the 1930s and its continued growth as a machinery of war and geopolitics in Iran during and after the Second World War. Next, I argue that the Shah's decision to markedly expand radio broadcasting and infrastructure in the 1950's was informed by the observed military and propaganda applications of the medium during the Cold War and occurred amid changing socio-economic conditions and large-scale government initiatives that punctuated the next two decades.

The second half of the chapter looks at the influence of the US military in Iran's nascent radio and television sector. Drawing from new primary research, it tells the story of the Armed Forces Radio and Television Service (AFRTS) in Iran, and the birth and short life of *Televizion-e Iran* (*Iran Television*), the nation's first television service. It points to evidence that suggests that the US diplomatic and military mission played a role in the demise of Iran's commercial television industry and in the regime's decision to create the state television and radio monopoly, National Iranian Radio and Television (NIRT).

Radio and War

War, and specifically foreign military operations on Iranian soil, colored the nation's early encounter with radio technology. While the German military used long-wave radio in their operations in Iran as early as 1915, it was not until the 1930s that radio broadcasts reached the ears of the Iranian people, however few and elite. These broadcasts came from neighboring Turkey and, being in the Turkish language, were incomprehensible to most listeners.[3] Later in 1939, Radio Ankara began broadcasting a limited number of news bulletins in Persian. Those lucky enough to have access to a radio transistor set were able to tune into the Persian-language radio broadcasts that penetrated the country.[4]

Shah Reza Pahlavi is generally credited with creating the state's first radio service, which began limited broadcasts from Tehran on April 24, 1940. For five hours each day, Tehran Radio transmitted short newscasts in Iran in Persian. It also broadcast in French, English, German, Russian, Arabic, and Turkish.[5] The government was not the only entity broadcasting to the Iranian people. Far from it. According to US intelligence assessments from the period, no less than eight foreign governments were broadcasting into Iran during the Second World War.

Of all the propaganda operations on the ground in Iran, the German effort was considered the most influential.[6] Its success was in no small part attributable to its use of radio as a primary means of ideological dissemination. German radio broadcasts tapped into the public's growing resentment of their Soviet and British occupiers. "By far the most effective portion of the Berlin Persian program is the weekly twenty-minute talk repeated on each of the three daily news periods," a US military intelligence report noted. "A major reason for the effectiveness of these talks is their presentation from the Iranian point of view, only mentioning the Axis or Allies in so far as they impinge upon the interests of Iran itself."[7] Noting their disadvantage as occupying powers, the US intelligence report deemed British and Russian radio propaganda in Iran ineffective and overdone.[8]

It was not for want of trying. Britain understood the power of radio early on and launched an ambitious project aimed at dominating the Iranian information environment: BBC Persian Service. The launch of the Persian language radio station on December 28, 1940, may be alternatively interpreted as a prelude to the British occupation of Iran or an attempt to prevent it. Either way, Whitehall evidently concluded that the geopolitical situation demanded more than just information warfare; it required kinetic intervention. In August 1941, the UK announced its intention to occupy Iran and seize all apparatuses of the state. The threat of German propaganda and other enemy tactics driving the Shah to side with Axis powers was part of its rationale for invasion. The UK was not alone in this calculation (or in this excuse). The Soviet Union also launched a military operation to seize and control Iranian territory and offered a similar justification for invasion. Iran was divided between the Soviet Union and Britain under military occupation for the remainder of the war.[9]

Radio During Allied Occupation (1941–5)

Western literature tends to highlight the relative press freedom enjoyed by the Iranian populace during the Allied occupation of Iran from 1941 to 1945. For instance, according to the *Cambridge History of Iran*, the Soviet-British invasion of Iran as heralded an end to the "era of dictatorship" and the beginning of "a period of freedom" in which the Iranian populace enjoyed "a level of freedom of expression which has not been repeated since."[10] Yet despite this new, purportedly liberal press environment, print remained a limited communication medium. While the number and diversity of citizen-owned and operated print publications increased, the quality of their journalism was poor. Newspapers and magazines catered to narrow constituencies and tended to be vitriolic and parochial.[11]

Indeed, closer analysis reveals that tactical communication blackouts, newspaper censorship, and total silencing of domestic and international reporting were the norm, rather than the exception, in occupied Iran.[12] A massive communication blackout accompanied the first weeks of the Allied invasion of Iran in 1941. From the entry of foreign troops on August 25, through the abdication of the Shah nearly a month later, the radio airwaves were silent.[13] When Pahlavi fled the country to live the rest of his life in exile he passed his crown to his twenty-one-year-old son, Mohammad Reza Pahlavi. The new shah announced his accession to the throne on Radio Tehran. In Radio Tehran's first broadcast in over a month, the new monarch spoke the oath of accession and appealed to the Iranian people for support.

As the first truly popular medium, radio effectively expanded the architecture of popular information in Iran. The technology played an important role in the spread of opinions and creation of emotional attitudes regarding the development of the modern state.[14] The utility of radio as a means of mass communication only increased in the post-occupation years. By the end of the 1940s, radio was rapidly becoming a primary source of information for Iranians and a preferred mode of information operations for foreign powers engaged in a mounting Cold War.[15] At first a novel source of news and entertainment, radio quickly became a mainstay of everyday life. It also became a theater for domestic politics and an important tool for the government to cultivate public support for its actions, not the least of which was the nationalization of the petroleum sector in 1952. Indeed, it is not an exaggeration to say that that action, and the foreign reaction, changed the course of history. In the next section, I tell the story of the foreign conspiracy to undo the nationalization of the Anglo-Iranian Oil Company by removing its champion, Prime Minister Mohammad Mosaddegh, from office. The US engineered coup left an indelible mark on the nation's political trajectory and cast a long shadow over the politics of media in Iran, both under the shah and today.

The 1953 Coup d'État

In 1953, Iran was rocked by a coup d'état engineered by the United States and the United Kingdom that removed the democratically elected prime minister, Mohammad Mosaddegh, from power and returned the country to the autocratic rule of Shah Mohammad Reza Pahlavi. The coup, named Operation Ajax by its creators, was a turning point in the political evolution of the country and contextualizes the Shah's actions concerning media in the years that followed. It also offers insight into the historical roots of Iran's present, and very likely future, contentious relationship between Iran and the United States and the United Kingdom.[16]

The covert operation for regime change in 1953 was justified by its American and British architects as essential for preventing Soviet infiltration and domination of Iran via the socialist Tudeh Party, which had been rising to prominence. But there was another motive also: the return of potentially billions in lost capital. Indeed, the British government and titans of industry were still reeling from Iran's nationalization of the Anglo-Iranian Oil Company (AIOC) years earlier, in 1951. The extraction, refinement, and distribution enterprise went back to 1901 when Iran struck an agreement that allowed Britain to find and sell its vast untapped petroleum reserves. The profit-sharing relationship was not equal. The 1901 concession provided Iran with a paltry 16 percent of the profits from crude. A renegotiated deal in 1932 provided slightly better terms but retained the same lop-sided relationship between parties.[17]

Although it brought in comparatively small revenue (Iran made more money on carpets than it did on oil), AIOC had an outsized presence in the lives of many Iranians. The company was by far the largest employer in Iran. But work conditions were poor, with refinery employees living in shantytowns, and oil field workers living in desert tents. The company restricted the number of Iranians in management positions and for years, it imported semi-skilled workers from India and Palestine. It made a practice of hiring Iranians for temporary positions, thus denying them the dignity and security of a full-time job.[18] When a concession between the United States and Saudi Arabia was negotiated at a 50–50 split in profits, itself inspired by the "Venezuelan principle" of a 50–50 division of net profits gained from oil operations, Iranian lawmakers rightly wondered why they should not have the same.[19]

A member of parliament at the time, Mosaddegh championed a bill aimed at righting that wrong by nationalizing the industry. The bill, which was passed by the Majles to popular acclaim, helped propel Mosaddegh to the post of prime minister. But the British refused to recognize the new law, contending that the existing concession agreement could not be renounced unilaterally. Mosaddegh was unbending and Iranians across the country watched the state seize British controlled oil fields and infrastructure in their name. The UK instituted a retaliatory embargo and the relationship between the two nations crumbled. Britain's embassy was closed, its diplomats and nationals expelled. Lacking a base of operations inside the country, the British turned to America for help. Their objective was to return Iran to a veritable autocracy under the command of a Shah they were confident they could control and who would denationalize the petroleum industry and return Britain to its former place as master of Iran's massive oil reserves.[20]

Media Aspects of the CIA Operation

Authorized by Winston Churchill and the newly minted American president, Dwight Eisenhower, Operation Ajax was the first of what would become a string of similar operations executed by the CIA to overthrow regimes the United States deemed a communist threat or otherwise inimical to US interests. Ajax had a media and economic warfare component and a martial component. On the former, recently declassified documents detail efforts to co-opt, buy, or otherwise commandeer Iranian media outlets. The aim was to prime the public against the prime minister, who would be painted as increasingly power-hungry, and to create the perception of popular support for his ouster. The effort also sought to generate unrest in the streets with dueling demonstrations of pro-Mosaddegh and pro-Shah agitators.[21]

Most of the propaganda and disinformation during the days leading up to and during the coup was circulated in the print press, which was comparatively robust and diverse. Regulations regarding licensing and content were loosely enforced. Radio, on the other hand, remained relatively untouched by CIA efforts. Indeed, Mosaddegh retained his command of the medium, which in the past, he had used quite successfully. Throughout the struggle, radio announcers read news stories and commentary from a diverse collection of newspapers, each reflecting the views of the political and ideological factions that backed them. It was only later, with the final martial operation and the arrest of Mosaddegh, that CIA-backed operatives took control of Radio Tehran and announced the failure of the coup and the imminent return of the king.[22]

The Legacy of the Coup d'État of 28 Mordad

Mosaddegh was at the vanguard of the country's transition from an absolute monarchy to a constitutional parliamentary democracy. The coup stopped the nation's hard-fought progress towards democracy in its tracks and replaced it with the increasingly autocratic rule of the Shah. It returned government decision-making authority to the monarch, returned income from petroleum sales to British coffers, and allowed American and British businesses in Iran to operate freely.

But the intervention had less visible but no less consequential impacts also. The story of the clandestine American intervention became part of the collective memory and a reference point for subsequent generations demanding aggressive action to free Iran from the hidden hand of imperialist powers and determine its own destiny. This discourse of discontent would simmer beneath the surface in the years following the coup only to reemerge in new form under the press of economic and cultural dislocation brought by the White Revolution, the oil boom, and the gathering tide of opposition to the monarchy in the 1970s. Years later, Ruhollah Khomeini would try to use the myth of Mosaddegh to legitimate his Islamist nationalist project, positing it as part of a historical struggle against tyranny and for self-determination.[23]

Although the nationalization of AIOC was short lived, that it happened at all was an important proof of concept. It showed the Shah and the men that dethroned him that the state had the power to seize control of its natural resources. The lesson could be carried over to other industries as well. Indeed, the nationalization of AIOC showed that government seizure of businesses and cornering of the market to the point of monopoly was both possible and advantageous. Iran's leaders would continue to use nationalization as a strategy of power consolidation over the decades.

The nationalist discourse that grew up from Mosaddegh's National Front and his nationalization project only intensified in the aftermath of the coup, both as a reaction to foreign meddling and as a consequence of the Shah's decision to seek détente, if not alliance, with Iranian nationalists in the years that followed. It is in this subsequent period, with the Shah's top-down modernization drive and the rapid expansion of the bureaucratic state, that we see radio truly become a medium for mass communication.

The Growth of Radio in the Late 1950s

The Shah was not idle after returning to Iran. With the coup behind him and the modernization project on the horizon, the Shah and his representatives and advisors embarked on a project to create a national radio service. Radio enjoyed widespread geographic and socio-economic distribution in Iranian society. Even the poorest of villages had at least one radio. While ownership was "concentrated in larger cities and in tea houses along bus and trucking routes," radios could also be found in "outlying villages, in homes of wealthy landlords and tribal leaders and in taxicabs and private automobiles." By 1958, there were an estimated 800,000 radio sets in operation.[24]

Two factors played into the Shah's decision to improve and expand the national radio service. The first had to do with its economic potential. The stream of foreign-made radio equipment indicated radio's rising popularity and demand. If Iran were to manufacture its own equipment, the Shah's advisors likely argued, it would generate revenue and make it easier and cheaper for Iranians to buy their own radios. There was a second, equally important, factor at play: the deluge of propaganda radio broadcasts into the country from neighboring states. Indeed, one can understand the drive to bolster the national radio system and create a foreign service as a reaction to such broadcasts and their perceived threat to the regime.

The Soviet Union was a major source of broadcasts into the country, and by extension, the Shah's ire. Like his American and British backers, Pahlavi considered the USSR's brand of socialism antithetical to the Western-oriented, capitalist modernity he envisioned. A strong national and international radio service would, it was reasoned, drown out such broadcasts through programs that promoted capitalism, consumerism, and the benign rule of the Shah. But it was not ideological competition alone that was the problem. It was, perhaps more importantly, the fact that much of USSR programming took aim at the Shah's claim to legitimate power, asserting that the monarch did not enjoy broad consent to his rule. This may have been more of a figment of imagination than of reality. Even so, for the Shah, the very existence of anti-regime radio stations was proof that there were formidable opposition groups working within and without his boarders. With appellations like "Voice of the Iranian Patriots," the names of Soviet-sponsored stations enhanced this impression, suggesting they were the authentic project of dissident Iranians, not a foreign power.

Communist and socialist radio broadcasts aroused the concern of Iranian officials as early as 1957, when intelligence reported that the USSR was making "extensive use of radio" for propaganda in the region. Communist radio stations broadcast in Persian, Azerbaijani, Tajik, and Armenian on a daily basis. In addition to the Soviet Union and its satellite stations, communist China was also reported to be broadcasting in Persian to Iran.[25] The broadcasts criticized the monarchical system and promoted socialist and anti-capitalist values. They encouraged resistance to "Western imperialism," as evidenced by the material and cultural products promoted by the Iranian government and its foreign benefactors. Even when they fell short of calling for the overthrow of the regime, the broadcasts undermined the Shah's authority by propagating an alternative ideology to that of the regime.

So much was the perceived threat that the Shah dispatched his trusted deputy, General Hassan Alavi-Kai, to Bonn to hire a propaganda advisor "to help with the ideological fight against the communists." The general enlisted the help of Dr. Eberhard Taubert in February. Known as "Dr. Anti," Taubert was a virulent antisemite who had served the Third Reich as Joseph Goebbels's screenwriter. In postwar Germany, he made a name for himself as an authority on anti-Bolshevik propaganda.[26] In addition to the perceived threat emanating from socialist radio propaganda, the regime's actions were catalyzed by the influx of pan-Arab and Arab-nationalist propaganda from neighboring states.

Iranian officials brought their concerns to the country's American benefactors. On October 9, 1958, the newly appointed Iranian ambassador to Washington, Ali Gholi Ardalan, raised the issue of Arab propaganda in a routine courtesy call on the US Undersecretary of State Robert Murphy. Murphy had recently returned from a trip to Cairo where he met with the new president, Gamal Abdel Nasser. Nasser had risen to power following the deposal of the Egyptian monarchy in June 1953. In his meeting with Murphy, Ardalan complained of the destabilizing effect of the Egyptian coup for the region, no doubt fearing Nasser's rising popularity would inspire a similar movement to overthrow the Iranian monarchy. He referenced the problem of hostile foreign radio broadcasts from Egypt and Iraq in particular. "Ambassador Ardalan referred to the continued activities of Radio Cairo and Radio Baghdad directing propaganda attacks toward people of other countries of the Middle East," a US State Department memorandum read. The pan-Arab nationalist broadcasts targeting areas in Iran with large Arab and Kurdish populations were of particular concern, the memo continued, as they had the potential to re-invigorate ethnic separatism, which could, in turn, undermine Iran's territorial integrity.[27]

The perceived threat to regime hegemony posed by anti-Iranian Arab nationalist radio broadcasts only grew in the years that followed. In 1960, the Egyptian government commissioned a special unit to direct radio propaganda efforts targeting the Pahlavi regime. The resulting radio station, *Sowt al Arab* (Voice of the Arabs), broadcast from Cairo in Persian.[28] Pahlavi sought to counter the propaganda from Cairo and Baghdad, in part, by entering into a covert partnership with Tel Aviv to stand up a propagandistic radio station targeting Muslim populations in Iran and the region. Broadcasting in Arabic from Iran's Khuzestan province, the station ran programs critical of Nasser and his radical brand of nationalism.[29]

The Shah's modernization project was an additional driver, as well as beneficiary, of the expansion of Iranian radio. In 1963, the Shah announced a sweeping campaign for social and economic modernization and reform, dubbed the "White Revolution." It consisted of a six-point program of land reform, nationalization of forests, profit-sharing for industrial workers, sale of state factories, suffrage for women, and creation of a Literacy Corps. The aspirations of the White Revolution grew in subsequent years, and by the late 1970s, it included seventeen separate initiatives.[30]

The regime saw radio as a means to propagate the White Revolution's vision of Western-style capitalist modernity to the masses. An early step was the centralization of control of the national radio service, which had until then been subjected to political infighting and successive take-overs by rival government agencies, under the remit of the Ministry of Information in 1964. It concomitantly worked to expand the reach of the service to parts of the country that rarely felt the presence of the national government. These measures, along with increased funding and prioritization, showed rapid results. By 1966, Iran had twenty-two transmitters broadcasting for thirteen hours a day. Twelve provincial radio stations relayed news broadcasts from Tehran. The provincial stations also carried programs of local or regional interest, often in appropriate dialects or in Arabic and Kurdish.[31]

The US Role in Building Iranian Radio Infrastructure

The US mission in Iran was one of the first stops of regime emissaries in search of the funds, equipment, and communication expertise needed to establish a new foreign broadcasting service and a more powerful domestic one. In meetings with US military and diplomatic officials, the Shah's emissaries argued that military aid alone was insufficient to support Iran against the Soviet threat. A strong radio network was needed to project national power and thereby deter foreign aggression. One US official summarized the Iranian position as thus: "Although Iran was grateful for military aid, assistance in the radio field [was] even more vital."[32]

The Shah took every opportunity to enlist Washington's sympathy and support for the project. He presented the problem of foreign radio propaganda through his emissaries in Tehran and Washington. He also made a personal overture to the US president. Seeking to appeal to Eisenhower's pre-occupation with the Soviet threat and the spread of communism, the Shah highlighted the problem of Soviet radio broadcasts in a letter to the president in 1959. The tactic drew a personal response from the American president, and an indirect pledge of radio aid. Eisenhower wrote back to say that he was fully aware of the "Soviet propaganda broadcasts" to his country and assure him that America would "use any opportunity" to cease the "vicious campaign." Later, when Pahlavi raised the issue during a personal meeting with the president, Eisenhower indicated that America would be willing to provide Iran with radio assistance.[33]

While Eisenhower certainly promised the Shah radio assistance, it soon became clear that the two leaders differed on what such support would entail. It was the opinion of the United States that radio assistance would be best spent supporting regime security by bolstering Iran's domestic service. National Iranian Radio should be used to shore up public support for the Shah and his projects, the Americans argued. The Shah had other designs. He thought US aid was most needed and best spent on the establishment of a foreign radio service. Such an international broadcasting capacity would enhance Iran's security by projecting power and countering anti-regime propaganda. "The Shah's first interest had initially been in initiating propaganda broadcasts to Arab countries to offset Radio-Cairo," wrote Anderson, an officer at the US Embassy in Tehran. "The American thought had been in terms of VOA [Voice of America] relay."

Tehran attempted to assuage Washington's concerns by proposing that the radio service could air VOA content directed to Iranian listeners as well as offer Iranian government produced content aimed at foreign audiences. Ultimately, Washington declined to provide the regime aid for its foreign radio project "on the grounds that Iran should concentrate on its local audience rather than on foreign propaganda broadcasts."[34]

The exchange, memorialized on now declassified US government documents, revealed both the American military's hesitancy to aid the foreign propaganda initiative and its hand in building the original national radio infrastructure that the Shah now sought to update and expand. The monarch's demand for additional radio aid was a reoccurring theme in bilateral meetings. "Both the Shah and Mr. Zolfaghari … feel Iran had been promised something in the radio field and will feel let down if nothing is forthcoming. Already American aid to Turkey and India is being frequently thrown at us."[35] Still, as dissenting embassy and U.S. Army Mission in Iran/Military Assistance Advisory Group (ARMISH-MAAG) officials pointed out, the United States had already provided significant development aid as well as direct military assistance on radio infrastructure projects. For fiscal years 1957 and 1958, US expenditure on Iranian communication (including telephone) projects totaled $4.7 million USD.[36] ARMISH-MAAG officials complained that the US military had spent more than a year building a radio transmitter in Tehran, only to see the equipment neglected and the transmitter operated at a fraction of capacity: "The transmitting set we have installed in Tehran is poorly maintained and never has operated at peak capacity unless an American engineer was on the job."[37] After the US military declined to sponsor the additional improvements, the monarch looked to the US commercial sector to make the sought-after updates. American manufacturers were happy to oblige.

In 1958, the Shah put his ministers to work purchasing equipment and technical advice on the US commercial market. In November, a US Information Service (USIS) officer in Tehran drafted a memo to Washington reporting that the Shah had "undertaken to conclude contracts for a considerable amount of radio transmitting equipment."[38] The officer's colleagues at the embassy protested the tenor of the telegram, arguing that it overstated the immediacy of the contract negotiations. But the officer's assessment soon proved accurate. Contract negotiations were quickly concluded, and by early December 1958, Iranian officials had begun planning for the transport of thirty-six tons of radio equipment from the United States. Tehran had purchased two 100-kilowatt radio transmitters from Radio Corporation of America (RCA) and needed the help of the US military to transport it. "The question has been raised by the Iranians as to whether these could be brought in by US military aircraft to save time." The request was granted.[39]

By the mid-1960s, the Shah had achieved his goal of creating a powerful nationwide radio network and foreign radio service. He did so largely through the import of US commercial radio equipment as well as previous US military aid and labor. While the US contribution to the development of the state radio network was subsidiary, its impact on the formation of the Iranian television industry was more direct. The rise of television, the anti-competitive influence of the US government, and the formation of the modern broadcasting monopoly as a strategy of state power is examined below.

The Life and Death of Commercial Television, 1958–76

The preponderance of the literature credits either the Iranian monarch, Mohammad Reza Pahlavi, or an enterprising businessman, Habibollah Sabet Pasal, for the founding of the Iranian television industry.[40] Yet deeper analysis along with new details from declassified US government records paint a different picture. In the following pages, I tell the untold story of the US Armed Forces Radio and Television Service (AFRTS) in Iran. I point to evidence that suggests that anti-competitive practices by the United States helped usher the demise of the first commercial television station and informed the Shah's decison to nationalize the industry and create the state television and radio monopoly.

However, the anti-competitive influence of AFRTS is only one part of the puzzle. The geopolitical circumstances surrounding the creation of the state television and radio monopoly must also be considered. In the latter half of this section, I argue that the Shah's decision to seize control of Sabet's commercial project was indicative of his appreciation of the danger and potential of broadcast media for regime security.

The Dual Rise of Commercial and Military Television

On June 5, 1958, a special meeting of the Iran Country Team was called to address the "pending problem of the Armed Forces TV station."[41] The gathering was composed of top representatives of the American military, diplomatic and intelligence establishments in Iran.[42] This was a "special" meeting, outside the similarly composed interagency working group which met regularly to share information and coordinate action between the various government agencies.[43] At issue was the imminent launch of Armed Forces Television, a project with a budget of $50 to $60 million USD and the mission of bringing "a little taste of home" to servicemembers and their families deployed in Iran.[44] The US military had begun terrestrial radio broadcast operations in the country in 1948 with the establishment of Armed Forces Radio and the Tehran based Radio 1555.[45] Television came ten years later with the launch of Armed Forces Television. Iran was to join a handful of countries that hosted the service. At the time of the deliberations, Armed Forces Television could be found in US forward operating bases and diplomatic missions in Germany, Japan, Iceland, and Saudi Arabia.[46]

The creation of a television service specifically for and by the US military was driven, in part, by the problem of morale. For officers and enlisted men serving in postwar Europe and elsewhere, life on a military base away from one's family and the modern conveniences of home was lonely and dull. Television offered an expedient, relatively inexpensive solution to the "morale problem," in that it would provide servicemembers with "a little bit of home" while stationed abroad. In other words, Armed Forces Television would make life on base more comfortable. Plus, its proponents reasoned, it would help with the problem of force retention: "To deprive service men and women such an accustomed source of entertainment would affect the morale of enlistments and retention of trained personnel," the US Army history of Armed Forces Radio and Television averred.[47] The idea was not far-fetched by American standards. Indeed, by the 1950s, television had become so popular in the United States that most Americans—including those on foreign deployments—considered their TV set a household staple and the consumption of television programming a ritual of everyday life. In this way, the push to add a television component to the radio service that was already in operation was to be expected.

The prospective benefits of Armed Forces Television were particularly relevant to ARMISH- MAAG leadership. At the time, the assistance mission in Iran was considered within military circles one of the least desirable assignments one could get. Far from the fighting in South Asia, it offered little opportunity for an officer or enlisted man to gain the combat experience considered necessary for his advancement in the military ranks.[48] Iran, in short, was a career backwater. It was perhaps because of this reputation—and the low morale it engendered—that Iran was among the early beneficiaries of Armed Forces TV.

The project to bring television to Iran was not without its detractors. Earlier that year, the US ambassador to Iran, Selden Chapin, received a letter of protest from the powerful businessman, Habibollah Sabet Pasal. Sabet, alternately referred to as the "Iranian capitalist" and the "Iranian industrialist" in embassy documents, complained that the Armed Forces Television project was at odds with his own plans for establishing a private, commercial television service called *Televizion-e Iran*. The military station would have an unfair advantage over his commercial start-up, he argued, as the Army station would have the full weight and resources of the United States government behind it, while Televizion-e Iran, as a commercial enterprise, would be restricted by limited resources and the demands of meeting the business' bottom line.[49] "[Sabet] argues that the more desirable presentations of the Army station will decrease his potential audience," Paul Strum, First Secretary and Counselor in the embassy's Political Affairs Office, wrote in June 1958. "He says that his is a private enterprise which is being competed with by a foreign government."[50]

While ARMISH-MAAG representative General Hoy voiced strong support for Armed Forces TV from the start, the position of his diplomatic counterparts proved fluid. At first, Ambassador Chaplin was sympathetic. At the meeting in May, the Chief of Mission reiterated Sabet's concerns about the anti-competitive nature of the US enterprise: "Sabet has a strong argument on the grounds of alleged potential foreign government competition."[51] The Country Team discussed ways to remedy the situation short of terminating the project.

A discussion captured in State Department documents provides a window into group's deliberations. In the Philippines, Anderson noted, the government ordered the US military to reduce the power of its television transmitter so that the signal would be limited to the vicinity of the American base there. General Hoy assured the group that to do something similar in Iran was impossible. Another Country Team member raised the idea of removing the digit seven, the channel number that was assigned to Armed Forces Television by the Iranian Army's chief signal officer in March 1957, on the dials of all television sets sold to the Iranian public. This too was ruled out.[52] The ambassador raised a second point of argument in favor of Sabet's position. Armed Forces Television might undercut US commercial activities in the Iranian information communications market. Chapin specifically referenced the "possible harm to the American firm, RCA, in respect to decreased potential sale of TV receiving sets."[53]

Yet it was not the validity of Sabet's complaint, but his perceived power in society and ties to the Shah, that likely drew the attention of the ambassador and retained his involvement in the negotiations throughout the spring. Sabet was a powerful industrialist. His was one of a handful of families favored by the Shah with proprietary access to Iranian markets. He started his first business, a taxi service, in 1919 and went on to found more than forty corporations before retiring to Paris in 1974.[54] Sabet's enterprises spanned numerous industries, including banking, trucking, and furniture manufacturing.[55] Hailed as the father of the "Pepsi Generation," his Firuz Trading Company imported many of the most iconic and popular American products – from soft drinks to cars, washing machines, and television sets. The Sabet family franchise holdings included General Electric, Westinghouse, Kelvinar, Electrolux, and Pepsi-Cola.[56] Sabet was "politically powerful," Ambassador Chaplin told the County Team. "The US establishment in Iran could be in difficulty unless it succeeds in mollifying him, which it should seek to do."[57]

Despite the arguments in Sabet's favor, not all members of the Country Team were willing to take his objections at face value. Some questioned the timing of the letter. "Sabet has known for many months that the Armed Forces TV station was in prospect. Why should he at this late date complain?" an unnamed participant mused. "There must be some factor in this case which is not presently known to us."[58] It was decided that the ambassador would invite the businessman to the embassy to discuss the issue, which he did soon after.

The meeting between Sabet and the ambassador seemed fruitful at first. A tentative compromise had been reached. The United States would scrap its plans to establish an independent Armed Forces Television. In exchange, Sabet would air some of the US government produced content intended for Armed Forces Television on Televizion-e Iran. Sabet, said an embassy memorandum of the meeting, was "willing to make time available free of charge to ARMISH-MAAG to show films provided through Army Special Services channels."[59]

While the Sabet family patriarch may have reached an agreement in private negotiations, his was not the final word on the subject. More crucial was his son, Iraj, who ran the company. One of two boys born to Sabet, Iraj attended Harvard Business School in the 1950s.[60] While at Harvard, he wrote his thesis on the establishment of a commercial television station in Iran.[61] When Iraj graduated and returned to Iran to take a place in the family business, he did so determined to realize his vision for Televizion-e Iran.[62] In subsequent discussions with ARMISH-MAAG officials, Iraj made his intentions clear. The United States would receive no free or proprietary access from the broadcaster. It would be expected to pay for airtime just like any other customer.[63]

Thus, when embassy officials walked into a special meeting on the matter on June 5, they were doubtless displeased with Sabet for his seeming inconsistency, if not outright duplicity, in the negotiations. As Strum acidly noted: while it was originally understood that Televizion-e Iran would carry Armed Forces Television content free of charge, "later discussion ... revealed that 'free' time works out to between $55,000 and $110,00 a year."[64] Economic Affairs Counselor Taylor distributed the embassy's latest draft of a joint Embassy-MAAG telegram to Washington on the subject. The memorandum summarized Sabet's objection to Armed Forces Television and the terms of Iraj Sabet's proposed compromise. The memorandum advised Washington to reject the terms and continue with Armed Forces Television as planned. "Whereas members of the Embassy staff particularly had felt earlier that a reasonable compromise was possible, there was general agreement... that no compromise could now be reached with Sabet."[65] The decision meant that the private station would have to compete with the US military station from its start. In just a few weeks, the font of sympathy for Sabet and his television project had run dry.

In informing Iraj Sabet of the Country Team's decision, Counselor Taylor offered the businessman a minor consolation: the United States would be willing "to delay the opening of Armed Forces TV for a reasonable period (two to six weeks)."[66] By delaying the launch of Armed Forces Television by a few weeks (which was easy, as all indications show it could not, logistically, start broadcasting for months), Sabet would be able to claim credit for bringing television to Iran, which he did on October 5, 1958.[67] Still, the gesture was small recompense for the founder of Televizion-e Iran. The message in the tea leaves was clear: the fate of Iran's nascent commercial television industry was subordinate to the interests of the US military mission.

The First Ten Years

In its first decade of existence, the Iranian television industry was composed of just two services: Televizion-e Iran and Armed Forces TV. At first glance, there was little daylight between the two. The stations were nearly identical in terms of organization, content, and methodology. They used the same industry techniques, organizational model, and American produced content.[68] Televizion-e Iran was even managed by an American named Vance Hallack. It used the US broadcasting standard of 525 lines.

Domestic production, which consisted largely of live telecasts, as the studios did not have the technology to make film recordings, was heavily influenced by the American format. For example, quiz shows were sponsored by advertisers and featured consumer durables as prizes for contestants. The state news agency Pars News provided content for domestic news reports. The US Information Service provided international news content and reports were sponsored by Pan Am Airlines.[69] But the Army had a fundamental advantage over Sabet, who was, after all, a businessman beholden to his investors and his company's bottom line. It had ready access to American produced content and operated commercial free, without the burden of revenue generation.[70]

The American station derived its program content from the United States through kinescope, a process by which technicians would record the programs as they were broadcast on television in the United States.[71] They would then embark on the arduous task of cutting the footage to remove all commercial advertising before it was deemed suitable for distribution to Armed Forces Television stations abroad.[72] Instead, Armed Forces Television in Iran would air a popular show such as Bonanza and between programs, instead of a commercial, it would run government-produced "educational content," such as tips on hygiene or how to interact with civilians of the host country.

In short time, Armed Forces TV began outperforming Televizion-e Iran both in audience share and broadcasting time. As early as December 1958, there were indications that Sabet was struggling to buy program content. "Mr. Sabet's TV station is using Soviet cultural material," Counselor Taylor informed his colleagues in December 1958.[73] "It was recalled that Sabet once said he would not use Soviet material but had later indicated he might have to because of the scarcity of Iranian, American, or other program material."[74]

By 1962, Televizion-e Iran was losing money. As of March 23, it had lost about 60 million rials (approximately $800,000 USD). The television station located in Abadan in Khuzestan province was failing to generate sufficient advertising revenue. Sabet feared he would be forced to reduce programming from three hours to one hour a day. Armed Forces Television, meanwhile, was broadcasting forty hours a week.[75] By the time the Shah moved to close Televizion-e Iran in 1969, Sabet's enterprise was in a significantly weakened state. When the notion of nationalizing the industry was first put forward in the National Assembly, Sabet had little economic incentive to put up a fight.

The impact of Armed Forces TV on the fate of Sabet's television station is largely unremarked upon in the historiography in both Iran and the West. The repercussions of the US military station on the industry and on the US-Iran relationship remain similarly unexplored. What would have happened if the US Country Team had decided to assuage Sabet and cancel plans for Armed Forces Television all together? Without the presence of Armed Forces Television, Televizion-e Iran would likely have prospered. The success of the private enterprise, in turn, may have helped establish a precedent for commercial competition in broadcasting. Sabet's television enterprise might even have grown strong enough to resist the state's efforts to close Televizion-e Iran and nationalize the industry. Moreover, without the presence of Armed Forces Television, the association between television and propaganda and television and state power might not have grown as acute. Without the shadow of a foreign military and hegemonic power behind it, television might have gained currency among the Iranian public as a medium for information, commercial exchange, and even artistic expression.

The Nationalization of Televizion-e Iran

In July 1969, the Iranian government seized Televizion-e Iran's Tehran and Abadan stations and its Ahvaz relay station, along with all of its equipment. The closure not only meant the end of Sabet's television enterprise but the end of the first and only commercial television station in the Middle East. Sabet appealed to the Shah personally in an effort to stop the shutdown. He argued that Televizion-e Iran and the new government station (authorized by the legislature in 1966–7) should be allowed to operate side- by -side and that the resultant competition would be beneficial for both enterprises. The appeal failed, however, and Sabet was forced to sell his share of Televizion-e Iran to the Iranian government.[76] The family was despondent. "The television network was like my child," Iraj Sabet lamented in an interview with Abbas Milani in 2002.[77] Sabet reportedly received 20 million toman for the company, a fraction of his original 70 million investment.[78]

The incident raises a number of questions. One query has to do with the parliament's decision to extend the company's tax exemption for another five years. A kind of government subsidy, the tax break would allow the company to continue operations while also making longer term investments in infrastructure and production. Why would the Iranian government close Televizion-e Iran after having just renewed its tax exemption?[79]

While the rationale for the government's take-over of Sabet's television station has never been fully explained, various theories have been proffered.[80] For instance, Sreberny and Mohammadi suggest that a primary motivation for the Shah's closure of the broadcaster was fear of the development of an autonomous base of power within the commercial sector. The significant growth of private industry produced great wealth, which rivaled his own.[81]

Another hypothesis relates to the family's religious affiliation. Sabet's father was a Jew who converted to Baha'ism. The businessman is described by numerous sources as a leader of the Baha'i community.[82] Under this reasoning, the regime targeted Sabet for his potential to unify the Baha'i as a political force. Sreberny points to a growing intolerance of the influence of the group in domestic politics. A number of Baha'i either served in the top echelons of the government or occupied a prominent place within wealthy elite society. Acting contrary to the "internationalist" and non-political reputation cultivated by the persecuted Baha'i, Sabet was among several members of the sect actively involved in domestic politics.[83]

If true, such action would be consistent with previous patterns of discrimination against Baha'i. In 1955 and 1956, intolerance turned to unrest as a wave of anti-Baha'i rioting raked the Capitol. Historian Michael Fischer credits Mohammad Taghi Falsafi for whipping up hysteria about the Baha'i threat, while top officials such as the Iranian prime minister and the military governor of Tehran tolerated and even facilitated the violence and persecution.[84]

Other sources suggest that it was the success of Televizion-e Iran and the demonstrated power of the medium that motivated the regime's decision to quash the private broadcaster and launch a state-run station in its stead. As one account of the period explains: "The success of [Televizion-e Iran] and the turning of the medium into a tool for promotion of culture and publicity prompted the government to seriously consider the establishment of a TV institution."[85]

Another explanation places the closure of Televizion-e Iran in the context of the massive expansion of the bureaucratic state in the early 1960s, contemporaneous with the state's push to expand into major, profit producing industries—in effect, extending the government's reach into virtually all aspects of everyday life.[86] The state bureaucracy grew enormously between 1963 and 1977. In just fourteen years, the central government grew from twelve ministries with some 150,000 civil servants to nineteen ministries and some 304,000 civil servants.[87] The closure of Sabet's television enterprise was, therefore, a symptom of the growth of the centralized, bureaucratic state.

While each of these theories is a helpful partial explanation of the Iranian government's decision to forcibly close the region's first and only private broadcaster, the decision gains new perspective in light of previous government action in the field of radio. This illuminates a pattern in which the Iranian monarch's threat perception contributed to his defensive actions aimed at consolidating control over what he perceived as the essential levers of state power.

One of these levers was the military. Indeed, the period under examination saw a massive increase in government spending on military weaponry and personnel.

Mass communication media was another lever of state power, with the potential to enhance regime security and influence on the national and international stage. The Shah's actions followed a logic in which television, like radio, became both an extension of hegemonic power and an important tool for regime security. As with national radio, which grew to include both a foreign and domestic propaganda division, television increasingly became intertwined with the security priorities and functions of the state. While ostensibly an independent agency, NIRT routinely featured programs by the internal security service, SAVAK. Parviz Sabeti, who headed the service and served as a key national security advisor to the Shah, used the medium to reinforce the power of the regime and highlight the consequences of crossing it. Among other things, he used television to air forced confessions of political dissidents (amoung other people) and showcase the perils of disobedience and dissent.[88]

The Creation of National Iranian Radio and Television

By the time the government took over Televizion-e Iran, it was already three years into its own television project. The Shah had begun the process of establishing a national television service in August 1966, with Project Number 4613 of the Seven Year Organization Plan.[89] The project allocated 180 million rials for construction of a headquarters in Northern Tehran and 35 million rials for basic maintenance of the station.[90] Less than six months later, the Shah commissioned the development of a nationwide television system based on the European SECAM broadcasting standard. The *Compagnie de Telegraphie Sans Fil* (Wireless Telegraphy Company) announced the signing of a $10 million USD contract with Tehran for the supply, installation, and start-up of a national telecasting system on January 10, 1967.[91] On July 2 of that same year, the National Assembly passed a bill establishing National Television as an independent government agency.

After the closure of Televizion-e Iran in 1969, the state embarked on a rapid expansion of the national telecasting infrastructure and activities. *Televizion-e Melli-ye Iran* (National Iran Television) began with 183 employees, one studio, and three cameras.[92] In its first year of operations, television broadcast coverage more than doubled, increasing from an initial 2.1 to 4.8 million people. By the end of 1971, the state broadcaster presided over fourteen television production and transmission stations. Its satellite and terrestrial broadcasts reached approximately 70 percent of the country.[93] By 1974, NIRT reached roughly half of the total population.[94]

Broadcasting remained a priority despite intensifying economic stress and the decline of the consumer market in the latter half of the decade. Even as the government was making across-the-board budget cuts in 1975–6, the budget for NIRT increased by 20 percent.[95] The exponential growth of NIRT may have been an indication of the short horizon that the Shah placed on his time in power. Unbeknown to his US allies and many members of his inner circle, the Shah's health was in rapid decline. In 1974, Pahlavi began receiving treatment for lymphatic blood disease, an often terminal form of cancer.

For the Shah and his advisors, national television was attractive for a number of reasons. For one, entry into the business of television was a relatively inexpensive proposal. The upfront investment for infrastructure and technical expertise was comparatively low, especially in light of military expenditures, and the potential return on investment was high. As far as the Shah was concerned, foreign governments had been in the business of broadcasting in Iran for years. The participation of the Iranian government was both appropriate and overdue.

Moreover, national television service could be used as a tool to advance the government's sweeping reform and development goals and help foster national unity and collective identity across disparate ethno-linguistic territories, in part by promoting Persian as the common national language. It would also serve an educational function. An entire channel was dedicated to educational programming for children.

Finally, the national television and radio network likely appealed to the Shah's pride and global power aspirations. International norms held that the development of a national telecommunication system was a key indicator of national progress in modernizing countries; it was one of the aspects that differentiated "developed" and "modernized" international powers from "developing," "third world" countries. Thus, the national broadcasting network helped fulfill the symbolic and institutional criteria necessary to join the club of "modern" nations.

One of the benefits of national television and radio, in theory, was that it would serve to enhance and reinforce regime authority by disseminating and enforcing a dominant ideology in areas otherwise untouched by the central government, and therefore susceptible to the malign influence of propaganda from internal opposition groups and neighboring states. In practice, however, NIRT had far different results. Dominated by foreign, mostly American entertainment programs dubbed into Persian, the state television and radio service often worked to exacerbate feelings of economic injustice among the poor and working class. Audience members across the economic spectrum were less than approving of the programming decisions made by NIRT staff. Indeed, NIRT Director Reza Ghotbi is generally seen to have had mishandled the service.[96]

The Western bent of the programs was a major area of contention. Even Minister of Women's Affairs, Mahnaz Afkhami, a regime loyalist, was critical of the national broadcaster. Afkhami complained that NIRT's primetime television news program was broadcast entirely in English and reported only international news.[97] Moreover, for many Iranians, NIRT news products bore scant relation to what a newspaper reader would consider domestic news. Television and radio programs routinely led with accounts of the latest appearance of the Shah and the activities of the royal family, rather than with substantive domestic reporting. Sunny domestic economic news reports only exposed the hollowness of the Shah's claim of nationwide economic growth. Commercial content added to the sense of inequity. In 1973, for example, while many Iranians struggled to eke out a basic existence amid rampant inflation, a commercial on state television urged viewers to use Travelers Checks on their next weekend getaway to Paris.[98]

+++

If the Shah's intention of gaining dominion over all broadcast media was not apparent with the nationalization of Televizion-e Iran, it became unmistakable five years later, when he ordered the closure of all foreign television and radio stations operating on Iranian soil. Only one foreign broadcaster was affected by the decree: AFRT. On October 25, 1976, after twenty years of radio and seventeen of television, AFRT issued its last broadcast. The following day, the Shah inaugurated the "international" service of National Iranian Television and Radio, Channel 5.[99] The new state television network was designed to serve Iran's English speaking foreign residents, the same audience served by AFRT. The new state-run radio station that replaced Radio 1555 was similarly positioned. It broadcast popular Western music as well as world news in French, German, Russian, and English.[100]

The nationalization of Televizion-e Iran, the creation of Armed Forces Radio and Television, and later, its closure, cemented the state's monopoly over mass communications media. This monopoly would endure, if imperfectly, through the overthrow of the regime and the inception of the Islamic Republic.

2

MASS COMMUNICATION IN REVOLUTION AND REGIME BUILDING

The French Revolution convinced us that in order to destroy a ruler one must destroy faith in the regime thus destroying its legitimacy.
—Richard Sennett[1]

You must know this and you must tell it to your government. This country is lost because the Shah cannot make up his mind.
—U.S. Ambassador William Sullivan[2]

The mass communication monopoly created under Mohammed Reza Pahlavi was intended to support regime security and the state's top-down modernization agenda. Yet paradoxically, it served to undermine regime authority in part by centralizing communicative power in the hands of those who dominated it. Simultaneously, the state media system exacerbated the mounting crisis of legitimacy by spotlighting the weakness of the leadership and the oscillation of the Shah's policy positions.

This chapter considers the role of media in the revolution of 1978–9. I examine how the imposition of military control in 1978 combined with state employee strikes and the suppression of newspapers served to legitimat key revolutionaries and delegitimize the incumbent regime. I go on to explore the role of mass communication in the struggle for power within the opposition movement and its evolution in the first decade of the Islamic Republic.

Martial Law and the End of the Regime

In late August 1978, facing ongoing civil unrest and waging a private battle to beat cancer and reclaim his health, the Shah appointed former aide and former prime minister (1960–1) Jafar Sharif-Emami to head a caretaker government. The decision was a mistake, as Emami's policies, and in particular his approach to media, exacerbated the erosion of the central government's power. Believing that the popular unrest stemmed from the dissident clerics in Qom, the prime minister immediately set into motion a bold set of policy changes aimed at appeasing the clerical opposition.[3] He announced sweeping reforms to counter the liberalization and modernization associated with the White Revolution. Virtually overnight, gambling and pornography became illegal and the Ministry of Women's Affairs was dissolved. The government announced a plan to replace the Imperial calendar, the official timekeeping method of the Pahlavi regime with quasi-historical ties to Cyrus the Great, with the Islamic calendar.

Ironically, the prime minister's exceptional unilateral action to appease the clerical opposition undid any last vestige of the regime's claim to legal legitimacy— that is, the belief in and adherence to the rule of law. Certainly, his actions did little to change the dynamics of the situation. If anything, they buoyed the religious nationalist opposition. When the protests reached new fervor during the month of Ramadan, Emami announced the wholesale ban on public demonstrations and established martial law in Tehran and eleven other cities.[4] Along with martial law, the administration imposed heavy restrictions on media. Newsrooms were informed of a new policy in which all journalists had to submit any domestic and foreign news stories to administration officials for clearance before going to print. Understanding the policy for what it was—censorship—journalists refused to abide and continued to strike. A number of major newspapers announced the decision to stop publication to protest the policy.[5]

The new media regime was short-lived, as Emami's resolve, or his hold on power, wavered under the continued pressure of public unrest and the non-compliance of some newsrooms and journalists. Just days after announcing the new oppressive media regime, Emami made a dramatic policy reversal, releasing a communiqué outlining a sweeping liberalization of press law and new, enhanced press freedoms. For a brief period, between October 15 and November 6, 1978, Iranian news media operated in remarkable freedom and were able to report on opposition protests and government failures without censorship. Instead of an information blackout, NIRT audiences were privy to graphic, unadulterated accounts of public dissent, regime brutality, and government forces unable to compel obedience.[6] Rather than creating more confidence and support for the government, the effect was to further erode the legitimacy of the Shah's regime.[7] Just two months after his appointment as prime minister, Emami announced his resignation.

On November 6, 1978, the Shah appointed General Gholam Reza Azhari to oversee the establishment of a martial governorship.[8] Azhari's first target was the state broadcasting monopoly, NIRT. The same day the military government was announced, the national television service in Tehran aired footage of deadly clashes between military forces and civilians at Tehran University. Early the next morning, soldiers and tanks converged on NIRT headquarters. The state television and radio monopoly was placed under military command and soldiers were deployed to oversee operations in its central headquarters.[9]

The military occupation came with a number of benefits. The most important was that it gave the martial government a hand on the spigot of information, images, videos, and news accounts. When NIRT reportage was deemed unhelpful to the mission, it was taken off the airwaves. When the content was deemed beneficial to mission, the military would afford it ample airtime. But military control of NIRT brought with it a new set of hazards and blowback. One of the most consequential was the tensions that it created between the soldiers and NIRT staff. These tensions came into the open little more than two weeks after troops first stepped foot on the NIRT campus.

On November 30, a group of soldiers tried to cut in front of a line of employees in the cafeteria. Fighting ensued. "Soldiers were beaten up, and troop reinforcements moved into NIRT, roughing up employees," read a then classified US intelligence account of the incident. The outcome was far from helpful for Azhari's government. Whether enraged or demoralized by the incident (perhaps both), NIRT workers walked out en masse and declared a general strike that was to last until December 17.[10] The strike joined a steady drum beat of government sector strikes throughout the country.

As the revolutionary fervor mounted on Tehran's streets, tensions within NIRT headquarters grew. The few remaining staff now joined the ranks of NIRT strikers.[11] The broadcaster's military overseers now found themselves under staffed, under resourced, and without the requisite technical expertise, forcing them to slash NIRT's broadcast schedule nationwide.[12]

The mounting information and public communication deficit introduced by the occupation of NIRT, the strike of NIRT workers, and the nationwide reduction of programming was compounded by the regime's concomitant closure of many newspapers. "The capital's press was paralyzed by censorship today and several journalists were arrested following the Army's restoration of order," Radio Tehran reported the day the military government was announced. "Sources here said military authorities had apparently banned publication of the newspapers until their content was satisfactory to officials."[13]

With the suppression of the print press and the imposition of content restrictions on national television and radio, foreign media filled the information vacuum. The BBC Persian Service, in particular, benefited from the absence of competitors inside Iran. Shahriar Radpur, who was a BBC Persian Service reporter during the revolution, attributed the service's marked increase in both content and listenership from 1978 to 1979 to the growing momentum of the opposition movement as well as the public relations acumen of the movement's leading activists:

> At this stage, there was a lot to report since the opposition was gathering momentum and they were contacting us in the BBC with news. It was not just the Islamic activists but also the National Front (*Jebheh-ye Melli-ye Iran*, founded by the embattled former prime minister Mohammad Mossadegh) and left activists of a variety of colors. They would call us daily giving us details of demonstrations, gatherings, and their political statements. So we had a lot to report.[14]

As Radpur's recollection suggests, opposition leaders understood the utility of foreign media coverage. In the absence of access to domestic outlets, the international press corps provided a means of disseminating information about what was going on inside the country, exerting pressure on the regime itself through public shaming. Influenced by opposition narratives spoon-fed to them through interviews and photo opportunities, such foreign press coverage poked holes in the Shah's carefully crafted image of father of the nation and hero of the people.[15] The multinational expatriate group the Confederation of Iranian Students, for example, used the Shah's trips to America and Europe as an opportunity to win headlines in the international media. The existence of international support for the cause only added to the enthusiasm of the people in their revolutionary mission.[16]

Foreign clandestine radio also filled the information vacuum created by the military government.[17] The Soviet-sponsored radio station the Voice of Iran used Soviet-controlled Azerbaijan as a base from which to broadcast anti-regime content into East Azerbaijan. The broadcasts built upon decades of activity to destabilize the regime through information warfare. The broadcasts began in the late 1950s and were regularly charged with socialist, nationalist, and anti-imperialist rhetoric. But as the opposition movement grew and began to take hold in the late 1970s, the somewhat veiled messages in opposition to the Shah turned into explicit calls for the overthrow of the regime.[18]

In sum, the evidence suggests that—contrary to the Shah's expectations—the imposition of military control in 1978 combined with public sector strikes and the intermittent suppression of the press undermined the authority and legitimacy of the Pahlavi regime and its military caretaker government. At the same time, the international press coverage helped amplify the voices of a number of leaders and groups within the popular opposition and set the stage for their claim to power when the revolution was successful.

Media and the Legitimation of Khomeini

While media worked to undermine the authority of the Pahlavi regime by propagating and amplifying images and symbols of popular dissent, it also helped create the impression of widespread consent to Khomeini as leader of the post-revolutionary government. The cleric's return to Iran on February 1, 1979, after fifteen years of exile was masterfully choreographed. Images and news accounts depicted a man of quite strength and pious asceticism returning home at long last. It told an overlapping story of a man of the people whose fiery speeches and revolutionary ideas inspired a downtrodden people to take back their country from a tyrannical ruler and his foreign overlords. Both stories about the man ended with the same historic scene—that of a single Muslim cleric enveloped in the passionate embrace of a massive, joyous crowd. It was a media moment like no other, and it helped secure Khomeini's place as leader-cum-savior of the Iranian nation. In the following paragraphs, I tell the media-centric story of the Ayatollah's return.

The Spectacle of the Ayatollah's Return

From his landing outside Tehran to his travel to Behesht Zahra Cemetery twenty miles away, Khomeini's appearance was ingeniously stage managed to give the maximum impression of popular support. More than one thousand people showed up at Mehrabad Airport where a privately chartered Air France Jet delivered from France Khomeini, a small contingent of supporters, and reportedly 150 members of the international press. On the tarmac, Khomeini gave a few remarks to reporters. He praised those who died and suffered in the revolution, blaming the bloodshed on the Shah and those who "destroyed our culture and turned it into a colonial culture." He spoke of the expansiveness of the opposition movement, from the clergy and bazaar merchants to workers and students, and lashed out at foreigners inside the country. This was not without irony given his domicile in Paris and undeniable embrace of the foreign press.[19]

Khomeini's first destination upon deplaning was Behesht Zahra Cemetery, the burial place of recent victims of the demonstrations. An estimated 5 million people greeted Khomeini. "So heavy was the crush of people along the route to the cemetery that Khomeini had to be airlifted from his motorcade and flown the last mile by helicopter," a *Time Magazine* correspondent observed. There, in Lot 17, Khomeini prayed and delivered a thirty-minute address, again blaming the Shah for the fatalities during the demonstrations. "Is it human rights," Khomeini asked the ebullient crowd, "when we say we want to name a government and we get a cemetery full of people?" After the speech, a boys' chorus sang: "May every drop of their blood turn to tulips and grow forever. Arise! Arise! Arise!"[20]

Khomeini's homecoming was the clearest signal yet of the public's overwhelming support for his leadership of the post-Pahlavi state. The newspaper of the National Front deemed the large-scale demonstrations against the Pahlavi regime on December 10, 1979, no less than a popular vote for Khomeini.[21] In its coverage of the event, the newspaper endowed the fiery cleric with the voice and will of an entire people: "Ayatollah al-uzma Imam Khomeini is the leader of the people; [his] wishes are the wishes of the entire people, and this march constitutes affirmation of the vote of confidence that has eagerly been given him several times over."[22] Contemporary accounts of the revolution similarly refer to the December 8–10 demonstrations as a "popular vote" for Khomeini, as if a mass demonstration could in and of itself constitute a legitimate conferral of sovereign authority from the people to Khomeini as the leader of the post-revolutionary state.

NIRT in the Battle for Power within the Opposition Movement

In the critical last months before Khomeini's return and the proclaimed victory of the revolution, the leadership of the various factions within the popular opposition movement took pains to display a united front against the Shah. Their profession of unity and alignment of values continued after the Shah fled and a provisional government was instated ahead of formal elections.

One faction of the opposition, the Marxist Tudeh, was largely sympathetic, even sycophantic, towards Khomeini and his religious-nationalist faction. In 1978 and early 1979, the Tudeh leadership announced their support for Khomeini as head of the new regime. In an attempt to highlight the groups' shared objective of improving the lot of the working class, they credited Khomeini with coining what was clearly a communist-socialist term: *mostaz'afin* (alternatively translated as the deprived, the downtrodden, the oppressed). The first secretary of the Tudeh Central Committee described the group's mission as "fundamentally changing for the better the living standards of millions of plundered people." The other components of the Tudeh platform were "eliminating the domination of imperialism in Iran; ending the murderous regime…[and] plundering, SAVAKist royal Pahlavi dynasty," and "procuring democracy for the people of Iran."[23]

Perhaps sensing the popular appeal of Khomeini as a Weberian-style charismatic leader, the leadership of the secular nationalist National Front and the Tudeh sought to minimize their political and ideological differences with Khomeini. These differences were in reality deep cleavages between and among the revolutionary opposition movement that deposed the Shah—cleavages that would become increasingly apparent in the tumultuous first year of the Islamic Republic. But in these early days, the leaders of the secular nationalist and Marxist groups chose not to contest the growing power of the seminary. Instead, they tolerated, and at crucial points publicly embraced, the Ayatollah and his activist clerics as part of the emerging power structure.

This tolerance and profession of unity yeilded a bitter bounty in the late summer and fall of 1979, as Khomeini's religious-nationalist faction moved to consolidate control over the government formation process. The unity witnessed during the revolution was quickly superseded by political infighting and factional warfare. While secular nationalist and socialist discourse tended to reflect a more sympathetic, even enthusiastic framing of political Islam earlier in the revolution, this dispensation changed as groups became increasingly convinced that they were being marginalized.

In late September 1979, the National Front published an open letter to the Iranian people denouncing Khomeini's emergent political order. The statement was particularly strong in its condemnation of the imposition of religious law, deeming the formation of special courts of "Islamic turban wearers" the first step in the creation of a "religious elitist oligarchy."[24] It warned of a future Iran in which a "religious clique" exercised "supreme" civil, religious, and legal authority.[25] Similarly, in a press conference on October 8, the leaders of the Tudeh Party charged that "a serious attack has been mounted by the right wing monopoly group in Iran to restrict freedoms," evidence of which was the "Kordestan incidents, and the banning of the newspaper *Mardom* and the attack on the Tudeh central club."[26] Both the National Front and Tudeh leadership warned the public that recent political developments were taking the country down the path of dictatorship. They were well on the way to establishing a new oligarchy in which a religious minority enjoyed a monopoly on governmental power. The National Front's argument was this: while the religious community should be able to participate in politics, it should not be allowed to "monopolize all regulations and laws in the name of religion and to reject or exclude any matter which does not [fall] within the framework of religion or runs counter to the lofty meaning of Islam." To be allowed to do so, the Front argued, would result in "government becoming the monopoly of the religious elements, with the creation of a religious elite."[27]

Despite these complaints, the work of creating a new class of 'clerical elites' continued. A new constitution was drafted that would institutionalize and codify much of Khomeni's vision into law. The constitution was ratified by popular vote on December 2 and 3, 1979. While what lies within the pages of text is important, it is equally important to examine the months leading up to the vote and soon after. In the following pages, I explore one piece of that story. It is a media-centric look at a major fracture from within religious community.

Resistance from Within

While outside factions spoke out in opposition to the emergent order, it was arguably the public dissent from within the religious establishment that posed a more serious threat. The resistance came in the form of public dissent of Grand Ayatollah Kazem Shari'atmadari and his followers in Tabriz. Shari'atmadari was a longtime ally of Khomeini and played a key role in mobilizing the opposition movement within Iran against the Shah and in support of the soon to be Supreme Leader in exile. In the soot and embers of the victorious revolution, however, the two men came into disagreement about the fundamentals of the new state. Grand Ayatollah Shari'atmadari had long indicated his concern about the concept of absolute rule championed by Khomeini and his followers. A leading *marja'e taqlid* (or *marja* for short, translated as "source of emulation"), Shari'atmadari opposed Khomeini's interpretation of *velayat-e faqih* as an organizing theory of Islamic government in the modern state. Instead, he envisioned a governing system in which *'ulama* (religious scholars; clerics) played a minimal role except on legal issues and questions directly related to Islam. He had deep concerns about the draft Constitution as it would codify Khamenei's unorthodox vision of *velayat-e faqih* and establish a clerical ruling class that would operate outside and above civil government and its laws and oversight mechanisms. His increasing outspokenness shattered the facade of consensus within the seminary.[28]

Shari'atmadari group, the Muslim People's Republic Party (*Hezb-e Jomhuri-ye Kalq-e Mosalman-e Iran*, or MPRP) criticized what it saw as the religious establishment's rising monopolization of power in Tehran. It complained about its expropriation of the state media broadcaster, calling its products "totally one-sided and biased propaganda," and criticizing it for "improper and discriminatory use of radio and television."

In his classic book on the revolution, *The Turban for the Crown*, Said Amir Arjomand points to the irony of the criticism, which took aim at the religious establishment headed by Khomeini without identifying anyone specifically. Not only did it not identify the persons behind the censorship and persecution, it denied that Khomeini was responsible. "The insurrectionists wanted the director of the National Radio and Television Network executed because of the vicious censorship he imposed," writes Arjomand, "they wanted the dictatorial constitution repealed, but Khomeini, they said, was their Imam!"[29]

On 2 December 1979, Shari'atmadari spoke out against the constitution as championed by Khomeini. Calling the document legally incoherent and contradictory, he signaled his (and therefore his followers') intention to abstain from participation in the referendum vote. Likely in retribution for his outcry, the Grand Ayatollah was the target of a failed assassination plot on 5 December. The attack on the cleric in his home in Qom did the opposite of the aggressor's intention. The MPRP redoubled their resistance activities. Rallying behind their marja in opposition to the constitution, they organized demonstrations and general strikes throughout Tabriz.[30]

Soon after, members of the MPRP took control of a number of government buildings, including, significantly, the provincial headquarters of the national radio and television service.[31] The occupation (and use) of the station became an important part of Shari'atmadari final push for the realization of his more democratic and religiously orthodox vision for the new Iranian state and his party's mission to broaden their base of support beyond their religious constituency. On December 7, MPRP used the station to broadcast what would become a series of last ditch appeals for unity against the rapidly consolidating Khomeini government in Tehran. In it, Shari'atmadari called on the National Front and all who wanted democratic governance to join him in opposition to Khomeini and his flawed constitution.[32] The message was broadcast three times on the Tabriz radio station, but to little avail.[33]

On December 8, the group again used its occupation of the regional headquarters to mass communicate its appeal for support and collaboration. This time the broadcast came in the form of an open letter to the regional government. Claiming to represent the sentiment of the majority of the population of Tabriz and Azerbaijan, the letter demanded that the "inadequate and flawed Constitution … be revised and amended as soon as possible." The authors took responsibility for the Tabriz unrest and the seizure of the provincial NIRT headquarters and rejected the assertion made by Soviet-linked clandestine radio, the Tudeh, and Khomeini's lieutenants that the unrest was the work of foreign conspirators.[34]

The action received a rapid, decisive response from Tehran. In a speech to the national television and broadcasting organization the next day, Khomeini called the events in Tabriz an "uprising against Islam," and "deserving of punishment of great magnitude."[35] The same day, armed guerillas descended upon the Tabriz radio and television station and forcibly removed the occupiers, thus eliminating an important means of mass communication for the religious democratic movement.[36]

Soon after, Shari'atmadari issued a statement withdrawing his criticism of the new constitution and the new order it created and signaled he would no longer support the MPRP and its demonstrations of dissent. The motivation for his decision is unclear. Saeid Saffari suggests that he called a halt to the resistance movement in Tabriz because he feared that the fighting would get out of control and could jeopardize the success of the religious government.[37] Mohsen Milani connects the Grand Ayatollah's choice to the slander against him and his organization, which, Shari'atmadari explained, was a tactic applied to other factions of the revolution as well. "And the point that I should tell you, dear gentlemen, is that with the current policy of the regime, by labeling political parties as American, Zionist, and un-Islamic, will gradually dissolve all of them." Another hypothesis is that he was cowed by the threat of violence against him and his loved ones. What is clear, regardless, is that Shari'atmadari paid dearly for his public dissent. He was put into what amounted to house arrest and found his authority as a religious leader under systematic assault. The defamation campaign reached its pinnacle in 1982, when a number of leading seminarians from Qom, apparently under the encouragement, if not direction, of the Supreme Leader, issued a *fatwa* (religious edict) rescinding his title of marja.[38]

But the systematic assault did not stop there. The regime made a concerted effort to erase the collective memory of Shari'atmadari including his critical role in putting Khomeini in power by building the religious opposition movement within Iran while Khomeini remained in exile, as well as his criticism of *Velayat-e Faqih* and the Tabriz resistance movement he headed. In the place of this true history, the regime constructed an alternative history of the man and his works. Today one can find an abundance of material—articles, reenactments, documentaries, even published and bound "historical documents"—detailing Shari'atmadari anti-revolutionary activity and political subterfuge.[39]

But the ayatollah's co-revolutionaries suffered far worst fates. Those deemed a threat to the realization of the new regime were purged from government and other stations of influence. Secular nationalists, socialists, and communists were systematically repressed and persecuted. Even individuals with demonstrated revolutionary credentials did not escape persecution. Far from it.[40]

The experience of the Reza'i family is an example of such treatment. When Mr. and Mrs. Reza'i learned that their children, both members of the *Mojahedin-e Khalq* (MEK), had been arrested, they issued a statement to the press appealing for their release. Their children were loyal revolutionaries, the Reza'i family argued. The statement went on to summon their children's participation in an assassination plot targeting "two American advisors" as evidence of their allegiance. Although the family most likely knew that their children had been imprisoned by Khomeini loyalists, they understood that to say so would be counterproductive, even deadly. Instead, they blamed "some monopolistic gentlemen who have based their power on the blood of the martyrs since the start of the revolution," thus providing a measure of political cover for their children's captors should they decide to release them. While the fate of the young Marxist revolutionaries is unknown, they may have been among the many victims of Khomeini's bloody push to consolidate power. One estimate put the number of MEK activists imprisoned at 800 with another 198 killed by execution or other causes while detained.[41]

From National Radio and Television to Voice and Vision of the Islamic Republic

On February 11, 1979, in what the official history has deemed the "most important conquest of the revolution," revolutionaries aligned with Khomeini's religious nationalist faction seized control of NIRT headquarters, and with it, control of all Tehran-based broadcast operations (Figure 1). The building had been under military occupation for a number of weeks.[42] Many NIRT employees who had been on strike participated in the seizure. One such worker, Mirali Hosseini, took to the airwaves to announce the opposition's victory at six o'clock that evening.[43] The primetime broadcast was accompanied by footage taken earlier that day of military tanks leaving NIRT headquarters. Not without irony, the national television and radio agency that was created by the Pahlavi state now exuberantly proclaimed its demise. "This is the voice of Tehran, the voice of true Iran, the voice of revolution," Hosseini said.[44] If it was indeed orchestrated by Khomeini's supporters as suggested in the official literature, it was an ingenious move, and arguably instrumental to his rapid consolidation of power.[45]

Khomeini's views of the organization and the role of media, and television and radio in particular, were articulated during the revolution and throughout his time as Supreme Leader. In 1984, his remarks were collected and published in a book entitled

Figure 1 Capture of National Iranian Radio and Television by Iranian revolutionaries.
Source: AP/Herve Merliac.

Seda va Sima dar Kalam-e Emam Khomeini (*Radio and Television in the Words of Imam Khomeini*). Khomeini emphasized the importance of radio and television above all other communication mediums. He considered the state monopoly broadcaster to be a central means through which Iranians could achieve spiritual enlightenment, as well as cultural and economic independence from the West:

> The importance of radio and television is more than any other media … This apparatus must be such that after a couple of years it makes the nation well-informed; fosters them to be combative, reflective, independent, and free-natured. It should send them out of Westoxification and give people independence.[46]

Ratified by popular vote in December 1979, the Constitution of the Islamic Republic placed the "mass communication media" at the center of the new nation-state. In its preamble statement, the Constitution established the primacy of media in the durability of the revolutionary project through the ages:

> The mass communication media, radio and television, must serve the diffusion of Islamic culture in pursuit of the evolutionary course of the Islamic Revolution. To this end, the media should be used as a forum for the healthy encounter of different ideas, but they must strictly refrain from diffusion and propagation of destructive and anti-Islamic practices.[47]

The national television and radio service was renamed "Voice and Vision of Islamic Republic."[48] Sadegh Ghotbzadeh, a Khomeini aide who had joined the exiled leader in Paris, was picked to head the organization. A proven loyalist, Ghotbzadeh used his first televised appearance to announce his intentions for the agency. He pledged to make television a forum for the common man, the "barefoot people" who made the revolution possible, and not the voice of government.[49]

While Khomeini formally announced the militant Islamization of Iranian universities by his intellectual devotees—what they called a "cultural revolution"—on March 21, 1979, Ghotbzadeh's work began months earlier, with the "cleansing" of the state broadcasting agency.[50] Among his first acts was to purge a number of NIRT executives, producers, and managers from the organization.[51] The forcible removal or retirement of NIRT employees was pursued irrespective of the individual's support for the revolution. Indeed, there appears to have been strong support for Khomeini and the opposition movement within the agency, as indicated by the fact that broadcasting was shut down or severally limited when NIRT staff joined other government workers in what amounted to nearly three months of strikes.[52]

The content of television and radio programs also came under scrutiny. Shows made by the West were at first completely removed, and later highly restricted and selected based on adherence to Islamic morals. "Television was becoming more and more a broadcasting pulpit," write media scholars Sreberny and Mohammadi, who were eyewitnesses to the events. "The style of programming was quickly Islamized …. the screen was dominated by turbaned talking heads who, in the best clerical style, could sermonize for hours."[53] In the seminal months following the seizure of NIRT headquarters, state television underwent a major aesthetic transformation.[54]

That Khomeini would seek to conquer every aspect of television, from its institutions to its content, is further evidence of the media–ideology–hegemony nexus. Still, this new broadcasting style can only be partially explained by the message of religiosity and material asceticism that Ghotbzadeh and the new clerical administration sought to convey.[55] It may also be attributed to the highly reduced technical capacity and management expertise that resulted from the dismissal of at least 179 NIRT employees by a "purification committee" (komite-ye paksazi) in August 1979.[56] Many NIRT workers left without waiting for forcible removal.[57] Others, including the head of public affairs and news analysis, Parviz Nik'khah and the first deputy director of political affairs and head of Pars News Agency, Mahmud Jafarian, were executed in February 1979.[58]

Ghotbzadeh was able to affect a number of changes to the organization during his tenure. He oversaw the rebranding of NIRT to Islamic Republic of Iran Broadcasting (IRIB), for instance, and cut and dismantled several subdivisions and research projects. Yet despite these cosmetic changes, his effectiveness as a reformer and advocate for the "barefoot people" was limited. Significantly, he failed to address the issue at the heart of opposition criticism of state television and radio during the revolution: the predominance of Western, "un- Islamic" programs and themes. In the absence of domestically produced content, Ghotbzadeh was forced to use some Western content. Too often, such content he believed to be morally appropriate contained what his critics deemed immodest scenes. In one such instance, the broadcast was unceremoniously cut off, and the television went blank.[59] For this reason, Ghotbzadeh came under increasing criticism from Khomeini supporters inside and outside the establishment elite.[60] Ghotbzadeh also came into conflict with the broadcaster's professional staff, who were dismayed by the rapid changes to the organization under the new, inexperienced management.[61]

The Closure of Newspapers and "Islamization" of Government Agencies

Upon his homecoming, Khomeini and his followers immediately set to work establishing control over the print press. The newspaper *Ettellaʿat* carried a front-page report that the interim government had ordered the closure of forty-one newspapers and magazines across the country.[62] The paper also published a list of eleven additional publications slated for closure by the prosecutor's office for being "against Islam." All of the newspapers cited were organs of political groups, mostly socialist or communist, although one student' and two women's union papers were also closed.[63] A new press law was passed with little debate.

A full blown effort to remove the remaining vestiges of the Shah's leadership circle and all government employees that might be loyal to him began in March. The work reached new heights following the electoral success of Khomeini's Islamic Republic Party (*Hezb-e Jomhuri-ye Eslami*, IRP) in the Majles in August. By that time, over 150 purge committees were in operation; the purges were particularly extensive in the military and the Ministry of Education.⁶⁴ Even IRIB did not escape their deleterious hand. Indeed, the criticism of Ghotbzadeh for airing "Islamic" content appears to have caught up with him, as, following a brief period of dual leadership with Mohammad Hashemi Rafsanjani, Ghotbzadeh was relieved of his post. In 1981, Hashemi Rafsanjani, a Khomeini loyalist, was made director.⁶⁵

If the publicity skills of Khomeini's dedicated followers were not evident in the spectacle of the Ayatollah's return, it was made abundantly clear months later, with the seizure of the American embassy on November 4, 1979. The hostage crisis was significant both for the politics of the time and for its imprint on the future. In the following section, I discuss the communication aspects of the event as it unfolded. In this drama-filled, internationally covered media event, we see a perceived inversion of power between the United States and Iran.

The US-Iran Hostage Crisis

When they climbed over the walls and broke down the gate of the US embassy in Tehran, it was hard to imagine that the 300 or so young militant Islamist nationalists calling themselves Muslim Students Following the Line of the Imam (*Daneshjuyan-e Peyrov-e Khatt-e Emam*) would occupy the embassy and hold its inhabitants' captive for 444 days. The actual conquest of the building was relatively easy. Most of the embassy's occupants had been evacuated. The skeleton crew of diplomats and support staff that remained greeted their captors with a calm obedience derived from the belief that the incident would follow the example of the prior embassy seizure on February 14 by the leftist MEK which ended diplomatically within days.⁶⁶ But the situation now, eight months later, was very different. The building of the new Islamic Republic was in full swing. Despite this progress, one problem had yet to be resolved in the minds of many of Khomeini's most ardent followers: the Shah had not been brought to justice, and it was the United States standing in the way.

Weeks earlier, the Carter administration had reluctantly accepted the Shah's request to enter the country for medical treatment. The deposed monarch had been receiving treatment for lymphocytic cancer for more than a year and his condition had deteriorated such that his doctors felt that he needed the expert medical attention that only the United States could provide. Outraged by the Americans' refusal to extradite Pahlavi and bent on punishing America and pleasing their spiritual leader, Khomeini, the militant student group plotted and executed the invasion of the embassy.

The Den of Spies

In addition to the immediate grievance of America protecting the Shah, the students were driven by the conviction that the embassy was a "den of spies," that must be exposed and eliminated. Like much of the conspiratorial discourse that grew up in the shadow of the 1953 coup, there was a kernel of truth to the claim. From the 1950s onward, the US embassy in Tehran served as a major base for American intelligence collection. It was from the two-story building on Taleqani Street that CIA operatives, under the guise of diplomats, collected information about Iranian citizens and revolutionaries.⁶⁷ The young revolutionaries scoured embassy offices and supply rooms for documents that would confirm their suspicions.⁶⁸ They found buckets of papers that had been shredded but not burned by officials and operatives in the dash to evacuate. They painstakingly reconstructed the documents, taping piece by shredded piece together while making public pronouncements about the espionage and treachery the pages contained. These meticulously reconstructed documents were later published in seventy-seven volumes (Figure 2).⁶⁹

Most scholars agree that Khomeini did not plan the embassy seizure and may not have been notified of the intentions of the assailants in advance. But as time progressed, Khomeini clearly saw the benefit that a prolonged stand-off with the United States would have for his cause, and watched—and later directed—what quickly became a made-for-TV spectacle.

The student group announced their intention to continue to hold the embassy and the beleaguered diplomatic staff inside before a gaggle of international press. Later, they paraded their captives, blindfolded and with hands bound, in front of television cameras broadcasting live. Infused with symbols of conquest and piety, such mass mediated displays spoke to the world of the significance of the Islamic Revolution and its triumph over America. But the embassy seizure bore another message as

Figure 2 Paper shredder with piles of shredded classified documents left behind by US embassy staff in their rush to evacuate. Normally such files would be shredded and then burned.
Source: Author's personal archive.

well—that the Iranian revolution was an international movement of the oppressed (*mostaz'afin*) against the oppressors (*mostakberin*).⁷⁰ Soon after the initial hostage taking, the captors announced in front of the cameras that they were releasing women and African American embassy staff. It was another theatrical act, likely ordered by Khomeini himself, intended to display to domestic and international audiences Iran's new role as a liberator and champion of oppressed people of the world.

Of course, the significance of the event was different for different audiences. For the domestic audience—Iranians who watched the events on television and followed them on the radio and in newspapers—it demonstrated the power of the militant Islamist faction of the revolution. It signaled that by following Khomeini and his vision of an Islamic government, Iran could triumph over the "Great Satan," humiliate it on the global stage, and claim a degree of revenge for decades under its thumb. For the international audience, the spectacle signaled that the Islamic revolution was powerful and would not break under the pressure of foreign powers. Most important, though, was the message it sent to the American people and government: the era of US hegemony in Iran was over and the US–Iran relationship was severed.

The dramatic failure of Operation Eagle Claw, the secret mission President Carter deployed to rescue the hostages, only sharpened the impression of Khomeini's omnipotence and America's impotence. The rescue mission was aborted after a helicopter loaded with special operations forces got caught in a sandstorm causing it to malfunction and veer into an accompanying transport plane.⁷¹ The collision killed eight servicemen and scattered survivors and wreckage across the Iranian desert.⁷²

The image of Khomeini's power was reinforced when, after negotiations to resolve the crisis through Algerian intermediaries were successful, Iran released the hostages on January 20, 1981. The Iranians clearly staged the release of the fifty-two captives to occur on the very day—indeed, the very hour—of the inauguration of Ronald Reagan as president, thus denying Carter the ability to claim credit for ending the crisis under his tenure. Describing "the incredible manipulation of this day in history," anchor Ted Koppel chronicled Carter's last, agonized efforts to secure the return of the hostages in detail on Nightline.⁷³

The mass-mediated release of the hostages added to the impression established by the hostage taking, suggesting that Khomeini had the power to decide the outcome of the US presidential election, bringing down one president and bringing another one into power. While that is an exaggeration of the truth, Carter's continued failure to free the hostages was indeed seen as contributing to his failure to win reelection.⁷⁴ The release of the hostages in exchange for a ransom of $3 billion and immunity from prosecution was further evidence of Khomeini's power and the potential of the revolution to upend the international order by challenging the dominance of world powers. The message communicated throughout Iran was that Imam Khomeini, under the blessing of Allah, had brought America to its knees. It was a masterfully orchestrated ending to a high-stakes, mass-mediated international relations crisis and an important political victory for the newly anointed Supreme Leader facing what would arguably be the greatest, most persistent challenge of his tenure: war with Iraq.

The Iran–Iraq War

War colored the first decade of the Islamic Republic. Referred to as the "imposed war" (*jang-e tahmili*) by the Iranian state and many of its citizens, the war between Iran and Iraq has been called the longest conventional war of the twentieth century.[75] It commenced with the Iraqi invasion of Iran on September 22, 1980, and ended with the bilateral acceptance of UN Security Council Resolution 598 on July 20, 1988.

This book is designed to investigate a number of inflection points in Iranian media history, where an inflection point may be understood as a fundamental disruption to the dominant media system. While the war catalyzed innovation in cinematic representations of the battlefront and everyday life, it did not feature the type of system level technological communicative disruption that is at interest in this study. For this reason, I will touch only briefly upon the media during the Iran–Iraq war.[76]

While the monetary and human costs of the war for the Iranian nation remain the subject of dispute among historians, the impact of the war on the media industry is more readily observed. The imperatives of a war-time economy retarded the advancement of the state broadcast monopoly and prevented new communication technologies from gaining a foothold. Despite the barrage of Iraqi radio broadcasting from outside Iran, the state maintained its dominance of the industry from within.

The institutional structure of television and radio service under the revolutionary government was a facsimile of the institutional structure of NIRT under Mohammad Reza Pahlavi. The educational mandate of IRIB was also the same. Under Khomeini's political philosophy, radio, television, and cinema were to serve a pedagogic purpose: to educate the people toward forming a virtuous society.[77]

While mass communication remained an important aspect of state power, "small" media—such as wartime posters, headbands, murals, and billboards—appear to have been the preferred mode of ideology transmission during the war. Visual artistry and sloganeering rather than television and radio absorbed the majority of the attention of the nation's culture officials. Television and radio broadcasting joined print media and murals in a traditional propaganda capacity. Such media was aimed at motivating and mobilizing Iranian soldiers and their families to rally to the "holy defense" (*defa'-e moqaddas*) and to overlook or accept the deteriorating economic conditions caused by war, international isolation, and embargo.[78] All in all, the enterprise of mass communication during the Iran–Iraq war was relatively static. If anything, the conflict worked to reinforce the prerevolutionary media system in which the state enjoyed exclusive access to, and dominion over, the industry.

Part II

A Different Sort of War: The Crisis of Satellite TV

3

PRELUDE TO A CRISIS

> The satellite is the West's weapon against Islam. They say this themselves. It is a weapon for them because the guns have fallen silent now. Today's war is different, today's war is over thought; war today is stealing hearts and minds.
> —Ayatollah Mohammad Emami Kashani, 1995[1]

In 1988, a UN-brokered ceasefire gave way to the formal end of the Iran's war with Iraq. The Supreme Leader grew ill soon after. When the charismatic founder of the Islamic Republic died on June 3, 1989, the political elite moved quickly to fill the leadership vacuum. The morning after his death, the Assembly of Experts met and elected Sayyed Ali Khamenei as successor, conferring on him all of Khomeini's titles and honors except the title of Imam. Little more than a month later, the people elected Ali Akbar Hashemi Rafsanjani as the fourth president of the Islamic Republic.[2] The ballot also included a referendum on a number of amendments to the Constitution. The amendments were overwhelmingly approved.

One of the amendments passed through the referendum was to Article 5, which assigned oversight of Islamic Republic of Iran Broadcasting (IRIB), also known as Voice and Vision of the Islamic Republic of Iran (*Seda va Sima-ye Jomhuri-ye Eslami-ye Iran*), and the appointment of its director to the supervisory body, the Voice and Vision Policy Making Council. Like the supervisory council before it under Pahlavi, the council had representatives from all three branches of government.[3] The amendment to Article 5 eliminated the body and placed IRIB under the singular remit of the Office of the Supreme Leader. Khamenei was given full command of IRIB, with the power to hire and fire its leadership and make decisions on its editorial policy.

That August, the Supreme Leader reappointed President Rafsanjani's brother, Mohammad Hashemi Rafsanjani (henceforth Hashemi) as general director of the state radio and television service. Hashemi had served in the position throughout the war period, beginning in 1981. In his letter of appointment, Khamenei reaffirmed Khomeini's vision of IRIB as a "public university ... responsible for the intellectual, cultural, and political growth of the nation." He urged Hashemi to go "on the offensive" against foreign propaganda.[4] He continued:

> The Voice and Vision should, through the presentation of our original, pure and rich culture, ideas, and art, promote and strengthen the ideological and practical independence of Iran, the systems of the Islamic Republic, and the principle of

neither East nor West. It should adopt a confrontational posture in the face of alien and imposed culture, art, and ideology.[5]

Khamenei also recognized, though indirectly, that audience preference should inform decisions regarding programming as well as any future improvements to the state broadcaster. He directed Hashemi to create "a research center to monitor and study the people's opinion on programs."[6]

The letter instructed Hashemi to develop content that appealed to Iranian youth, a booming population born under the ministrations of the wartime government. "I stress the importance of airing programs for the youths and teenagers, which in addition to having a sound foundation, should be interesting, healthy, and joyful," wrote Khamenei. He warned of the potential for programs to negatively influence malleable young minds. "In presenting and broadcasting [radio and television] it is necessary to avoid any subject that has a bad influence on their thinking and behavior so that this significant mass medium does not become a means of corruption and deviation."

Khamenei's concern for the nation's "youth" was well placed. Society had undergone significant demographic changes as a result of a major increase in birth rate throughout the 1980s. Over less than a decade, the size of the Iranian population effectively doubled. Official government census figures put the median age of the population in 1991 at just under eighteen years.[7]

The IRIB chief shared his brother's ideas about the role of IRIB in Iranian society. It was to serve as an "open university" catering to the "mental and psychological needs of society."[8] But Hashemi's vision for IRIB went beyond education and spiritual health to include news reporting, which he saw as a positive force in the country's development. Hashemi made this position clear at a meeting of bureau chiefs after his reappointment. It was important that IRIB programming compliment and reinforce the political and socioeconomic agenda of the state, Hashemi argued, and news reportage had an important role to play in "directing opinions and ideas" and creating "suitable incentives" in support of "reconstruction." It would encourage the growth of a politically developed populace, in part by exposing audiences to different viewpoints. A television or radio news item is more than simply a "political phenomenon," said Hashemi. Rather, it is a "comprehensive entity which can save society from viewing issues only from one angle and can prevent the occurrence of unrest."[9]

Hashemi's comments suggest an understanding of media as a potential agent for social progress, where information and news empower citizens to be more committed to the regime and less disposed to dissent and unrest. It points to the benefit of a common vision or understanding of "facts on the ground" not dissimilar to the Marxist *weltanschauung*, or worldview.

The Majles-Hashemi Stand-off

The Supreme Leader's 1989 warning about the potential for radio and television to become a source of "corruption" and religious and ideological "deviation" proved prescient, as discontent with IRIB grew in the years to come.[10] At first intermittent and indirect, the critiques steadily increased and ultimately spilled out from the seminary to the Majles and onto newspaper pages and radio and television airwaves.

Criticism of IRIB appears to have begun within the religious conservative faction aligned with Khamenei. In a sermon to worshipers in Qom in February 1990, Ayatollah Ali Meshkini took aim at the state broadcaster for "sensual" programs that were "making religious people unhappy." In a veiled reference to IRIB director Hashemi, Meshkini called on the "nation's high officials who supervise the Voice and Vision to resolve the problem with these people."[11] The Friday prayer leader described the current environment as one in which the greatest threat to the revolution and Islam came from the "deviated culture of the West." In this new security paradigm, cultural, spiritual, and material corruption replaced martial force as the preferred method of war against Iran. "The enemy has despaired of military measures," Meshkini told his congregants, "and they have taken up another path."[12]

> They are making harmful tapes and photographs, along with harmful narcotics and clothing, and spreading them among the youth. History shows that if a nation cannot win militarily, it will then seek victory through corruption. Take care and do not allow the enemy to get into the schools. The danger of an ordinary photograph or tape is no less than a kilogram of heroin.[13]

Ahmad Khomeini similarly decried the programs aired on IRIB and was even more explicit:

> One day everyone suddenly turns against radio and television and asks: why are they not doing anything? Radio and television propagate Western thoughts and air trite films. Everyone agrees ... the officials of Voice and Vision of the Islamic Republic of Iran should be asked to organize radio and television discussions to answer questions on why such films are shown and repeated.[14]

Members of the Majles launched a formal investigation. The Commission for Cultural and Islamic Guidance Affairs produced a 270-page report on the state of the national radio and television service which it presented to parliament in November 1993.[15] While the report analyzed everything from programming and content to finance, accounting, management, and staff, the television service and its Western-influenced programs was at the heart of the inquiry.[16]

The Majles investigation of IRIB coincided with Hashemi's unveiling of a dedicated leisure channel in December 1993. The mission of the new channel, Network 3, was to protect youth from "social disease" and to "create the appropriate conditions for the productive use of leisure time." President Rafsanjani endorsed the new leisure television network and presided over the opening ceremony in December. The president called the project "constructive ideological work" and praised the channel for "filling the people's leisure time in a constructive and effective way."[17] By all indications, the new channel was a core component of Hashemi's campaign to revitalize the ailing broadcaster and make it more palatable to young viewers amid an increasingly competitive and diverse media environment. It came alongside similar reforms to the IRIB radio service. A few months earlier, IRIB announced the expansion of the external radio service. It increased foreign-language broadcasts from twelve to eighteen languages and doubled its broadcast output from 540 to 1080 hours. The deputy chief of the Provincial Affairs Department of IRIB described the increase as an effort to build Iran's "international image to confront the West's cultural onslaught."[18]

Hashemi's efforts, as well as the backlash against them, occurred amidst a mounting stream of foreign broadcasting into Iran via satellite.[19] Satellite dishes increased public access to alternative sources of news and entertainment. Iranians had more choice than ever before; those with access to satellite dish receivers could choose from up to fifteen free, largely entertainment-focused foreign satellite channels. IRIB was in jeopardy of losing its audience.[20]

By all indications, Hashemi was well aware of the threat that changing global technology standards and the entry of foreign satellite television posed to the state mass communications monopoly. His remarks in an interview at a Qom seminary in March 1990 are particularly telling:

> Moderator: It has been said that the United States is about to broadcast television programs to Iran and the Middle East. If so, what action has been taken?
>
> Hashemi: The United States is already broadcasting these programs, not only in the Middle East but all over the world. Technically speaking [the broadcasts] can be received using the advanced equipment now existing in the communication company [IRIB] or the Foreign Ministry, and on certain occasions they are received... The world is moving toward DBS, that is the direct satellite service system. It broadcasts the programs via satellite to anyone able to receive them... This means that the international borders now existing for the airwaves will be removed.[21]

Here, Hashemi acknowledged both the existence of the US government's broadcasting into Iran and the fact that IRIB as well as other government agencies had satellite television. His remarks suggest a deeper comprehension of the ramifications of Direct Broadcast Satellite for the state monopoly broadcaster and the globalizing power of communication technologies.

The Majles Report on IRIB

The Majles committee report can be summarized into three major criticisms of IRIB: ineffective communication of ideology, an abundance of Western content, and improper veiling and relations between the sexes. Each of these criticisms, as well as the IRIB response, are examined here.

Foremost in the committee's list of complaints against the IRIB was that it failed to effectively communicate the ideology of the Islamic Republic.[22] It found that 95 percent of Network 1 programs related to Islam and the revolution took the form of direct messages such as the recitation of reports and news, prayers, speeches, and lectures, with no programming in the form of films and serials.[23] The committee's examination of Network 2 produced similar findings. "[P]rograms related to Islam and revolution are produced 98 percent as direct messages, that is, at low cost and ineffectively, whereas programs indifferent, neutral, and even deviant to Islam are higher in quality, attractiveness, and effectiveness." The report found that between 1985 and 1992, the share of Islamic programs decreased by 17 percent. Serials unrelated to Islam were largely Western produced (79 percent), but perhaps more worrying for the report's authors, 21 percent of the non-Islamic content was Iranian made. It concluded that the IRIB was using precious resources to produce content that was neither Islamic nor ideological. "Despite the storming cultural invasion of the enemy, television does not have the power to produce films and serials in defense of Islam."

Moreover, the report argued that the few films and serials which the IRIB did produce were expensive and not properly vetted from the outset. This meant that full scale productions required significant retroactive cuts to remove un-Islamic content. They were then aired in a choppy, abbreviated form.[24] The television show *Crocodile Tears* was a case in point. The serial was "produced at an incredible cost, but because of certain problems of deviation, many parts of it are cut out," the report's authors lamented. "But even parts that are shown are the target of widespread protest by the people."[25]

IRIB did not take the criticism lightly. On the contrary, it posted a vigorous defense. In a formal response to the charges, IRIB representatives called the impartiality of the investigative committee members into question. They also attacked the substance of allegations, rejecting the premise that the series *Crocodile Tears* promoted Western values and was a source of moral and ideological "deviation." On the contrary, the show was "against liberals and the agents of the United States and was approved by the late Imam." The IRIB response explained that the programs fell into one of three operational buckets: guiding-instructional, information-educational, and entertainment-recreational. *Crocodile Tears* had a guiding-instructional function.[26]

A second major charge of the Majles report was that state radio and television—television, in particular—carried an abundance of "Western-"produced content and a small percentage of inferior, domestically produced content. Comparative analysis of the thematic content composition of Network 1 in 1363 and 1370 (in the Gregorian calendar 1984/1985 and 1991/1992, respectively) showed that in 1363, Iranian-produced serials comprised 14 percent of the content. That ratio decreased to 11.5 percent in 1370. Foreign films and serials comprised 24 percent and increased to 38 percent in the same time periods respectively. The report continued, "while Voice and Vision is more than 14 years old, our young people benefit 75 percent of the time from foreign culture and 25 percent from our own culture."[27]

IRIB disputed the report's findings regarding the ratio of foreign-to-domestic-produced content. It argued that, in fact, the opposite was true: the majority of IRIB content was Iranian made, with foreign programs only comprising 14 percent of all radio and television broadcasts. Of the foreign content broadcast, the majority was not "Western" in origin, but rather originated from Japan, China, and "Muslim" countries. It cited insufficient budgetary resources as justification for use of foreign content, arguing that IRIB's limited finances encumbered production of indigenous, high-quality programming. "The budget shortage ... created numerous problems for the organization. Among them, we can point to the lack of resources for production of serious programs, the creation of obligations and large financial debts, the lack of maximal use of studios and transmitters, deterioration of equipment, etc."

Indeed, the budget for the broadcaster decreased significantly immediately following the revolution and roughly corresponding to the war with Iraq. According to IRIB, the majority (75 percent) of the organization's budget went to employee payroll, with the remaining 25 percent allocated to a variety of activities, including program production and equipment repair and maintenance. The comparative increase in the IRIB budget from 1991 to 1992 did not result in an increase in program production or improvement of program quality. Rather, the additional funds were allocated to support the expansion of the hours and reach of existing television and radio service (Figure 3).

The third major complaint of the Majles investigative committee dealt with women and sexuality. The report repeatedly raised the issue of television programs encouraging "improper veiling" and acceptance of Western-style relationships between genders, especially among children. "By showing coeducational schools and very normal relationships between boys and girls in these schools, Iranian pre-collegiate men and women who have been prohibited from having relationships

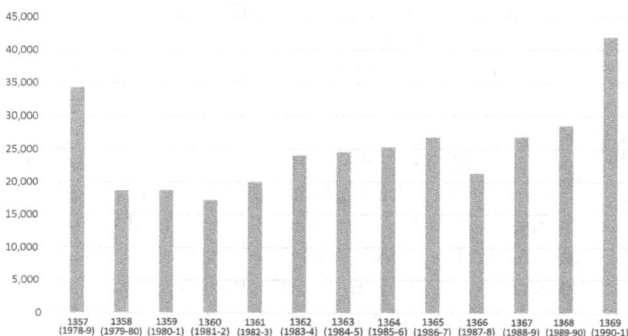

Figure 3 *Ratified Budget in Millions of Rials, FY 1357–69 (1978–91).* In Iran, the fiscal year usually starts on the 1st of Farvardin and concludes on the 29th or 30th of Esfand in the Jalali calendar which translates to March 20 or 21st on the Georgian calendar. The data for 1357 is the budget of the incumbent, NIRT. The Gregorian year is indicated in parenthesis.
Source: *Jomhuri ye Eslami.*

with the opposite sex begin to contemplate doing so." The authors describe a downward spiral like that of a gateway drug user becoming a heroin addict:

> Intrigued, they take a position against Islam, which prohibits such a relationship and becomes inclined towards Western culture. They become disinterested in veiling. The Islamic regime becomes condemned in their minds and their personality is formed in a manner that prepares the ground for rejecting divine Islamic values and accepting decadent Western values.[28]

The IRIB response sought to neutralize this criticism by appealing to the authority of the late Supreme Leader. It cited at length Khomeini's response to a letter from Esma'il Ferdosipur, a member of the Voice and Vision Supervisory Council, on 29 Azar 1366 (December 20, 1987) regarding constituent concerns that Western films carried on state television promoted a culture of deviance and improper veiling. The Imam responded:

> Watching such films is not a problem from a religious standpoint and many of them are instructional and their broadcast is no problem. Also, sports films or music are mostly no problem. Sometimes, violations can be seen, rarely, and more care must be taken.[29]

The IRIB response also took issue with the investigating committee's definition of what constituted proper Islamic dress: "Islamic cover is not only the *chador* (a semicircular cloak, usually black, enveloping the head, body, and sometimes the face), but any covering for women on the basis of the standards of the sacred religious law," it maintained.

The Majles report on IRIB was both comprehensive and damning. Bereft of attractive, entertaining programs that captivated the audience and infused young minds with "Islamic" ideology, the broadcaster was failing its most fundamental charge: to propagate and protect the ruling ideology and to educate the masses. In fact, the television service did quite the opposite, the authors persisted. Its channels were saturated with Western programs that disseminated Western ideology and Western sexual mores at the expense of Islamic values and national unity. The circulation of and public preference for Western cultural products like television programs, music, and film was an immense, perhaps insurmountable challenge, one that would continue to plague IRIB through the decades.

New Leadership

The charge that IRIB was a purveyor of Western culture was a scarlet letter that no amount of refutation could erase. So widespread was this opinion among the establishment that the veracity of the original charge became inconsequential. The "truth" of the matter was set, and Hashemi no longer had the support of the establishment. In short, IRIB was suffering a crisis of public confidence. The consensus was that IRIB was failing its organizational mandate, and in so doing, failing the ideals of the revolution and putting the hegemony of regime ideology in jeopardy.

And yet the problem IRIB faced went beyond ideology. The quality of its programs was poor. It was a problem that existed from its start in the early days of the Republic, a problem made worse with the elimination of music by fatwa in 1988.[30] Domestically produced content was for the most part unimaginative, austere, and doctrinaire. Even soon-to-be general director of IRIB, Ali Larijani, acknowledged the problem. In an interview with a Lebanese newspaper, Larijani accepted the charge that Iranian television contained "no joy and happiness, only wailing and weeping" and that Western television was, in comparison, more attractive to Iranian viewers.[31]

The challenge before IRIB was rendered all the more significant due to its status as the only legally sanctioned source of news, information, and entertainment on television and radio. As IRIB itself conceded in its response to the Majles inquiry:

> Various statistics and polls show that most of the criticism of Voice and Vision is due to different tastes, because the audience of Voice and Vision ranges from two-year-old children to the oldest members of society and from the illiterate to the most learned, in short, all of the state and people in society, as well as beyond [Iran's] borders, audiences who have different intellectual, political and social backgrounds.[32]

The state radio and television service was struggling to fulfill a sensitive, extremely challenging task: to produce content that upheld Islamic strictures and served to propagate and support regime ideology, while catering to the demands and expectations of a large and diverse audience—a national populace that ranged from the educated to the illiterate, the rural villager to the urban cosmopolitan, from the very old to the very young, the poor to the wealthy, and all those in between.

Despite his impassioned defense of his organization and efforts to continue work unfazed by the Majles inquiry and the harsh light of public criticism, Hashemi was fighting a losing battle. The president did what he could to bolster his brother's claim to the directorship, appearing with Hashemi in public and celebrating the growth of *Seda va Sima* under his nearly decade-long stewardship. But the pressure from Majles and other hardline conservative voices prevailed, and on February 12, 1994, the Supreme Leader announced the appointment of Ali Larijani as the new director of IRIB. From Tehran to Qom, voices once critical of the broadcaster under Hashemi now raised cries of approval.[33]

In his remarks to the press, Khamenei tacitly acknowledged the problem underpinning the challenges that Hashemi spoke about. While the geographic expansion of the service between 1989 and 1994 extended the reach of the state and, in theory, the penetration of regime ideology, it did so at the expense of program quality. The focus going forward, said Khamenei, should be on improving the substance of IRIB content and "confronting the cultural and news propaganda onslaught of arrogant [powers]."[34]

The Majles took steps to operationalize the Supreme Leader's instruction. Soon after the announcement of the change in IRIB leadership, Reza Taghavi, chief of the Majles Islamic Guidance and Art Commission, announced that an additional 1 percent of the general budget would be allocated to "fight the cultural invasion." Half of the estimated 7.5 billion toman would go to IRIB, said Taghavi. A committee comprised of the deputy vice president, the director of IRIB, the chief of the Islamic Propaganda Organization, and chaired by the Minister of Culture and Islamic Guidance would oversee the fund.[35]

Examining the episode from a purely political-factional lens, the ouster of Hashemi can be understood as the continuation of an effort by hardline conservatives to strip moderate and reformist voices from positions of power. The conflict was preceded by the resignation of the Minister of Culture and Islamic Guidance, Mohammad Khatami, in 1992. By many indications, Khatami's departure was not of his own free will, as the president later maintained, but the result of pressure by hardline factions critical of Khatami's liberal policies toward the press.[36] In a letter released to Iranian newspapers, Khatami framed his resignation as the result of the "rising retrograde and stagnant influence and the climate of insecurity that increasingly bedevils cultural activities." Citing lack of tolerance for debate and expression, he warned that the situation threatened to condemn "intellectuals, artists and even faithful friends of the Islamic revolution [to] indifference."[37]

While Hashemi can hardly be considered a reformist, his conception of the role of broadcast journalism in society and his efforts to reorganize IRIB television to respond to audience preference by creating a leisure and entertainment channel can be considered progressive. Hashemi's actions challenged conservative tenets of mass communication as a unidirectional transaction for the propagation of Islam and the maintenance of the status quo.

It may also be argued that the Hashemi–Majles standoff was symptomatic of the politicization of the cultural sphere. Culture and cultural production became a site of contestation, as control over the dissemination of "culture" was deemed necessary for ideological dominance. Indeed, culture was more of a lightning rod than ever before, with those who deigned to touch it doomed to failure and political chastisement.

Khatami was pressured to resign because of his "liberal" policies on print media, film, and the arts.[38] Less than two years later, Hashemi faced similar criticism, if indirectly. The Majles report charged Hashemi's IRIB with undermining Iran's Islamic culture and promoting deviant behavior through its dissemination of Western cultural products. This was no minor charge. That it resulted in the resignation of a man who had been appointed by the late Imam and had served the nation as IRIB director for over a decade was a testament to the power and poison of the cultural realm.

+++

As the Majles-Hashemi standoff was unfolding, satellite dishes were fast becoming a familiar feature of the urban landscape. Its ability to preserve the state broadcasting monopoly amid an increasingly globalized information-communications environment already in question, the broadcaster now had the nearly impossible task of communicating to a diverse populace through a limited and increasingly obsolete technology of transmission, Fixed Satellite Service (FSS), with flat or diminished fiscal resources while adhering to the strictures of Islam and regime ideology. By the spring of 1994, it was increasingly clear that IRIB was failing to meet the demands of its audience, the Iranian people, and its benefactors, the Iranian regime. The ruling establishment's dissatisfaction with IRIB, as well as the practical disconnect between IRIB capabilities and its mandate, continued to deepen as the lure of the next generation information communication technology, Direct Broadcast Satellite (DBS), grew. Satellite television would soon become the media of choice for a growing section of the population.

4

THE CRISIS OF SATELLITE TV

> The danger of an ordinary photograph or tape is no less than a kilogram of heroin.
> —Ayatollah Ali Meshkini[1]

> It is our duty to campaign against this problem as with rascals and rogues.
> —Ali Mohammad Besharati[2]

Marshall McLuhan famously wrote that the medium is the message.[3] The crisis of satellite TV shows the truth of that maxim. The big domed dishes poking out windows and perched on rooftops proclaimed a foreign technology had arrived, one that was funneling foreign messages and culture into the homes of Iranians across the country. This chapter examines the public debate over how to respond to the new technology, the market surrounding it, and the challenge it posed to a government intent on maintaining its long-coveted monopoly over the airways.

I begin with an overview of Direct Broadcast Satellite (DBS) technology and how it differed from Iran's existing system of terrestrial broadcasting. As a matter of background and context, I offer data points about the DBS market and the challenge it posed for the state television monopoly. Following a brief chronology of the public debate, I examine the arguments of those opposed to legislation that would prohibit satellite ownership and broadcasting, as well as those of its champions. The champions prevailed and legislation prohibiting dish ownership was passed in 1994. The chapter concludes by considering the challenge DBS posed to the existing power dynamic and the reforms aimed at making IRIB products more competitive in Iran's rapidly globalizing media marketplace.

The Technology of Direct Broadcast Satellite

Before the main discussion, it is necessary to consider the technical details of DBS and the broadcast television system that proceeded it. In the period under investigation, roughly 1991 to 1995, Iran's national television service broadcast through a first-generation information communication technology called Fixed Satellite Service (FSS). In FSS, a geostationary satellite carries a signal from one earth-based station to another. The terrestrial station receiving the signal then retransmits it to end users—television set owners—through the air or by cable.

Direct Broadcast Satellite is a second-generation information communication technology. In the DBS system, end users receive signals directly from the geostationary satellite. The signals are broadcast at microwave frequency.[4] This eliminates the need for an in-country ground station to transmit satellite signals originating from elsewhere in the country or abroad. The satellite dish is the essential instrument of DBS and enables its owner to receive a signal directly from a geostationary satellite.

The Market for DBS

In October 1991, the Hong Kong-based, American-owned conglomerate Satellite Television Asian Region (Star TV) began broadcasting its free-to-air services via Asia Sat 1.[5] Initially, Star TV consisted of five theme-based channels: one for music videos (MTV), one for sports, one for news (BBC World Service Television), one for family entertainment, and one channel broadcasting in Mandarin Chinese. All channels ran content twenty-four hours a day. With the exception of the Chinese language channel, Star TV carried predominantly Western programs obtained through contractual suppliers or the international market.

At first it was not possible to receive Star TV signals in Iran using anything smaller than a three-meter satellite dish. This limited reception to a handful of wealthy Iranians, some government agencies, international hotels, and embassies.[6] However, by 1993, the technology and signal strength had improved such that Iranians could receive Star TV channels using a 1.8-meter dish.[7] This expanded access to thousands of middle-class Iranians.

While the dishes and receivers that first came to the country were of Taiwanese manufacture, it was not long before Iranian manufacturers began utilizing the abundance of raw material available inside Iran and producing comparable equipment for domestic retail.[8] The price of a domestically manufactured satellite dish was lower than its foreign competitors, and the competition benefited consumers. Iranian-made dishes cost 230,000 rials for a 1.2-meter dish, and from 380,000 to 500,000 rials for a 2.4-meter dish, or $57.50 and $95 to $125 USD, respectively.[9] A receiver cost between 610,000 rials for a short tuner and 900,000 rials for a long tuner, or $152.50 and $252, respectively.

But few but the wealthy purchased such equipment for just themselves. Most Iranians pooled their money to buy a dish, in what may be described as a community access scheme. Access to foreign broadcasting was affordable—and after the initial down payment for the equipment, virtually free. The cost per household in a community access scheme with one central dish and a tuner was between 140,000 and 160,000 rials, or $33 to $40 USD. The cost per household in a scheme with a central dish only was even lower, at 80,000 to 100,000 rials, or $20 to $25 USD, respectively.[10]

In short, for many Iranians, satellite TV was an attractive, low-cost alternative to the free FSS Persian service offered by IRIB. Iranian audiences were generally able to access from ten to fifteen foreign satellite channels, primarily through Star TV, at no cost. But there was still the problem of translation. Most programs were in English or in an Indian or Chinese dialect and may or may not have had captions; there were no programs in Persian. (This problem would be solved, if imperfectly, through the years as an increasing number of English programs were dubbed in Persian.) Despite the undoubtable comprehension gap, an increasing number of Iranians were choosing to watch satellite television programs in a foreign tongue over state-run television in Persian.

The proliferation of the large gray and rust-colored discs on rooftops and skyscrapers was powered, if unintentionally, by the Rafsanjani administration's pro-trade, "free market" economic policies; rising household incomes; and a large, information-hungry, technology-savvy youth consumer population. Between 1993 and 1994, satellite dishes of all sizes and makes began emerging on high-rises and apartment blocks throughout Tehran, particularly in the more affluent North, Northwest, and West.[11] An aerial survey of Tehran conducted in 1994 gives us an idea of their popularity. Of the 95,415 buildings, 3 percent featured at least one satellite dish, with the number of satellite dishes in all buildings and homes in the Iranian capital estimated to be 29,460.[12] Satellite dishes soon spread to other large cities as well as to more remote areas of the country.

Once a product largely relegated to select government agencies and the more affluent people of Tehran, satellite dishes now grew more affordable by the month, propelling a once-limited communication technology to a popular information communication technology with the potential to speak to Iranians en masse. It is no wonder then, that in the nation's capital, a debate about how the government should respond to DBS was well underway.

Chronology of Satellite Dish Prohibition Law

If any single action could be credited with forcing government action on satellite dishes, it was the unilateral declaration of Interior Minister Ali Mohammad Besharati. On April 5, 1994, Besharati stood before a gaggle of press and announced the start of his campaign to eradicate all satellite dishes in Tehran. "Within two months' time, none of these dishes will be seen on [Tehran] rooftops," Besharati pledged. In response to the suggestion that such an action required legal authorization, the minister responded: "The campaign against satellite does not need law. It is our duty to campaign against this problem as with rascals and rogues."[13]

The decision was most likely unilateral and not in coordination with the president's office, the Parliament, or the Judiciary, where responses to the proclamation were decidedly cool. According to one source, the administration pressured Besharati to rescind his remarks, citing fears that opportunists would use the proclamation as a license to enter people's homes and steal their property under the pretext of collecting satellite dishes.[14] Perhaps as a result, Besharati moderated his stance in subsequent press interviews. "The use of satellite dishes is not illegal, but it will need to be authorized," Besharati told the *Tehran Times* a few days later. "The issue is under discussion by the cabinet and a comprehensive decision is to be made within a month."[15]

Despite the minister's pledge, a speedy resolution was not forthcoming. Indeed, what followed was nearly a year of deliberation over the appropriate government response to the intrusion of a powerful new commercial media system into an industry conceived as the singular province of the Iranian state. Government officials, academics, engineers, and clerical leaders weighed in on the issue in public forums, in newspapers and magazines, and on radio and television. The result was an exceptionally well-documented, multifaceted debate about how the Islamic Republic should receive a powerful new mass communication technology and media logic during a time of national transition.[16]

Ultimately the Majles passed a measure banning the "import, manufacture, distribution, transportation, repair, installation, maintenance, and utilization of satellite reception equipment."[17] Responsibility for enforcement was placed with the Ministry of the Interior. Article 8 of the law assigned penalties to those involved in the supply and distribution side of the satellite trade. First-time offenders were subject to a cash penalty of two to five times the value of the recovered equipment. Second-time offenders would receive fines from five to ten times the value of the commodity in addition to six months to three years imprisonment.[18] Article 9 established the penalties for consumers of satellite television, and specifically satellite dish owners. In addition to the confiscation of the equipment, the offender, just like the supplier or distributor, would be fined two to five times the price of the offending merchandise. Second-time offenders would be fined five to ten times the price.[19] The plan gave the public a one-week grace period during which they could surrender the equipment without penalty. Foreign embassies and research centers could keep the dishes provided they secured a special license.[20] Finally, the law was given a sunset clause of three years, after which the law could be extended.

The Majles passed the prohibition bill in late September 1994 with two-thirds of the 268-member body voting in approval. The measure was then amended after it was reviewed by the Guardian Council.[21] The final bill was ratified in January 1995. It contained some notable changes.[22] It extended the grace period for citizens to turn in their equipment or apply for a permit to one month, instead of one week. The cash penalties for offenses were also revised to up to 100 million rials for importers, producers, and distributors, from 1 to 3 million rials for users of satellite reception equipment, and from 1 to 5 million rials for those involved in the transport, maintenance, installation, and repair of DBS equipment. The penalty of jail time was removed entirely. Article 10 charged the Ministry of Culture and Islamic Guidance "with the duty, by using international and juridical levers, of taking necessary measures towards the preservation of the country's cultural boundaries and against frivolous and prosaic satellite programs."[23]

Even before the measure became law, the Basij began attempting to impose the spirit of the law in some areas of the country. A round-up of dishes was reported in Mashhad, for example, while clandestine opposition radio reported jamming of satellite signals in Tehran beginning in July.[24] Foreign press reported that some technically savvy Iranians were able to use decoders to subvert the electronic jamming that produced parallel lines across images transmitted over certain frequencies.[25] Following the passage of the law, Iranians were told they had until April 22 to voluntarily hand over equipment to IRIB, after which time officers with special identification would be going to homes suspected of harboring DBS contraband.

Not without irony, the interior minister made a distinction between use, which was illegal, and "possession" of satellite dishes, which was not. "Of course… no legal action will be taken against people just for possessing satellite dishes," Besharati told reporters.[26] Adding further obfuscation, the minister went on to suggest that mere possession of DBS equipment (versus use) would be tolerated and even praised by the government. "Keeping these dishes is okay at this stage. In other words, if the people themselves have dismantled their satellite dishes to keep them in their houses, we even praise and thank them. Law enforcement will not bother them."[27] Soon after the law went into effect, state media reported that the public was responding positively and that the measure was having a deterrent effect.[28] Ninety percent of satellite dish owners in Tehran dismantled their dishes voluntarily by the end of the first week, Interior Minister Besharati reported.[29]

Contours of the Debate

Domestic and foreign print media reflected a range of views on the appropriate government response to satellite television. Almost all voices within Iran's ruling establishment favored some sort of government action. For the purpose of discourse analysis, we can divide these voices into two buckets: those in opposition to the satellite dish prohibition bill and those who supported it. The media outlets that recorded and helped shape elite opinion on the issue can be similarly organized. Those newspapers opposing the prohibition in favor of non-regulation or a light touch approach by the government tended to come from the moderate conservative camp aligned with Rafsanjani's Executives of the Construction of Iran party (*Hezb-e Kargozaran-e Sazandegi-ye Iran*) whose constituency was generally urban, moderately educated, and belonging to the middle class and petite bourgeoisie. These news outlets include *Abrar, Hamshahri, Salam, Iran Times*, and *Tehran Times*. Voices supporting the prohibition of satellite dishes and the heavy hand of enforcement tended to come from the hardline camp associated with Khamenei. This constituency was also urban, moderately educated, and connected to the mercantile bourgeoisie. In contrast with the former group, however, this political camp mainly had religious or religiopolitical motivations.[30] Newspaper outlets that carried such views include *Jomhuri-ye Eslami, Resalat*, and *Kayhan*. Of course, the opinions circulated defy easy categorization, and many early voices in opposition to government intervention later revised their view. Nonetheless, within these two categories of discourse, a number of argumentative themes emerge. I will begin by examining those by groups and individuals who opposed the bill to ban satellite dishes.

Arguments in Opposition to Government Prohibition

Arguments opposing the bill to prohibit the use, trade, and ownership of satellite equipment followed several tracks. Three themes are particularly noteworthy: the unstoppable march of globalization, the positive potential of communication technology, and the need to strengthen the state-sponsored television service.

The Problem of Prohibition

Arguments opposing the prohibition bill tended to highlight the impracticality of the ban given the inevitable improvements to the technology as time went on. Moreover, enforcement requiring the physical removal of dishes was virtually impossible. DBS is here to stay, the argument went, and technology will only get better, with stronger and more discreet receiving antennae. The dishes will continue to shrink in size, making them increasingly difficult to detect by human or photographic surveillance. Majles deputy Shapour Marhaba put it this way: "Prevention of and the physical reaction to the use of satellite networks is not possible because satellites are waves that due to the growth of communication technology will find their way into homes." Instead of prohibition, said Marhaba, the government should turn the technology against itself. He urged the government to use satellites to "jam" the signals from the offending satellites as they broadcast into Iran, noting that such broadcasts were "clear aggression" and a violation of state sovereignty.[31]

In May, *Resalat* published an article written by an engineer named Mehrabi Bayan that claimed technical measures against satellites, including signal jamming, were feasible. Later, Bayan and three other engineers wrote a letter to Majles Speaker Ali Akbar Nategh-Nuri that repeating this claim and expressing their readiness to assist in the building of such a mechanism. "Some of our friends are now working on a project that employs a technical solution to the problem of unwanted satellite signals ... the progress is satisfactory, and the hope is to finalize the project within a minimum budget."[32]

Other voices in opposition to the prohibition bill focused their argument on the need to educate the people about the danger of satellite programs. "You cannot prevent satellite," Majles deputy Abbas Sheibani put simply. "Strengthen [state] radio and television and then nobody will watch satellite. When I, a Muslim, realize that satellite [television] is religiously forbidden, I will not watch it. You must educate us as Muslims."[33] Indeed, Sheibani's argument was an opinion shared with many voices in opposition to the prohibition bill and some in favor of it as well. They argued that the government should focus its efforts on improving the alternative to satellite television, IRIB. "You have weaknesses here, and you want to fix it somewhere else and say, prohibited, prohibited," said Sheibani. "Well, what will you replace it with?"[34] Banning DBS would only seed public curiosity about satellite television, he averred. "In my opinion, the proposal is very harmful and has attracted more people to satellite."[35]

Abrar criticized the prohibition proposal as ineffectual and pointed to the poor results of the ban on video recording devices.[36] The ban on Video Cassette Recordings (VCRs) was unsuccessful. Worse yet, it encouraged black-market trade, *Abrar* argued. The ban on satellite dishes would not solve the problem of foreign television and might even make satellite dish ownership more popular. The editorial went on to point out the hypocrisy of government efforts to ban satellite while simultaneously publishing a magazine dedicated to the subject, called "Video and Satellite."[37] Finally, *Abrar* questioned the timing of the bill. "While satellite dishes have been in Iran for years, why is the action only being considered now?" The paper noted that the Majles began considering prohibition only after "a certain Arab country" enacted a ban on satellite dishes. This was a reference to Iran's regional competitor, Saudi Arabia, which had, along with Malaysia, enacted a ban on satellite dishes. "Is this the way to combat satellite?" the editorial concluded. "Why are we still acting defensively?"[38]

The clandestine radio station of the opposition group, the Democratic Party of Iranian Kurdistan (*Ḥezb-e Demokrat-e Kordestan-e Iran*, or PDKI), presented a similar argument, although its criticism was more explicit than the necessarily veiled language of the domestically licensed newspaper *Abrar*. The Iraq-based radio station called the proposed ban on satellite dish ownership "a means of distracting from the regime's failures."[39] In an attempt to obscure its complicity in the larger problems of the economy and government, the station argued, the regime sought to shift blame to television, radio, and magazines as well as scapegoat loyal adherents. "To justify their repressive actions [they] have not even hesitated in sacrificing someone like Mohammad Hashemi, the head of the Islamic Republic's radio and television, who was one of the propagators of the reactionary clerical regime's thinking."[40]

Propaganda and Progress

Another theme within the opposition narrative emphasized the progressive, constructive potential of satellite communication technology. These voices advocated for the state's appropriation of the technology for the propagation of regime ideology globally. After outcompeting Western programs by producing superior content at home, the Islamic Republic could then "export our religious values, culture, and art through the same medium of communication to the rest of the world."[41] These voices channeled narratives within the ruling establishment that privileged science and self-sufficiency as central to the evangelizing of Iran's Islamic revolutionary ideology.

Conversely, according to this logic, those who opposed public access to DBS technology were against science and self-sufficiency. That Khamenei loyalist and then Friday prayer leader (a highly honored and powerful position) Ayatollah Amad Jannati deigned to refute this charge may be an indication of the argument's relevance and pervasiveness. In a Friday prayer sermon in May, Jannati rejected the charge that the prohibition bill was an effort to keep the people ignorant by limiting their access to information from external sources. "If satellite equipment is used in the service of science, morality, religion, piety, and all other virtues, we will be the first to promote and strengthen it by importing, distributing or even producing that equipment," said Jannati. "But if you, under the banner of the arts, culture, and progress, seek to spread corruption in families and bring moral decay to boys and girls as they sit in their own homes and before the eyes of their parents, then we will, with all our might, stand up against you and put a stop to your acts."[42]

Jannati went on to put forward an interesting, if revisionist, version of the revolution to explain Qom's changing position toward mass communication. In his telling, during the revolution and in the early days of the Islamic Republic the establishment sought to prohibit the use of television and radio by the masses. After the revolution, "when these problems were eliminated and schools, TV programs, and cinemas were made healthy," the clerical establishment embraced modern mass communication technology. In Jannati's account, he and his colleagues in the seminary were the first to promote the newly "Islamicised" radio and television media. "We ourselves pioneered action in these fields," Jannati said.[43]

Some proponents of the "technology is inevitable" argument came to embrace the ban as an interim measure. A temporary ban on DBS would provide IRIB the breathing space it needed to focus on improving the quality and attractiveness of its content, these voices contended. It would remove the competitive pressure currently posed by international television channels broadcasting into Iran.

The editorial board of the *Tehran Times*, for example, favored exploring the possibility of ban as a short-term fix. Assuming it took more than three to four years for new, undetectable satellite dishes to reach Iranian markets, the legislation could help prevent "unwanted programs from entering our households." In the longer term however, it was necessary to improve domestic content. "The long-term and logical way to combat cultural invasion is to improve domestic production of films and radio and television programs, thereby removing the incentive to watch Western products."[44]

Arguments in Support of Government Prohibition

Like those in opposition to the ban, the arguments in support of government prohibition of satellite dishes varied. Still, voices in favor of the ban tended to focus on a number of intersecting questions concerning program content, culture, and ontological security.[45]

Content and Message

A major line of argument in support of government prohibition related to the content of the programs being broadcast. At issue was not the technology (DBS) or the medium (television) but rather the content being relayed. "One of the tools in present technology is the satellite which is not prohibited. If used properly, it (satellite technology) is even desirable," the spokesman of the Islamic Guidance and Art Committee said in his introduction of the bill in Parliament. "No one opposes satellite, they oppose what is broadcast from satellite now, which in fact is an effective tool for bringing deviation to human societies."[46] In a story about the British Broadcasting Service (BBC) radio coverage of the Majles bill, *Resalat* singled out programs that carried "songs and dances" for particular criticism. In this narrative, music television (perhaps in reference to MTV) was a colonial force bent on the subjugation of Iran and its peers in the so-called Third World.

> All our complaints against satellite programs are due to this very repertoire of songs and dances. Those who have set the world on fire and are engaged in the plunder of the mines and reserves of the Third World and draw their swords against a nation every day do not have the right to celebrate such a system and dance and sing on the bodies of those killed![47]

The concern over content informed a sermon by Ayatollah Jannati soon after the interior minister's initial declaration about satellite dishes in April 1994. The cleric spoke about the effects on people's behavior and habits. Satellite television programs, Jannati argued, encouraged "lust" and specifically, "sexual lust, evil and animal lust." When a person falls prey to lust, they are "not satisfied" and want "more and more."[48] Left unchecked, such lust would consume and corrupt Iranian society. It would undermine the revolution, sully children's minds, and destroy the traditional family unit.

This line of argumentation rendered the satellite dish an antirevolutionary agent, not just contraband. Proliferation of DBS technology threatened to undo the new normative reality that he and the founding Islamic revolutionaries strove to put into place and replace it with the decadent, corrupt values associated with the "tyrant" regime of Shah Mohammad Reza Pahlavi. "The revolution came and truly caused an upheaval in attitudes, smashed the symbols of lust, and destroyed the sites that corrupted youngsters," Jannati said to his congregants. "We have to make sure this situation does not return."[49] Moreover, he argued that by providing an alternative to state television, satellite induced a public demand or expectation for more information and high-quality programs. Like lust, which makes a person "not satisfied" and wanting "more and more," satellite television threatened to disrupt the status quo by encouraging personal ambition and striving. In this way, it challenged the regime's idealized model of mass communication as a one-way transmission from the state to a homogenous mass of passive receivers.

Culture and Security

Defense against a cultural onslaught was another major theme in support of the satellite dish ban. This narrative associated satellite dishes with the cultural products they conveyed. It correlated television with foreign culture. Majles Judiciary head Ayatollah Mohammad Yazdi framed the satellite prohibition bill as a question of "retaining healthy minds and sustaining the campaign against cultural onslaught."[50] Allowing foreign satellite television to continue unabated was akin to opening the city gates to an enemy invader; to do nothing was to allow the unfettered assault on Iranian "Islamic" culture.

Ali Larijani, former minister of Culture and Islamic Guidance and current IRIB director, pointed to Europe as an example of what would happen if satellite television were allowed to penetrate Iranian society without restriction. "Today, the expansion and increased activity of satellite broadcasting has become a serious problem for Europeans because it will bring about the destruction of their cultural identities."[51] Similarly, the *Tehran Times* reported that European countries were "up in arms" about American films and television saturating the airwaves. France was considering limiting the amount of American content that could be shown on television after American distributors refused to "voluntarily cut down their imports to Europe."[52]

Sovereignty and security were closely connected to the theme of culture. In the narrative of proponents of government prohibition, satellite dishes were both an agent and a symbol of foreign domination. Satellite dishes represented a threat to moral and national security. Foreign powers sought to dominate Iranians by spreading cultural products that would erode the religious and social fabric of society. Mostafa Mir-Salim, Minister of Culture and Islamic Guidance, described satellite television as an attempt by foreign agents to "conquer the minds of the Asian societies and dominate them."[53]

In a Friday sermon, Ayatollah Mohammad Emami-Kashani described the proliferation of satellite dishes as part of a plan by foreign adversaries to weaken the Islamic Republic by encouraging moral and cultural decay:

> The satellite is the West's weapon against Islam. They say this themselves. It is a weapon for them because the guns have fallen silent now. Today's war is different, today's war is over thought; war today is stealing hearts and minds ... And this is why they brought the satellite about: first, moral corruption—to keep our children and youth busy with these films—and secondly, so that children become corrupt and seek shelter in heroin, corruption, and drugs and become unemployed, empty, worthless individuals. They will not then pursue their studies, they will forget science, education, and exams. These are the two aims pursued by the enemy.[54]

Indeed, a major justification for the prohibition bill was the threat DBS posed to the Iran's "moral" and "national" security. "What we oppose is the vulgar satellite programing, which has today undermined the moral security of the Muslim and martyred people, and is about to endanger our national security," said Firuz Ahmadi, a Majles member from Moghan. As a state under constant threat of infiltration and manipulation by "invisible hands," Iran must take defensive and preventative action against satellite television "so that moral security will be protected."⁵⁵

Almost a year earlier, in June 1993, presidential candidate Ahmad Tavakkoli spent nearly the entirety of his forty-five-minute slot on IRIB radio on the subject of cultural invasion. Using language that would become a familiar refrain of proponents of prohibition, Tavakkoli warned of the "western onslaught on Islam and Islamic revolution" through "extravagant consumerism," and by "arousing lust" and spreading "propaganda."⁵⁶ This argument tended to point to a foreign plot or conspiracy against Iran. "We are not talking about satellites," said Ahmadi. "We are talking about a profound cultural plot whose seeds were planted years ago and is now bearing fruit in Muslim youth." The threat to religion, national identity, and Iranian culture posed by satellite television served to justify the paternalistic call for the ceding of personal choice to the state. Once again, the government took the position of protector and patriarch, and the Iranian people were given the role of "Muslim youth" or passive subject. ⁵⁷

Some proponents of the ban took aim at the forces behind satellite television, arguing that the problem with satellite television was that it was controlled by Iran's foreign enemies. "What causes us concern is that this tool has fallen into the hands of those whose goal is to destroy all human values," said Majles member Zare'i Ghanavati. Satellite television was "a sharp blade in the hands of a drunken savage."⁵⁸ Those who controlled the medium had either ill intentions for the Iranian public or little moral or ethical discretion.

Stepping back, it becomes clear that Ghanavati and other proponents of the ban considered DBS, and specifically the information and ideas it conveyed, a direct threat to the ruling ideology upon which society was ordered. Allowing satellite dishes to proliferate would be to allow this order to be challenged and, perhaps, be destroyed. To permit unrestricted use of satellite dishes was to cede government control over the information the population received. It was essentially forfeiting autonomy over ideology through a means of its dissemination, satellite television. In elevating the judgment of the government over that of the people, this narrative reveals the paternalistic viewpoint underpinning conservative arguments in favor of prohibition.

In a sermon in Tehran, Ayatollah Jannati praised the extra-judicial collection of satellite dishes by the revolutionary court prosecutor in July, months before the bill became law. Calling it an act of "benevolence" and "charity," Jannati said that the Iranian people both desired and welcomed the prosecutors' action as "necessary to protect the revolution" and "to preserve our revolutionary fervor."⁵⁹ This frame presents a social distribution of power in which the people need, and indeed want, the ruling *fuqaha* (Islamic jurists) to intervene in the moral life of individuals and the affairs of the family for the good of society. The exercise of moral authority and enforcement of a moral social code were the prerogatives of the regime. Such a dynamic is consistent with Khomeini's conception of government authority in his system of velayat-e faqih in which the relationship between the leader and people is akin to that of parent and child. Authority and power are not bestowed by the child on the parent but are instead intrinsic at birth. In a liberal democracy, in contrast, the distribution of power is not permanent; government authority is bestowed by its subjects and can be taken away. In Iran's Islamic Republic model, hegemonic power is a "grave responsibility" and immutable. "The governance of the *faqih* is a rational and extrinsic matter; it exists only as a type of appointment, like the appointment of a guardian for a minor," said Khomeini. "With respect to duty and position, there is indeed no difference between the guardian of a nation and the guardian of a minor."[60]

The remarks of Reza Akrami, deputy from Semnan Province, reflect this paternalistic ideation.[61] Speaking before his colleagues in the Majles, Akrami presented the prohibition of satellite dishes as a responsibility of government and a right of the Iranian citizenry.

> Regarding the global satellites, whose planners are the oppressors of the world and who inculcate lies in the context of news, do we have the right to permit our people to be under the influence of such propaganda? Do we have no responsibility vis-à-vis the thoughts, ideas, and beliefs of the people? We are responsible for the people and the regime has the responsibility for their health, education, and treatment, as well as for their ideas and beliefs.[62]

In short, Akrami argued that Parliament had a "responsibility" to protect the Iranian people's interests and culture, and this meant creating an environment free from corrupting Western influences delivered via satellite television.

In a series of essays on the matter published in *Resalat*, Mohammad Javad Larijani similarly argued that the state had a responsibility to intercede in the burgeoning satellite market. His argument was rooted in his conception of the role of the state in Iranian society. "The state, in an Islamic system ... has the responsibility to combat false thoughts and guarantee the health of society." Larijani sought to place the proposed action in context, comparing it to other laws to establish and protect basic moral standards of a society. Not without irony, he compared the proposed action of the Iranian government to that of the United States in passing laws against prostitution and gambling:

> Even in democratic systems which are based on liberalism and the basically think the state should be neutral about [values], the issue of public modesty is exceptional. This is why in some American states gambling houses, bawdy [sic] houses and, to an extent, nakedness is prohibited. A man cannot be married at the same time to several women and vice versa.[63]

But perhaps his most forceful argument for the banning of DBS related to the fundamental role of the state as moral protector. Just because prohibition is impractical does not mean it should not be pursued, he argued:

> To talk about the impossibility of state control on the exercising of the law, there is doubt about both the premise and the syllogism! If the difficulty of enforcing the law could prevent the enacting of a prohibition mandate, then this should also prevent the state passing any mandate about drinking wine, adultery, debauchery, and venality.[64]

In other words, legal prohibition should be established based on the principle that satellite was immoral, and it was the state's responsibility to protect society from moral corruption.

A Message from Qom

In May, members of the hardline faction, the Society of Combatant Clergy (*Jame'eh-ye Ruhaniyyat-e Mobarez*) sought to settle the debate by referring the issue to the *mojtahed* (jurists qualified to express an independent opinion).[65] Grand Ayatollah Mohammad Ali Araki and three other scholars of the Qom Theoretical School received an *estefta'* (query seeking advice on a religious matter) from members of the Majles.[66] In response, Araki, as *Marja'e Taqlid*, issued the following fatwa:

> An installation of a satellite dish, which paves the way for penetration of strangers' frivolous culture into Islamic society and causes the destructive illness of the West to Muslims, is *haram* (prohibited by Islam).[67]

The fatwa presents the danger of the satellite dish to Islamic society as that of kryptonite to Superman. Others within the seminary agreed. Following Araki's pronouncement, several leading clerics also issued fatwas against satellite dishes.[68] The effect was to create the impression of a consensus among the leaders in Qom about the danger of satellite dishes and provide the religious legitimation necessary for the measure's backers to push its passage in Tehran.

It is interesting to note that at least one scholar puts Khamenei on the opposite side of the marja in this debate. According to Iran scholar Asghar Shirazi, in late May, just days after Araki issued his fatwa declaring satellite television forbidden, Khamenei issued a fatwa that pronounced the use of satellite antennae to receive foreign TV broadcasts permissible as long as it "caused no harm."[69] If such a fatwa was in fact issued, it appears to have had a limited influence in the Majles. Moreover, Khamenei seems to have changed his position in later years, as reflected by the opinion published on his official website.[70] Setting this aside, the decree by Araki and others likely worked to consolidate opinion within the Majles on the necessity of prohibition.

Some who had initially opposed the ban ultimately voted in favor of it based on the linkage of satellite technology to moral subversion and the rationale that the threat to religious values outweighed the potential benefits. One such Majles member explained his new position thus: "One cannot be careless about dangers which threaten our values just because its technology,."[71] In other words, the mission of protecting the moral health of society must take priority over technological advancement.

The ruling from Qom also lent renewed force to arguments that the state had a duty to prohibit satellite dish usage regardless of the impracticality of the ban. This argument drew on ecclesiastical writ as well as constitutional law. Specifically, Article 3 of the Constitution states: "[T]he government of the Islamic Republic of

Iran has the duty of directing all its resources to … the struggle against all forms of vice and corruption."

The debate ended when the Parliament voted for, and the Guardian Council subsequently approved, a law banning the use of satellite dishes. Exceptions were made for government entities that needed access to conduct their duties, foreign embassies, and Iranian companies that manufactured satellite parts. Fewer than one-third of the 268 members of the Fourth Majles voted against the ban.[72]

The public deliberations on and eventual passage of the bill to ban satellite dishes presaged a larger transformation within the media and communications sector. By 1995, the media environment had shifted from one characterized by scarcity and monopoly, where IRIB was the only provider and there were only three channels to choose from, to one characterized by quasi-competition and multiplicity, where there were a number of extra-national broadcasters and numerous channels from which to choose. The debate itself, though admittedly a footnote to a larger societal negotiation, revealed manifold tensions and contradictions within the establishment's ideology about media and how that ideology turned to praxis in the young Islamic Republic.

Now, nearly three decades later, the efficacy of the law is debatable.[73] If the intent of the law is to be taken at face value, one can argue that it has failed, as it has done little to stop the flow of foreign information and cultural products through the Iranian airwaves. But perhaps more important than the stated aim of the bill is the power it gives to government entities charged with enforcing it.[74] Indeed, over the years, we see pattern of behavior in which the law is enforced when it is in the interest of the security forces and other entities within the ruling establishment as a way to demonstrate the regime's hegemony over all people and all parts of one's life, even at home. Such state actors have also used it as a pretext to search homes, detain and interrogate dissenters, and fine "offenders" for financial gain. But this and other applications of the law is only one piece of the puzzle. Deeper understanding requires a more rigorous exploration of the satellite dish as symbol and signifier of power and legitimacy.

5

THE BIG DISH: DIRECT BROADCAST SATELLITE, SYMBOLISM, AND THE POLITICS OF CULTURE

In *Ideology and Modern Culture*, sociologist John Thompson argued that satellite television was a fundamental break with the existent system of mass communication where a powerful few sent messages to the consuming masses in a unidirectional exchange.[1] The world, said Thompson in 1991, was witnessing the rise of a "new modality ... of cultural transmission."[2] He named a number of features of Direct Broadcast Satellite (DBS) that made it a departure from traditional systems of cultural communication.[3]

Whereas traditional systems of television broadcasting offered a limited supply of channels (in some cases only two or three), DBS technology allowed the transmission of a greater number and variety of channels and content. "The traditional scarcity of channels is being rapidly replaced by a bewildering multiplicity," wrote Thompson.[4] The overall effect was to increase the amount and diversity of audiovisual material available, while retaining the speed and quality of the original system.[5] Perhaps even more important was the fact that DBS was, by nature and practice, transnational. Traveling through the air from an orbiting satellite, DBS signals knew no national boundaries. This was a significant change from the incumbent Fixed Satellite Service (FSS). The television signal had, until then, been relayed from one ground-based station to another. DBS removed the need for a terrestrial intermediary, thus circumventing the infrastructure that was previously required for television networks to broadcast and either owned or regulated by the state. While many nations were also grappling with these and other challenges posed by DBS in the 1990s, there were several features of the new system that made it especially disruptive in the Iranian context.

DBS as a System of Transmission

DBS was problematic for the regime, in part, because offered a new, arguably superior, system of information transmission. In the existing system, IRIB headquarters in north Tehran would relay a program to a satellite in fixed orbit, which would then relay the signal to ground stations across the county;

the ground station would then transmit the signal to peoples' homes. The ground station was thus a physical intermediary between the sender—the state-controlled radio and television service—and the receiver—the Iranian people. The state owned and controlled all aspects of the broadcast cycle, from production to transmission to reception. DBS upended this cycle. In DBS, a source, usually outside Iran's borders and thus outside the jurisdiction of the state, would broadcast content to an orbiting satellite that would then broadcast directly to any Iranian home with a satellite dish. As a technology of transmission, DBS removed the need for a terrestrial intermediary, thus circumventing the infrastructure that IRIB depended on for its monopoly over the airwaves. The Iranian people, likewise, could circumvent the iron shackles of the state that until then had controlled what Iranians could or could not watch on television.

This new system presented a number of advantages to the Iranian public. First, it allowed people to receive broadcasts who may otherwise have been out of range of a ground station. Second, it allowed a greater density of information to travel to the receiver, offering more channels and thus more choice in what television programs to watch. Finally, it allowed Iranians to access television content from sources outside national borders, as DBS technology could broadcast in a country without having a receiving ground station located there.

The advantages to the Iranian consumer were largely disadvantages to the regime. From a content perspective, the greatest disadvantage was loss of control over the messaging Iranians received. In the existing system of FSS, the regime leadership enjoyed a high degree of editorial control over broadcast content, as production and transmission were centralized within the institution of IRIB. Transmissions originated from a single, central entity in Tehran, which was under the jurisdiction of the Supreme Leader. Moreover, in the case of live broadcasts, FSS inserted a short delay between the time the broadcast signal was sent and the time it was received on the television set. This delay added to the eight- to fifteen-second delay already worked into the system to enable on-the-spot censorship of live broadcasts, giving the regime an additional degree of control.[6]

DBS as a Communicative Structure

There are notable parallels between the sociopolitical order of the state and the structure of the then status quo media system. In the system of velayat-e faqih, the ulema is the guardian of the Islamic faith on earth. The ulema, and particularly the marja and the velayat-e amr (the ruling jurist, now Supreme Leader Khamenei), has both the responsibility and the singular power to interpret the Quran and communicate the will of God and the teachings of the Prophet to the people.[7] In the absence of the return of the Twelfth Imam from occultation, the right to rule reverts to the Guardian Council. At least theoretically, these intermediaries have authority over all aspects of private and public life.[8]

The relationship between the Iranian state broadcaster and the people exhibits a similar communicative structure. Here, an institution of the state (IRIB) serves as the intermediary between message sender and receiver. It is no surprise, then, that DBS was seen as a threat to the clerical establishment, as it challenged the traditional hierarchy of mass communication by offering the possibility of message transference directly from the message producer (in this case, the amorphous "West") to the receiver, the Iranian people, and from life dictated by the Ayatollah to the possibility of life outside the repressive reality of post-revolutionary Iran.

DBS as a Challenge to the Regime's Media Ideology

DBS was disruptive to the ruling establishment in another way: it challenged the regime ideology *about* media. In the status quo system in which the state enjoyed a monopoly on mass communication, audience preference had little to do with determinations about form and content of television programming. Content decisions were made in service of the regime's ideological and political agenda, rather than according to audience taste, commercial imperatives, and advertiser demand. Program content was determined by IRIB personnel as directed by Supreme Leader and in accordance with the IRIB's institutional mandate as established by writ and by law.[9]

Indeed, if hegemony is built on the dominance of regime ideology, mass communication media was no more than a means to an end. It enforced a relationship embedded in the system itself and reinforced by the state at every opportunity in all manner of activities. In the case of national television and radio, messages and symbolic frames articulated and reinforced the establishment's dominion over the masses, rather than the people's interaction with the state; it expressed the people's duties and responsibilities, rather than their rights.

DBS challenged this media ideology. Facing competition from foreign satellite stations, IRIB officials and government leaders were forced to reexamine the way they thought about media and give greater credence to audience preference. One can see the rising sensitivity to the changing relationships of power in the Majles debate about satellite dishes, where there is a tug of-war between communicative philosophies—propaganda and monopoly versus internationalist multiplicity and audience preference—and between a regime built on populist legitimacy and the demands of the people needed to maintain it. But by 1995, it was abundantly clear that the time when the state controlled what their citizens watched had ended.

The Symbolism of Satellite Dishes

Given the clear impossibility of total eradication and the challenge and expense of enforcement, why would Tehran nevertheless elect to pass a law that made the use of a satellite dish illegal? Part of the answer rests in the symbolic message that the equipment conveyed. To work, satellite dishes must have an unobstructed path to the sky. Dishes therefore had to be situated in a place people could see: outside of homes, on top of buildings, and out apartment windows. Such prominence and publicness was problematic in part, because of the dish's association with foreign culture and globalization. The increasingly dense peppering of large gray discs across urban landscapes signified both the entry of Iran into the global economy and the entry of globalization's brand of Western capitalism and culture into Iranian society.

The satellite dish also symbolized public choice. The audience for broadcasting widened as result of the technology that could reach more people farther away. Their signal no longer tethered to a television tower, and Iranians were able to access foreign satellite television in more regions and with programs of better quality. Such a new norm raised people's expectations of the state broadcast service, ultimately leading some of the more vocal critics of IRIB to demand more channels and higher quality programs. Satellite dishes sprouted in windows and on rooftops like mushrooms and the fact that Iranians were choosing foreign programs, many in languages they could not understand, over IRIB could not be denied.

In a sociopolitical system that favored homogeneity of appearance and conduct in public spaces, the satellite dish, especially in the early days, was a public expression of non-compliance. Following the passage of the prohibition law, the act of owning a satellite dish became a political act as far as the nezam was concerned. One can go further and argue that by persisting to own and use the equipment, the Iranian offender was signaling his or her lack of consent to the law and the system that birthed it.

Finally, because satellite television was seen as a cultural product with political objectives, the spread of satellite dishes was interpreted by some as a sign of the population's preference for the alternative ideology of the liberal, democratic West. In essence, satellite dishes became an indication of the public's disinterest in state sponsored cultural products and proof of the falling resonance of its revolutionary ideology.[10]

The Politics of Culture

In *Media, Culture, and Society in Iran*, Mehdi Semati blames the failure of Western scholars to understand and anticipate developments in contemporary Iran on their "inadequate appreciation for the significant role of culture in Iranian society and its social and political antagonisms."[11] If one were to apply Semati's observation to American scholarship in particular, as opposed to Western scholarship in general, this defect may be partially understood as a by-product of the unique political-legal culture of the United States. In law and politics there are systems and norms designed to keep what is considered the sphere of culture and civil society separate, or protected from, what is considered the realm of the state. Although a cultural product or activity can overtly venture into the sphere of government and politics (e.g., an oil painting can have a political message), it is frowned upon and often illegal for a government official or agency to seek to regulate or participate in cultural production. Similarly, with a few exceptions, the US government is prohibited from imposing restrictions on news reporting or television production as such activities fall into the category of free speech and are constitutionally protected.

No such distinction is made in the government of the Islamic Republic of Iran. Quite to the contrary, participation, intervention, and regulation of the cultural sphere are the prerogative of the state. This view, which considers the location of the cultural within the realm of the political, is a cornerstone of regime ideology and *velayat-e faqih*. The Ministry of Guidance and Islamic Culture exists for this reason; it was conceived as the arbiter of matters pertaining to the exercise and expression of culture, from writing to theater, music, and film.[12] It should be noted that this overlap of politics and culture is not unique to the Islamic Republic. Arguably, it is something to which any number of states (usually autocratic) would subscribe. Moreover, while the inclusion of the cultural and religious realm in the jurisdiction of government is prohibited or else highly circumscribed in the United States, it is a common feature of many European governments.

It may be argued that the government's efforts to control the production and dissemination of symbolic goods through mass communication have had the effect of increasing or exacerbating the interweaving of the cultural and political realms. As Semati observes:

> In the context of restrictions in the political arena, weaknesses of non-state institutions and processes, uneven institutionalization of the exercise of power and the limited space for political expression and discourse, culture takes on considerable force. In other words, the scope of politics is wider in so far as politics is conterminous with culture.[13]

The result is that even the most benign endeavor is potentially political, and therefore potentially subversive. The very act of owning a satellite dish and watching Western satellite television becomes a political act against the regime.

Another outcome of the interconnection between culture and politics is that the attractiveness of Iranian culture and the pervasiveness of regime ideology are beholden to the agency of the state. If the culture fails to be attractive and demonstrate its attractiveness by its popularity within Iran, that failure is also seen as a failure of the state. If the culture of the Islamic Republic fails to engender popular adherence or consent, then the regime fails to achieve popular legitimacy. Therefore, the success of IRIB, as the premier distributor and manufacturer of cultural products through television broadcasting, becomes imperative for the maintenance of hegemonic power.

Postscript: Growth of the TV Monopoly, 1995–2011

In the decade following the ban, satellite television remained a prominent component of peoples everyday lives. The state embarked on a number of efforts to remain competitive and attractive in the new communication environment characterized by diversity, multiplicity, and consumer choice. This was no small feat. Over twenty Persian language channels broadcast into Iran using DBS technology. The stations were a combination of exile stations—a number based in Los Angeles and expressing anti-regime and pro-monarchist viewpoints—and

US and UK-sponsored television services. *Manoto* topped the list for viewership, followed by BBC Persian and Voice of America.

The Iranian state sought to confront this challenge in several ways. In addition to the prohibition of satellite receivers, it appropriated $2 million for "Protection Against Cultural Invasion." According to government reports, most of the money went to covering the technical cost of producing "parasites" (signal jamming) against foreign radio and television.[14] In 2010, officials announced a special committee "to investigate the invasion of foreign- based Persian-speaking TV networks that are targeting the foundations of Iranian families within the frameworks of a soft war." The group was tasked with drawing up a "strategic plan" for countering the soft war for the Cultural Council.[15] IRIB received an additional $500 million (USD) bursary for countering "enemy soft war in the cultural domain."[16]

In addition to signal jamming, the state sought to improve the attractiveness of the national television service by broadening its menu of domestic services. In the decade after the debate over the government policy on satellite dishes, the number of channels doubled. By 2011, there were seven national channels and thirty provincial channels.[17] The growth was accompanied by an increase in government investment. In 2011, the budget for IRIB reached $1.12 billion, an all-time high as a percentage of GDP.[18] Government investment in information and communication technology also showed upward trends.[19] Between 2000 and 2006, telecommunication expenditure increased almost four-fold, from 1.5 billion to 5.3 billion USD.[20]

Corporate strategy also evolved. Tehran's model of offering a limited number of channels with broad, generic appeal eventually gave way to a strategy of audience segmentation. This trend began with the launch of the dedicated "youth" channel, Network 3, in 1993 and continued with the launch of Network 4 (Knowledge Network), Network 5 (Tehran Network, dedicated to coverage of the country's capital), and Channel 6 (News Network). In 2011, IRIB introduced a digital TV network that included all of the provincial, national, and international channels, as well as iFilm, Shoma TV, Bazaar Channel, Drama Channel, and the Educational Channel.

The international service also enjoyed growth. By 2011, IRIB's menu of foreign channels had increased to seven: *Jam e Jam* Network (which included three channels), *Sahar TV*, *Al Kawthar*, *Al Alam*, *Qods TV*, *Press TV*, and *Hispan TV*.[21] According the its website, IRIB's international service broadcast in Chinese, Dari, English Armenian, Azeri, Bosnian, Japanese, Arabic, Hindi, Indonesian, Italian, Bengla, Hausa, Hebrew, Urdu, French, German, Turkish, Kiswahili, Pashtu, and Russian.[22] It also began streaming domestic and international channels on the internet.[23]

The international service developed a sizable audience in the Middle East and the Maghreb, with programming designed to target both Sunni and Shia populations in neighboring states such as Iraq, Lebanon, Syria, and Bahrain. It also broadcast programs via satellite to South America and Asia.[24] The creation of a new terrestrial service for Iraq was an early indication of Tehran's renewed interest in mass communication media as an instrument of extraterritorial influence and regime security. It also coincided with the rise in rhetorical sparring and minor military skirmishes between the United States and Iran.[25]

Internal and External Challenges

Following the scrutiny of IRIB in the Majles investigation of 1993–4 and again with the debate over the law to ban satellite dishes, IRIB director Larijani found himself under significant internal pressure to make IRIB channels available to other parts of the government. Likely in response to such pressure, in 1995, IRIB partnered with the Municipality of Tehran to launch a new IRIB Network, Channel 5.[26] (Tehran originally sought to launch its own channel, an idea that was soon quashed by Ershad in favor of a joint channel.) Although it was originally created by and for the city of Tehran, Ershad also wanted a piece of the action. It insisted that the new channel carry its ideological content, and later, routinely allocated its coveted share of airtime to the state's security, intelligence, and coercive apparatus. Channel 5 became a forum for the IRGC to air forced (many through torture) "confessions" of political prisoners.[27]

There are a handful other of other examples in which the state television monopoly found itself under pressure from within. In 2002, the Parliament passed legislation to allow private sector competition with IRIB. Despite the support of the Majles, the public, and the president, the measure never became law. The Guardian Council struck down the legislation, deeming it unconstitutional.[28]

Later in 2005, Majles speaker Mehdi Karroubi took it upon himself to challenge the television broadcasting monopoly by announcing plans to launch a private satellite channel, Saba TV. The channel, which was to begin broadcasting on December 21, would serve as the "free voice of the *Etemad-e Melli*" (National Trust Party). Karroubi established the party in an attempt to unite a number of moderate factions.[29] Saba TV was to produce content in Iran, cover Iranian politics, and cater to an Iranian audience, but it would operate and make transmissions from a headquarters in Dubai.

In establishing the channel outside of the country and broadcasting by satellite, Karroubi argued that the channel would not violate the state's television monopoly. He also argued that his action was appropriate given IRIB's violation of Article 41 of the Constitution, which guaranteed political factions equal access to mass communication media. As speaker of Parliament and candidate for president, Karroubi complained about unequal access to broadcast television and preferential treatment of other candidates.[30] Following the announcement, leaders of the Reformist Islamic Iran Participation Front (*Jebheh-ye Mosharekat-e Iran-e Eslami*) and the Iranian Hezbollah signaled their intentions to establish their own satellite television networks.[31] Iranian Hezbollah went as far as to announce that the channel would be called *Kheybar*, after a historic battle, and that it would be headquartered in Damascus.[32]

Just days before its inaugural broadcast, Saba TV was shuttered under pressure from the authorities. Government officials denounced the project as the illegal and the station's general manager was reportedly interrogated by intelligence officials. Ali Reza Shiravi, head of Arshad's Office of Correspondents and Foreign News Agencies, told Fars News:

> According to the constitution, pictorial media in Iran is government-controlled and only the state radio and television is allowed legally to cooperate with other countries in the creation of satellite Persian-language television networks … launching a private television network broadcasting from outside Iran is illegal.[33]

There are also indications that the government exerted diplomatic pressure to stop the channel. Iranian officials reportedly requested that the United Arab Emirates suspend Saba TV's operating license in Dubai.[34] The justification for the closure of Saba TV was, in part, that the existence of mass communication channels outside the state broadcaster would fuel factionalism and undermine national unity.[35] More likely, however, is that the emergence of an autonomous political voice was seen as a direct threat to the hegemony of the Supreme Leader as well as to the conservative faction aligned with Khamenei in the Parliament, Judiciary, and other centers of influence. "They have taken god's space from us," said Karroubi in reaction to the closure.[36]

The lure of privatization was not confined to the Reformist faction. Conservative leader Mahmoud Ahmadinejad appears to have harbored similar feelings. His criticism took shape amid a political falling-out with the Supreme Leader and in reaction to allegations that he was manipulating IRIB coverage of his presidency to give more publicity to his preferred successor, Mohsen Rezaei. Perhaps as a response to Ahmadinejad's manipulation of the system, and in reflection of the Supreme Leader's disfavor, IRIB reduced its news coverage of the president, its once glowing depictions now laced with subtle criticism. When Ahmadinejad delivered a speech at a rally in the province of Shiraz, for example, IRIB coverage took aim at his populist image by making it appear like there was low public turn out.[37] It was in this environment of mutual manipulation that Ahmadinejad called for the privatization of the industry. Since challenging IRIB was virtually impossible from a political as well as an economic standpoint (as IRIB employed thousands of Iranians), his remarks were likely meant as an affront to the Supreme Leader rather than a practical proposal.

Another challenge came in June 2013, when an Iranian football club announced the creation of a dedicated satellite television channel, *Persepolis TV*.[38] The Persepolis Television Network was launched under the banner of Iran's first private satellite television network. According to club manager Mohammad Rouyanian, the channel would carry programs "dedicated solely to Persepolis and Iranian culture, especially ethical issues dominating the sport."[39] The network was reported to broadcast coverage of the Persepolis club from within the country via the Hotbird satellite.[40] The fact that Persepolis TV was able to operate inside Iran lends credence to the argument that the satellite prohibition law was only enforced when it was economically or politically expedient. It may also be that as a sports channel, Persepolis TV did not pose the threat that an overtly political channel such as *Saba TV* posed. If correct, it provides further evidence of the system's emphasis on ideological propagation, as opposed to socialization or education.

Satellite TV and the "Cultural Confrontation of Modern Times"

In the 1990s, the narrative of Western cultural imperialism was expertly employed by those advocating prohibition of satellite dishes. The sermons of Ayatollah Jannati taped into themes of the third-world liberation movement, using narrative frames reminiscent of Franz Fanon's *Wretched of the Earth* and Pierre Fourier's *Pedagogy of the Oppressed*, in which oppressed peoples of the world would rise up against their colonialist overloads and shed the ideological, social, and economic bondage of the West.[41] In a collection of essays called *The Cultural Confrontation between Iran and the West in Modern Times*, Ali Davani wrote that America took up the war against Iran from the "colonialist British" following the nationalization of Iranian oil and now wages "*este'mar*" through cultural mediums. Satellite television was one such medium.[42]

It is no surprise, then, that well over a decade after the crisis, broadcast media continued to be a site of contestation. Like before, cultural imperialism was a favored framework for interpreting and controlling the communication products of the West. The IRIB organizational mission published on its website in 2010 is indicative of the broadcaster's evolution as proxy for this struggle. In it, IRIB described the media environment as a "battlefield" where an "intensifying media war" was raging, where "supranational waves and messages have trespassed the geographical and cultural borders," and where Iranians were confronting a "domineering empire of Western media," bent on "cultural conversion." IRIB's mission was to counter this threat by strengthening "cultural solidarity" and "national identity."[43]

Television programs routinely warned viewers of the incendiary effects of satellite television, deeming it a threat to personal identity, religious morals, and Iranian culture. For example, an investigative series about Western fashion aired on IRIB's twenty-four-hour news channel blamed foreign media for "transmitting corrupting influences." Entitled "Loss of Identity Among the Youth," the program featured what appeared to be unscripted interchanges between an IRIB reporter and pedestrians on the street.[44] Interview responses were presented as evidence of a larger enemy offensive against Iranian culture through satellite broadcasting. A voice-over described the situation in ominous terms:

> The enemies of the culture, history, and faith of the Iranian people began this cultural attack many years ago. We, the Iranians, are missing the opportunity to fight this, and to inform the general public and our youth of this. Perhaps it is already too late, but preserving and protecting our culture and faith is our duty as Iranian Muslims.

The program blamed the media for corrupting influences and presented images of women with "bad hijab" and beardless young men with form-fitting shirts as evidence of the Western cultural offensive. In case there was any question of whom or what was to blame, the reporter asked one young woman wearing heavy makeup and hair sprouting out from her headscarf where she got the inspiration for her deviant fashion:

Interviewer: How do you know when something is in fashion?

Woman: We see it outside, on the street, and we see it on Fashion TV.

Interviewer: On the satellite channel?

Woman: Yes.[45]

As this example shows, more than a decade and half after the satellite dish crisis, television continued to be the site of a Manichean struggle between Islam and the West, between Iran and the Great Satan (the US), and between national independence and subjugation. But satellite was not the only mode of the Western cultural offensive; the internet was fast outpacing television as a popular medium for information and entertainment. A new iteration of the cultural onslaught narrative, "soft war," emerged as the regime struggled to confront the next great challenge to its mass communication monopoly: the internet.

Part III

SOFT WAR: THE POLITICS OF THE INTERNET

6

ENTER THE INTERNET

Whereas the debate over satellite dishes exposed the problem of new communication media as a purveyor of foreign culture and ideology, the communications powered political upheaval of 2009 gave name to the problem: soft war (*jang-e narm*). Imminently flexible, soft war was a way for the state to both explain the public protests and justify their violent suppression. After the crisis, the term gained a new dimension, as military thinkers transformed soft war from a strategy of aggression used by Iran's enemies to a strategy of asymmetric warfare used by Iran against the West.

This chapter provides historical context to these developments. Drawing from new primary research, including an array of digital artifacts collected via the Internet Archive as well as expert interviews and records from the Internet Corporation for Assigned Names and Numbers (ICANN) and elsewhere, I offer a history of the internet from 1993 to 2003 and consider elite discourse concerning the internet as a public forum.

The Birth of the Internet in Iran

The first institution to establish an internet connection was the Institute for Studies in Theoretical Physics and Mathematics (IPM, henceforth the Institute) through its membership in the European Academic Research Network (EARN) in January 1993.[1] The connection consisted of a single 9600 baud leased line from the University of Vienna in Austria to the Institute in Niavaran, Iran.[2] The first email was sent in the form of a greeting from the Institute's Director, Mohammad Javad Larijani, to administrators at the University of Vienna.[3] The single line was expanded and developed with the aid of 500 IP addresses allocated through the Network's BITNET system to Iran. At this early stage and with no internal data networks, the Institute was completely dependent on the lines provided through EARN for its connectivity.[4] No doubt cognoscente of the limitations of such an arrangement in the longer term, in 1993, the High Council of Informatics and the state telecommunication monopoly, Telecommunication Company of Iran (*Sherkat-e Mokhaberat-e Iran,* hereafter TCI) began discussion about using the country's telephone lines for internet connectivity, but action was delayed due to lack of investment by TCI and the absence of any clear government policy or impetus.⁵ It was not until 1995, after the establishment of a number of privately run and funded ISPs, that the government took action to develop TCI as the primary ISP of the government.⁶

Around the same time, IRANNET (the Information and Communication Network of Iran) came into operation. Created in 1993, IRANET was born in the cradle of the university as a large virtual bulletin board where scientists could collaborate and communicate. As an internet service provider, it provided access to the web and also offered e-mail services, electronic publishing and website design. Perhaps because of its academic roots, IRANET operated largely without government intervention. The network, along with other emerging ISPs operated with little regulation, riding the wave of the post Iraq war reconstruction economy under President Akbar Rafsanjani, whose pro-business, pro-development philosophy prized scientific and economic advancement over state control, at least for a time.

In a pattern reminiscent of the early years of television, where commercial and state broadcasters operated side by side, in the early stages of the internet, the government held TCI was just one of a number of ISPs Iranians could choose from for connection to the web. The handful of commercial ISP's soon grew by the hundreds and then to over a thousand as internet cafes proliferated in response to consumer demand.

As the technology and popularity of the internet progressed, TCI found itself increasingly pushed to the sidelines—becoming no more than an observer and third string player in the burgeoning internet society. By 2001, it was clear that the private sector competition was having an impact on both its profit margins and infrastructure. Part of the problem was that ISPs were using the national telephone system to provide cheap international calls through the internet. Cyber cafes, many with their own ISPs, competed for customers by offering economy packages of ten–to twenty-hour blocs of internet access, which then would be used to make international calls over the internet, known as voice-over IP. This drove down the price of international calls and lured away TCI customers using its (more expensive) service.

Thus, even as people's access to the telephone network increased threefold between 1998 and 2002, TCI profits decreased by 32 million.⁷ In order to stave off the losses, TCI was forced to reduce its rates for international calls. The government also cracked down on ISPs and internet cafes that offered voice-over IP services. In a large-scale operation in 2001, the police reportedly closed over 400 internet cafes for this reason.⁸

For the first half decade, the internet was almost entirely the province of the academy and the commercial sector.⁹ Efforts to consolidate state control over internet can be traced to a speech by the Supreme Leader and codified by a series of decrees issued by the Supreme Council of the Cultural Revolution in December 2001.¹⁰ Significantly, a directive required all private ISPs in Iran that offered internet connectivity to the Iranian public to route their services through the state telecommunication monopoly, TCI. The directive also required all ISPs to employ filtering systems.¹¹

The effect of these policies was to place all internet access points under a singular gateway owned and operated by the Iranian government. A report on internet filtering by the OpenNet Initiative aptly describes the logic of the move: "Designing the internet infrastructure around a government-managed gateway—rare for a country with this many internet users—offers a central point of control that facilitates the implementation of internet filtering and monitoring of internet use."[12] Not only did the reorganization enable state surveillance and gatekeeping, it also provided the state with the option of "shutting down" the internet in one fell swoop, the existence of a competitive, commercial ISP market in Iran notwithstanding.

Growth of the Internet, 1997–2003

Between 1993 and 2003, lack of adequate investment in infrastructure, high cost of access, and limited technical expertise and education hindered the development of the internet as a mass communication medium. Despite these limitations, Iran had one of the highest internet growth rates in the world.[13]

In 2003, seeing the potential benefit of infrastructural improvements to the Iranian economy both in terms domestic commerce as well as foreign investment, the government began to take steps to expand the nation's infrastructure. It commissioned the French telecommunication company, Alcatel, to install 100,000 Asymmetrical Digital Subscriber Lines (ADSL) in Tehran over three years.[14] By 2004, Iran reported 27,850 kilometers of fiber optic lines in place. The number of private ISPs operating in Iran ballooned to 650, including twelve major certified ISPs and eighteen internet content providers.[15] The state-owned Data Communication Company of Iran was the largest ISP and the provider through which most ISPs obtained internet connectivity.[16]

As the popularity of the internet increased, so too did its use as a forum for political organizing. Some media scholars credit the 1997 presidential elections for bringing the internet to popular awareness, as all three candidates established campaign websites.[17] The student demonstrations of 2 Khordad (May 23, the day Khatami was elected) were also organized on the internet.[18] Others point to the online publication of investigative reports such as those by journalist Akbar Ganji in 2003 as a revelatory moment for Iranian journalism.[19]

One of the earliest instances in which the internet served as a forum to challenge the government monopoly occurred in 2000, with the online publication of the memoirs of Ayatollah Ali Montazeri. The cleric was one of a cadre of leaders of the revolution and successor-designate of Supreme Leader Khomeini. But in the years following the founding of the republic, Montazeri grew increasingly critical of Khomeini's leadership and his concept of *velayat-e faqih*. In 1989, incensed by Montazeri's public intransigence, Khomeini issued a letter formally removing his designation of successor and stripping him of the title of *marja* (source of emulation). Khomeini died soon after. The requirement that Khomeini's successor be a marja was removed, and the then minor cleric, Ali Khamenei, was elevated to Ayatollah and inaugurated the new Supreme Leader.

Despite the intended affront and formal loss of standing, Montazeri remained a popular and influential voice in his home province of Tabriz. He continued to speak critically of the system and its clerical leadership, this time focusing on Khamenei himself. It is no surprise then, that in 1997, amid the state's violent crackdown on Reformist media, the regime placed Montazeri under house arrest. Khamenei justified the move as necessary to protect the Montazeri from assault by hardline critics.

The publication of Montazeri's memoirs in 2000 must be understood within this context. After two years of confinement to his home, virtually cut-off from society, his followers, and the press, Montazeri, with the aid of his son, published his memoirs on the internet for the world to read. The document was no less than an alternative history of the founding and ideals of the Islamic Republic. Even after the website was taken down, sections of the memoir remained in cyberspace, having been republished and quoted by both Iranian and international news outlets and blogs.

The publication of Montazeri's memoirs was an early case in which the internet served as an alternative means of conveying ideas and information outside the established mediums and methods monopolized by the Iranian state.[20] It is also one of the earliest recorded instances in which the government was accused of filtering or blocking of web content. Indeed, in a story published December 14th, the London-based *Al-Sharq al-Awsar* reported that Iranian government authorities had begun "jamming" Montazeri's website "to deny the Iranian people and world public access to his memoirs."[21] The site was removed a week later, presumably due to the technical interference and other pressures from the state.[22] Despite such interventions, the reach of the internet continued to expand. As connectivity increased, so too did public use of the internet as a means of communication. "Web logs", what later became known as "blogs," proved the most popular format and served as the first crisis point in which the Iranian government was forced to recognize the internet as more than a technology of government and universities, but as a potential means of mass communication.

The Rise of the Persian Blogosphere, 2004–8

The year 2004 marked the beginning of the heyday of the Persian language blogosphere. By 2007, Persian was the tenth most popular language on the internet.[23] The Persian language blogosphere ranked the fourth largest in the world.[24] According to one poll in 2004, Iranians considered the internet, over any other media, the most trustworthy source of information and news.[25] The period featured a rapid proliferation of Persian language blogs. The second most popular hosting service, PersianBlog, had 600,000 users.[26] Other popular platforms (also known as "blog farms") included: blogspot.com, blogdrive.com, modblog.com, livejournal.com, 20six.fr, and myblog.de.[27]

As the popularity of blogs became obvious to even the most insulated regime insider, a debate emerged within the print media about how the government should respond. While this discourse was nowhere as extensive as the discourse on satellite dish ownership in the 1990s, it does offer clues about the regime's early thinking about the internet as a potential medium for mass communication. How should the Islamic Republic react to blogs as a popular medium? Should the "Iranian blogosphere" be embraced as a victory for Iranian culture or rejected as a threat? Such questions were at the heart of establishment debate about the internet in the first decade of the twenty-first century. Unsurprisingly, opinions within the regime differed. I will consider positive and negative lines of argumentation regarding blogs now.

Opportunity

A number of newspapers and commentators from both sides of the political spectrum greeted the rise of the Persian blogosphere with open arms. These voices argued that blogs (and by extension the internet) presented a golden opportunity for the Islamic Republic to propagate its faith, ideology, and international leadership. Mohammad Mehdi Mousavi, in a commentary entitled "Writing Web Logs: An Opportunity to Safeguard the Revolution," argued that the government should do more to expand internet connectivity and support blogging. Calling the internet and the rise of the Persian blogosphere an "ideal opportunity that we Iranians must make the most of," Mousavi wrote:

> Considering that web log is an easily accessible, simple and comprehensible form of media, it could play an effective role in giving direction to public opinion. Web logs, as independent communication media that have no ideological affiliation with any particular source, nowadays provide a place in virtual environments for presenting different views and ideas. So by properly utilizing this opportunity and carrying out good plans, we will be able to propagate our revolutionary views and messages first throughout the region and then in the whole world, and in this way we can somehow safeguard our Islamic and revolutionary principles.[28]

While supporting the monitoring of blogs by the government, Mousavi emphasized the need to balance security and "cultural work." He cautioned against the assumption that the government could or should monitor all blogs all the time. To make his point, Mousavi quoted Dr. Hamid Shahriyari, Chairman of the Computer Research Center of Humanities and the Secretary of the State Supreme Council on Transmission of Information, at length:

> This practice that they say the government must control all web logs is, in my opinion, not doable because first of all the government's limited resources would not allow it to do this, and second, this task would basically not accomplish anything important. Let me bring an example to clarify the issue. Suppose that two people who are ordinary citizens of the country are walking down the street

and criticizing the government. Their talks are neither much important, nor do they pose any sort of threat to the future of the system.[29]

Because the communication was between two individuals (as opposed to communication from one individual to many individuals), Shahriyari and Mousavi argued, blogs did not "pose any sort of threat to the future of the system."[30]

By 2005, Iran's leadership was publicly embracing the internet as a means to advance national interests. In his remarks to the High Council on Information Technology, President Ahmadinejad highlighted his country's participation in an upcoming international conference on IT and pledged that Iran would continue to "make use of information technology in line with the national interest and promoting Islamic culture."[31]

State and religious institutions started using the internet to disseminate information and answer religious questions. The Institute for Preserving and Publishing Works of the Supreme Leader Khamenei was among the first to establish an online presence. Others soon followed suit.[32] In 2007, a number of seminaries in Qom announced the publication of the complete texts of many of Islam's leading theologians online.[33]

As early as 2006, some institutions were using a form of instant messaging to communicate directly with religious followers. In a commentary in the conservative paper, *Siyasat-e Ruz*, Mehdi Ahmadi noted that some cultural centers, including the Islamic Communication Organization and the Fatima Masumeh and Imam Reza shrines, Imam Reza had begun to conduct outreach to Iranian youth via the internet through chat rooms and instant messaging. The reach of these institutions was limited, however, because they used the Iranian platform "Paltalk," as opposed to the "free and public chat rooms" frequented by the country's youth.

Another narrative within the public discourse on the internet and blogs pertained to the potential benefits to the government in the provision of services and the creation of public policy. Here, the argument focused on the popularity of blogs among Iranian youth. Identifying Yahoo, MSN, and AOL as the "most famous chat programs," Ahmadi outlined a plan for institutions to use Yahoo Messenger, which he deemed the most popular with Iranian youth, for their online propagation and guidance activities.[34] Blogs also offered the potential to communicate with and to better understand this large portion of the Iranian population, it was argued. The internet had become the "media of choice of the young generation of Iranians," wrote Mousavi; it must be used to the benefit of both teachers and students.

This line of reasoning highlighted the value of the blog as a mechanism for multimodal feedback. Proponents said the blog should be embraced as a pedagogical device, allowing for the strengthening of religious observance in youth and encouraging the path toward religious jurisprudence. In his editorial, Mousavi pointed to the experience of an (unnamed) theology student from a small village who wrote about his studies in a popular blog. The blog allowed his followers to speak to him directly and for him to respond. As a result, according to Mousavi, the student "discovered the needs of [his] audience" and improved his writing and thinking about religious jurisprudence.

A commentary in the Reformist newspaper *E'temad* argued that the medium should be embraced as a means to strengthen the connection between the state and population. Blogs encouraged public feedback and interaction, and as such, should be viewed as a source of information about the interests and opinions of the public. Rather than a threat to regime authority, the blog should be seen as a valuable opportunity for the Iranian leadership "to assess and understand the people's demands and desires and even to adjust and regulate affairs and decide priorities."[35]

Threat

A major counter narrative linked the internet and blogs to ideological security, and by extension, to the security of the state and the nezam. For the hard-liners and conservatives around Khamenei that took up this line of argument, the internet was a soft spot in the national armor, a means through which opponents of the Islamic Republic could disrupt national unity and undermine regime ideology. The internet joined television and radio as a vehicle for the dissemination of foreign ideas and values. "A young person on this side of the world, by means of a small device, can readily receive the thoughts, notions, dreams, intellectual suggestions, and scientific ideas of any other person—even an evil one—from the other side of the world," said Khamenei in a speech on the subject in 2005. On the internet, the ideas of the Islamic Republic could be examined and contrasted with other ideologies in the world. The internet, like satellite broadcasting, was a battlefield—a place where different ideologies were not just in contact, but in competition for saliency, or even truth.

> Today, with the internet, satellites, and the wide variety of communication technologies that are available, words easily spread to every part of the world. This arena where people and the pious present their ideas is a battlefield between different thoughts. Today, we are in a war zone where an intellectual battle is going on.[36]

Like DBS, the internet became a site of epistemic confrontation. The question of taking action against blogs became a choice between winning and losing the battle for ideological supremacy. For a regime that saw its hegemony bound up with its ability to maintain the dominance of its ideology, it was a threat that could not be ignored.

The metaphor of war was extended to a complimentary and supporting narrative about the internet as a threat from within. In this narrative, the internet was a weapon that could be used by Iran's enemies to foment unrest and carry out regime change. One hardline newspaper, playing upon long held concerns about separatists in within Iran boarders, claimed that Arab separatists had created thousands of blogs to inspire separatist movements in the northwestern province near the Turkmenistan border. Thirty-eight thousand websites and blogs created for the "provocation of ethnic minorities" were shut down by the government, the newspaper reported, with 700 made specifically to rally "Turkmen into opposition to the Islamic system."[37]

Soft War

In the course of the debate, the language of cultural imperialism took on a new brand: "soft war" (jang-e narm). Early on, the term was levied to describe the perceived danger posed by the changing communications environment. In this media centric frame, bloggers were no less than an inside threat. The most prolific were deemed traitors, spies, and pawns of foreign adversaries. In one notable example, the Iranian government accused Hossein Derakhshan, whom Sbreberny and Khiabani once deemed the father of Iranian bloggers, of spying for Israel on the grounds that he wrote newspaper articles that "expressed views different from his past viewpoints" after visiting the country.[38] Soft war was used simultaneously as a call for action. In 2006, for example, the head of the state news outlet, IRNA, announced an initiative to recruit "soldiers of soft war" to counter Western information communication activities.[39] Derakhshan was ultimately apprehended and jailed based on a bevy of charges, including: propagating against the regime, co-operating with hostile states, promoting counter-revolutionary groups, insulting Islamic thought and religious figures, and managing obscene websites.[40]

Conservative and hardline outlets used similar framing in reports about political opponents during the 2008 Majles elections. They dubbed the Reformist faction associated with Khatami, the "party of bloggers." One particularly scathing commentary described the internet as a "spider's web" of conspiracy in which Reformist bloggers were working with foreign governments and Iranian exiles to undermine the government.[41] The regime continued to use the frame in later years. In 2017 "Operation Spider" and "Operation Spider 2" targeted a number of fashion models with popular Facebook and Instagram pages. The models were arrested, and their social media accounts were blocked.

A related discourse advocated government action to restrict and regulate speech on the internet, including blogs, due to the dangers the medium presented to Iranian culture and national unity. The need for a gatekeeper to censor content was a premise of many, if not all of the commentary on the subject and employed and accepted by even the most liberal-minded enthusiast of the internet and blogs. According to this narrative, it was the responsibility of the government to restrict access to certain content and information deemed solicitous, blasphemous, or otherwise in violation of the legal and religious strictures of the Islamic Republic.

In conclusion, I have argued that the rise of the Persian blogosphere revealed an internal disagreement within ruling establishment regarding the implications of the popularization of the internet for regime hegemony. Some contended that the internet and blogs should be embraced and utilized for the propagation of regime ideology. Others pointed to the danger such an open access, multidirectional communication medium. These voices argued that the internet was no less than a gaping hole in the nations cultural and ideological armor—a shining invitation to foreign agents to meddle in domestic politics. That there was a debate at all is indicative of just how disruptive the technology was or could be. By 2008, even the most aloof members of the ruling elite had come to recognize the popularity of blogs and the power and potency of the internet as a communication medium. In the years that followed, the establishment would come to recognize just how much it challenged—indeed upended–the incumbent media system.

Early Policy Responses

The government did not wait for the debate over blogs to find its conclusion. In fact, the public and internal argument within the establishment was still underway, when the government began taking steps to assert greater autonomy over the internet and the communication processes it enabled. The major government policies established in response to the internet and blogs between 2001 and 2008 is discussed here.

Registration

One policy response to the concerns raised by members of the establishment arrived in 2007 in the form of a national blog and website registry. The Ministry of Culture and Islamic Guidance described the project as a means to both supervise the activities of blogs and websites and to collect information about the number of government and private sites in various fields.[42] A spokesperson for the Ministry presented the registry as a practical measure that would benefit both internet users and the government. It would give websites and blogs that became subject to a complaint or investigation the opportunity to respond to the charges against them. "Anyone whose site has a known address, whose identity has been made known can be informed if they commit an offense. They can be told: 'Sir, this or that has happened, correct it,' or someone may have a complaint, people have a right [to complain]," said Deputy Culture Minister for Press Affairs Ali Reza Mokhtarpur in an interview with Voice of the Islamic Republic, the state radio service. In other words, by providing his or her name and contact information to the government, the blog or website owner would have the benefit of being forewarned when/if an investigation or legal charge was imminent.[43]

The rationale was put into practice in 2007 with the closure of the online newspaper and news aggregate, *Baztab*.[44] The seizure of the website and revocation of its press license was justified by the fact that the website had not registered with the Ministry and the Ministry did not know who to contact when the investigation was taking place. *Baztab*, in an article detailing the official justification for the closure, indicated with many examples that the Ministry did, in fact, know the owners of *Baztab* and had met with them and corresponded with them on many occasions. "In addition to (Minister of Culture and Islamic Guidance) Saffar-Harandi, other officials of the Guidance Ministry, such as the ministry's deputy head of the press department—who is also the secretary of a group that determines the sites that are illegal—have known *Baztab*'s owners for a long time."⁴⁵

While the plan to register websites and blogs was formally announced in January 2007, the idea had been under consideration and discussion within the ruling establishment for years.⁴⁶ According to some scholars, the notion dates back to 2000–2001, with the policy framework articulated in a speech by the Supreme Leader and subsequent directives of the Supreme Council of the Cultural Revolution.⁴⁷ The announcement of the plan drew immediate criticism from the blogger community as well as from members of the establishment. It was criticized as unrealistic and impractical. One editorial called the scheme to regulate websites and blogs "persisting in the impossible."⁴⁸

Filtering

Yet the plan to register blogs was far from the only strategy employed by the state during this period. A central strategy, one which Iran had been practicing since at least 2000, was the filtering of websites based on text keywords. In 2002, an interagency body was created to set the criteria for identifying unauthorized web sites to be blocked, called the Committee in Charge of Determining Unauthorized Sites.⁴⁹ While the Committee was charged with identifying sites and content to be filtered, the Information Technology Company of Iran was charged with implementing the decisions. Another agency, the Communication Infrastructure Company, was tasked with unifying filtering efforts across Iran.⁵⁰

Still, by 2003, the bite of the filtering was not yet widely felt and the Iranian internet was very much an unregulated space. Khamenei was no doubt aware of the problem. In a question and answer session with Basij members, a young man asked: "Why is it that China, which is a communist country, severely censors the internet but the same does not happen in Islamic Iran?" To this Khamenei responded:

> Of course, there are filters for the Internet in all parts of the world … Every country in keeping with its beliefs, proclivities and interests places filters. This is natural. In our country, there was a period of inattention, but the officials are doing something about it. And they must do it and it is right to do so.⁵¹

The Supreme Leader's answer was both a justification for filtering, which he described as common practice and "natural," and an indication that the work of developing or acquiring a filtering software had already begun. Indeed, Iran acquired filtering software from the US company Secure Computing and began using it in 2005.⁵² As a contemporaneous report by the internet-monitoring group Open Net Initiative (ONI) read:

> Iran has recently acknowledged, as our testing confirms, that it uses the commercial filtering package SmartFilter—made by the US-based company,

Secure Computing —as the primary technical engine of its filtering system. This commercial software product is configured as part of the Iranian filtering system to block both internationally-hosted sites in English and sites in local languages.[53]

The report continued: "SmartFilter, as with all commercial filtering software packages, is prone to over-blocking, errors, and a near-total lack of transparency. In effect, Iran outsources many of the decisions for what its citizens can access on the internet to a United States company, which in turn profits from its complicity in such a regime." Ironically, the publication of the report and the response by the US government likely informed the Iranian government's decision to commission the development of its own filtering software, thus removing Iran's reliance on the United States for its filtering needs.[54]

The government's strategy of filtering, which was in essence the selective blocking of websites Iranians could access on the web using key words, was not without criticism. Take, for example, Rauf Pishvar's scathing commentary on the futility of blocking websites in the newspaper *E'temad*:

> The money spent for this job is unbelievable to the extent that the job itself is unimaginable when one knows all the blocked websites have been able to appear on the internet with new addresses or their users have been able to find access to them by using numerous 'unblocking' programs. Websites (and blogs, accordingly), including Iranian websites, use servers (hosts) 98 percent of which are located in America, and America's laws govern them.[55]

Indeed, as the writer pointed out, the primary complication with applying the tactics used on satellite television of "blocking" or "jamming" an offending website was the fact that many of the websites were hosted on servers outside of Iran, and therefore outside the control of the state. As the technological advancements and workaround referenced by Pishvar suggests, the goal of preventing illicit internet use was a near impossible task. Like the game "whack-a-mole," it required tremendous energy and resources and generated little tangible returns.

Reduced Speed

Another government tactic of control was placing limits on connection speed. In October 2006, the Ministry of Information and Communications Technology ordered all ISPs in Iran to limit their download speed to 128 Kbps for home users and internet cafes, and 512 Kbps for commercial users and government offices.[56] This policy, which restricted the ability of internet users to download multimedia content, was likely intended, in part, to reduce the circulation of entertainment videos and other content that would compete with state sponsored products for audience attention.[57]

Intelligence and Police

Filtering and reduced speed were two technological components of the government's effort to rein in the internet. As time went on, it became clear that the human, bureaucratic, and legalistic components were equally important. A number of intelligence and enforcement organizations tasked with policing the internet were created. Perhaps most important was the Center for Inspecting Organized Crime, a special department within the IRGC dedicated to investigating organized crime, terrorism, espionage, and social and economic crimes on the internet in cyberspace. The department's investigative force, *Gerdab*, has been called one of the largest cyber armies in the world.[58]

In the coming years, a high court and governing oversight body would be created, thus completing the legal and bureaucratic infrastructure needed for a comprehensive internet censorship regime. At the same time as the government was working to restrict and dilute the potency of the internet, President Mahmood Ahmadinejad was harnessing the power of the internet for political ends. We turn now to the 2009 election contest, and our next inflection point.

7

THE 2009 ELECTION CRISIS

The aim is to defend the Islamic system and the Islamic Republic against a full-fledged movement dependent on oppression, hypocrisy, money and huge and advanced scientific and media capabilities.
—Supreme Leader Ali Khamenei, 2009[1]

Variously deemed the "Twitter Revolution" and the "Green Revolution," the large-scale protests that began in response to the fraudulent presidential election in 2009 were initially celebrated in the West as a victory for the people of Iran and proof of the democratizing potential of the internet and social media in authoritarian states. For some Western neo-conservatives and liberal internationalists, it was evidence of widespread discontent with the ruling regime.[2] The event coincided with a trend in Western scholarship that held up "new media" as a liberation technology and credited it for kicking off the domino-like wave of antigovernment protests and uprisings known as the "Arab Spring" in early 2010. The basic argument was that the internet created a "virtual public sphere" where social movements were born.[3] What Marwan Kraidy later called "hypermedia," the global, digitally networked technology of the internet and mobile telephony allowed publics to bypass government censors and organize mass protests.[4]

The internet was, indeed, a critical site of contestation in the post-election crisis. Historian Ali Ansari aptly describes the period in Iran as "the first example of mass social protest in which the internet played a central role."[5] Although understanding the strategies and tactics of the opposition movement is essential for decoding the political and social dynamics of this period, my analysis is primarily concerned with the regime's handling of the demonstrations and unrest following the announcement of the ballot results.[6]

This chapter begins with a short chronology of the election crisis. It goes on to explore what we will come to understand as the Janus-faced nature of the internet in Iran as both a potent cudgel for repression and persecution used by the state and a tool for delegitimization used by those whose collective power posed, at the time, the most serious challenge to the regime's hold on power since the founding of the Islamic Republic up to that date.

Chronology of the Crisis

On June 12, 2009, Iran held its tenth presidential election. Four candidates competed for the presidency: the incumbent and first-term President Mahmoud Ahmadinejad, former prime minister Mir Hossein Mousavi, former Islamic Revolutionary Guard Corps (IRGC) commander and head of the Expediency Council, Mohsen Rezaei, and former Majles speaker Mehdi Karoubi. Under law, campaign season is restricted to eighteen days and campaign activity must cease the day before the vote. During this short window, the candidates competed for public support through a range of media forums, from national television to Facebook. They exchanged views in the country's first live, nationally televised debates.[7] The candidates and their supporters were also allowed to congregate (provided the candidates secured a license) in public spaces for rallies and events.

Domestic and foreign media followed the election day with much anticipation.[8] And for good reason. By any measure voter turnout was immense, as was the enthusiasm of voters of all persuasions at polling sites across the country. The level of participation was so high, according to the state, that voting hours had to be extended in some localities.[9]

While the majority of eligible voters were in Tehran and so the vote tallies could be sent to the Interior Ministry by courier, results from polling locations in the other provinces had to be sent via fax.[10] It was generally agreed that because of the unusually high voter turnout in conjunction with the inefficacies and complexities built into Iran's paper balloting system (in which a voter must legibly and accurately write in the name and number of the candidate), the results would not be known for a day or more. It was, therefore, a major surprise when state media reported the results soon after the polls closed.[11] The final tally, issued by the Ministry of the Interior, showed Ahmadinejad winning by a large majority, with 63 percent of the vote. The Reformist favorite, Mousavi, was reported to have won only 34 percent, with Rezaei and Karroubi wining 2 and 1 percent, respectively.[12] Given the large mobilization of voters in opposition to Ahmadinejad, the percentages, and the speed with which the votes were tallied, many observers, including members of the ruling establishment such as the conservative presidential contender Mohsen Rezaei, raised questions about the validity of the results. Each new detail and piece of data that emerged strengthened the case— spearheaded by the defeated opposition candidates Mousavi and Karroubi—that there were serious irregularities in the voting process and counting of ballots. In the days following the election, scholars examined the data released by the Interior Ministry in an effort to deduce whether fraud had taken place, and if so, if it was extensive enough to invalidate the results. The answer was affirmative on both counts.

The overtness of the fraud and the obstinacy of the authorities in response were doubtless a driver of many of the first demonstrations.[13] People took to the streets to declare their outrage. The streets of Tehran and other major metropolises filled with protesters, and "where is my vote?" became a popular rallying cry.[14] Almost every day that followed saw large-scale, nonviolent demonstrations. Estimates of participants number up to 3 million.[15] It was in these circumstances that a loose coalition of people and groups began to emerge. The protesters were in different locations but joined in the conviction that the election was rigged and they must publicly demand what their nominal leader, Mousavi, called the "people's denied rights." The activism would soon become known the world over as the Green Movement.

The government responded relatively swiftly. Mousavi and Karroubi were apprehended by security officials and imprisoned within hours of the announcement of Ahmadinejad 's victory.[16] Within days, the foreign press, many of whom were granted visas to cover the election, found their licenses revoked and visas invalidated, forcing them to leave the country with all possible speed. Members of the domestic print and online media became targets of surveillance, intimidation, and threats. Other journalists were seized from their place of work or residence and subjected to prolonged interrogation, solitary confinement, and physical and psychological abuse. Some reporters and bloggers were imprisoned for days, weeks, months, or even years.

A week later, on June 19, 2009, the Supreme Leader took to the *minibar* (a pulpit or podium where a cleric leads prayers) to call for an end to the demonstrations, which were at that time occurring almost daily in capitals across the country. In a speech to congregants broadcast live to the nation on radio and television, Khamenei signaled that he would no longer tolerate the public questioning of the election results. Those who continued to protest would face "consequences."

> Street challenges after the elections are not the right thing to do. This is, in fact, challenging the principle of elections and democracy. I want everyone to end this sort of action. If they do not end it then the consequences lie with them.[17]

The Supreme Leader's remarks proved the opening salvo in a large-scale campaign to silence opposition parties and clamp down on public expressions of dissent.[18] These measures were accompanied by show trials of Reformist members of the political elite; televised forced confessions of dual-national academics and journalists; and the mass imprisonment of student activists, civil society leaders, and anyone who happened to get caught up in the maelstrom.[19]

Media Inflection Point

The 2009 election crisis was an inflection point both in the political history of the Islamic Republic and in the pattern of regime domination of mass communication media. Indeed, as the following pages will argue, the Green Movement revealed the extent to which the internet challenged the state-dominated mass communication paradigm. Paradoxically, while many in the ruling establishment considered the internet a threat to regime power, it ultimately proved an asset in the struggle to suppress the opposition movement and project hegemony.

A Liberation Technology

As a media for ideology transmission, the internet presented a unique challenge for a regime that cut its teeth on the traditional propaganda of billboards and film during the Iran-Iraq War and the not-too-subtle art of signal jamming satellite television in the 1990s. Part of the challenge related to the internet's global, decentralized nature, where every user can contribute content and report on events and information and such information can be accessed and exchanged almost instantaneously by users all over the world. Another contributing factor was the comparatively low barrier to entry. All that was required was access to a computer or mobile phone with a connection to the internet via the national telecommunication system. Although the cost for accessing the web was low, the benefit was not. For many people the internet offered the only opportunity to escape the rigid strictures of state-imposed Islam and communicate authentically in the safety of anonymous communities and protective avatars. Iranians posted art and amateur journalism, argued about politics, and exchanged cooking recipes in what was fast becoming the virtual public square.[20] It was precisely this open and relatively anonymous forum that made it so difficult for the regime to police. The internet, in short, undermined the government's well-worn role of information moderator, censurer, and manipulator, and, in the early days of the post-election crisis, complicated the state's efforts to identify and apprehend protesters.

Pointing to these new challenges and the internet's ability to reach millions of people across the country, some Iranian intellectuals foresaw an age in which the internet transformed the way that social movements were organized. Writing in *Mardom Salari* six years earlier, Mohammad Hossein Adib predicted that the internet would create a "third-wave society" in Iran. Deeming the internet the "hero of democracy," Adib argued that the internet would bring about a fundamental reordering of power relations within society. In the Iran of the past, wrote Adib, the public was confined to expressing its desires through proxy "intellectuals." Not so in the internet society.

> The intellectuals used to be the heroes in the exchange of ideas and news, the ones who used to break the restrictions imposed by the state on the exchange of news and ideas. However, in the third-wave society, the hero of democracy is the internet, which makes the exchange of thoughts and news possible among the citizens without the control of the state.[21]

The internet empowered individuals to express ideas and influence public policy directly and continually, Adib argued. Unlike social movements of the past, no single intellectual or group would lead the third-wave society. All Iranians could lead and contribute. Adib's argument implies that such a movement, via the internet, would be immune to regime efforts to stifle speech and arrest the march of sociopolitical change. A leaderless movement, the third-wave society could not be debilitated by the removal or suppression of a single person or party.

Adib's prediction about the challenge the internet would pose to the regime's inherently conservative impulse bent on self-preservation and the maintenance of the status quo proved prescient. Mere hours after the Supreme Leader's June 19 speech, Reformist candidates Karroubi and Mousavi were apprehended by the powerful intelligence and national security force, the Islamic Revolutionary Guard Corps (*Sepah-e Pasdaran-e Enqelab-e Eslami*, also known as IRGC). They were not alone. Hundreds of intellectuals, public leaders, journalists, and campaign staff were swept up in the government dragnet in the days that followed and ultimately put on trial.[22] Yet the street demonstrations continued. The seemingly organic growth and horizontal power structure of the opposition movement meant that the removal of the traditionally centripetal node of power—the candidate and campaign—did not demonstrably affect the pace and voraciousness of the political activities conducted in their name. Nor did the government's imprisonment of student activists, website administrators, and bloggers—at least at first. Even the security forces' arrest of Ahmadinejad's Reformist opponents was no match for the web, it seemed. After Mousavi was taken into custody, for example, one of his devotees in Germany who ran the presidential candidate's Facebook page continued to make posts and facilitate the organization of protests.[23]

Despite the intimidation and arrest of activists (or anyone suspected of participating in the protest movement), information about fast-breaking events continued to circulate. Mobile phones connected to the internet circulated information about upcoming protests that newspapers refused to print. Iran scholars Mohammad Hadi Sohrabi-Haghighat and Hadi Mansuri describe the cycle of communication and action on the internet as such:

> There was a cycle between the streets and the Net: people planned a demonstration, discussed the slogans and strategies on the web, actualized the plans in the streets and confronted security forces, then tuned back to the internet and published the pictures, news and videos of the incidents, discussed the outcomes and prepared for the next demonstration.[24]

Websites and blogs became a forum through which an alternative account of events could be communicated and recorded. Iranians took to the web to challenge the election data, discuss abnormalities in the tallies, and report personal observations and experience at the polls. The internet also allowed citizens to fill the void of information and reporting created by the lack of coverage of the protests by state television and the exodus of the international press. Amid this information vacuum, anyone with a cell phone and access to the internet became a citizen reporter with the ability to inform the world about events. With mottos such as "every Iranian, one media," and "you are the media," Iranians used the internet to broadcast a torrent of news, images, and video across the country and the world.[25]

Importantly, social media (largely Twitter and Facebook) proved vital tools to document and publicize the violent repression of peaceful demonstrations. During the protests of June 15, demonstrators and witnesses took to social media to report on and document the dispatch of Basij and law enforcement personnel to violently confront protesters. One can argue that the international media grew dependent on such internet-savvy Iranians to provide information and footage about developments that their reporters, having been expelled from the county, could not. For example, the postscript of one BBC News article reads:

> Are you in Iran? Have you witnessed any demonstrations? Are you attending any celebration gatherings? Send your videos and pictures to yourpics@bbc.co.uk or text them to +44 7725 100 100. If you have a large file, you can upload it here.[26]

Neda and the Sting of Foreign Scrutiny

The Islamic Republic has proved time and again its sensitivity to foreign opinion despite assertions of independence and self-sufficiency embodied in the post-revolutionary slogan "neither East nor West." Public images of police brutality, government injustice, and election fraud aroused serious concern within the regime, particularly as it played in public opinion of its constituencies in the region as well as on the "Arab street." The concern about loss of face among these populations on the world stage in general may have made the regime more circumspect in its persecution and been a restraining factor preventing more state-sponsored violence.[27] The opinion of the international community mattered to the regime not so much because of the censure and sanctions that could be inflicted for its actions, but in terms of prestige, bruising its self-image as a legitimate world power, leader of the Islamic world, and defender of the downtrodden.

In a retrospective interview, former head of IRIB Ezatollah Zarghami acknowledged the negative impact of the Green Movement on the legitimacy of the Islamic Republic in the eyes of the international community.

> Had the Sedition [the post-election protests] not taken place, the international reputation and the strength of the system would have become more powerful and more successful than ever before due to the high percentage of people who took part in the election, and the revolution would have moved forward with a stronger backing.[28]

The murder of Neda Agha-Soltan on June 20 was perhaps the most infamous example of regime brutality and the power of the internet to generate global outrage. Agha-Soltan, accompanied by her music teacher, was walking down the street with other protesters when a sniper from a rooftop shot her in the head. She fell to the ground. A British-trained doctor witnessed the event and tried to help her but it was too late. Agha-Soltan died almost instantly. The event in its entirety was caught in grisly detail in a video taken by a bystander with his mobile phone. The man sent the footage to a handful of trusted friends in Europe and the United States. Within twenty-four hours the video had gone viral on YouTube and was being covered by major international media outlets.

The Iranian government was slow to respond to the allegation that a plainclothes member of the security forces fired the deadly sniper shot. Despite the fact that the event had made it to the front pages of many international newspapers, national television and radio made no mention of the event. IRIB leadership and its state overseers likely calculated that the story would soon fade from interest amid the deluge of other stories and the state's lack of acknowledgment of the incident.[29]

Yet the attention did not flicker out and die. Quite to the contrary. The incident attracted new scrutiny by foreign governments and drew tens of thousands of people to the streets all over the world to demand accountability from the Iranian government and to express solidarity with young people like Agha-Soltan who continued to protest despite such egregious acts of persecution and butchery.[30] While the shooting and the accompanying and subsequent vandalism and violence was attributed to the Green Movement by the regime, in reality, it was largely the work of the IRGC and the Basij and men hired to masquerade as protesters.

This incident became a powerful example of the use of technology to expose the human rights violations of the Iranian government and the power of such coverage to affect the domestic political discourse of the ruling elite. The violent suppression of the demonstrations resulted in a number of fatalities (estimates vary from nineteen to over seventy), thousands of arrests, untold hours of interrogation and harassment, and numerous reports of the torture and rape of prison detainees.[31]

A Repression Technology

While the internet aided protesters against the regime, it also served the regime as a means of silencing opponents and asserting its hegemony. The regime utilized the communicative power and intelligence-gathering potential of the internet to its advantage during the crisis. State intelligence agents found some success in infiltrating online forums activists used for organizing. Such virtual networks had emerged as the population of disaffected, underemployed youth grew and the space for civil society constricted thanks to state policies and religious edicts that pushed more and more political and social activity into the gender-segregated cloisters of the Majles, madrassa, and mosque. Indeed, one of the first steps the architects of the revolution took once in power was to eliminate a number of civil society organizations like student unions, which had been instrumental to the success of the revolution but were now feared for their potential to unseat the new regime. In the absence of such public forums, young people turned their energy and attention to the virtual world of Facebook and its Iranian equivalent *Orkut*. It made sense then that these websites became almost by default the major outlet for disaffected Iranians to express dissent and organize Green Movement protests.

The regime put intensive effort into filtering and blocking such websites in the hope of stopping who they deemed counter-revolutionaries from plotting against the regime. The practice proved minimally effective, as filters were routinely circumvented by VPNs and other techniques. The regime had better success when it came to monitoring and surveillance. Such activity thwarted a major Green Movement demonstration planned for February 11, 2010. In the weeks prior,

Facebook and blogs were abuzz with discussions and planning for the protests. It was to be held on the 22 Bahman, the anniversary of the founding of the Islamic Republic. The date was chosen for its pragmatic advantages as much as symbolic effect. As a government holiday, the public were expected and encouraged to be on the streets celebrating and so the government relaxed strictures on public congregation.

The Green Movement online activists circulated instructions for a "Trojan horse strategy," in which people would come to 22 Bahman ceremonies in regular clothes under the guise of ordinary, regime-loving citizens. Then, at the given signal, they would take out green scarves and bandanas in a collective (and cinematic) message of dissent.[32] Clued in on the plan through its clandestine patrol of blogs and social networking sites, the state wielded the joint cudgels of intimidation and suppression. While some skirmishes, arrests, and government violence were reported, the authorities were largely successful in preventing a stand-off between the regime and Green Movement activists and effectively stopped the demonstrations before they started.[33]

The government dispatched thousands of security officers to Freedom Square (*Meydan-e Azadi*) the night before the holiday to intimidate the opposition and to block it from organizing. The Ministry of Information reportedly sent text messages to opposition activists reading "rioters would be killed today," while government employees were instructed to take part in the festivities as pro-government demonstrators.[34] The authorities complemented such defensive maneuvers with a media campaign to promote public participation. Government and religious leaders encouraged followers to attend, extolling the event as "a historic referendum in response to opponents and enemies of the state and the country's Islamic Revolution."[35] The move appears to have had the desired effect, as organizers called off the rally. Those who insisted on showing up at Azadi found themselves overwhelmed by regime supporters and unable to congregate.

In addition to its value for surveillance and infiltration of Green Movement forums, the internet was also valuable as a tool for the outsourcing of intelligence and police enforcement activities. The strategy was on full display during the Green Movement protests with the publication of over thirty photos of Green Movement protesters on the website of the Office for Investigating Organized Crime, *Gerdab*. The photos, many of which were taken from social media posts of participants and spectators and showed the faces of individuals wanted by the authorities circled in red, were circulated online and published in Iranian newspapers. In posting the photos, the Office for Investigating Organized Crime said that the identified individuals were wanted for "acts of sedition." Anyone with information relating to the identity of the individuals pictured was asked to contact the authorities through a Gerdab email address and telephone number provided.[36]

The impact of this online strategy of intimidation, public shaming, and intelligence collection defies easy measurement. However, what is clear is that the tactic was threatening enough to elicit a retributive response from Green Movement activists.[37] The digitally empowered opposition and their diaspora sympathizers countered the regime's actions by creating a similar website aimed at identifying Iranian regime operatives, while outside technologists advised activists of how to shut down the Gerdab website through distributed denial-of-service (DDoS) attacks.[38]

Another regime tactic was to target individuals associated with online news media (some with print newspaper affiliates) deemed unacceptably critical of the election process and the government's handling of the opposition movement. IRGC forces aligned with Ahmadinejad and the Supreme Leader arrested and interrogated the owners and staff of online news outlets, forcing the sites to close and redacting their license to operate, which in turn forced the online newspapers to apply for a new license under a different name and construct their news service anew.[39] This delayed the reappearance of alternative news outlets, reduced the number of information sources, and discouraged investigative journalism. While the closing of online news outlets individually would only provide a short respite from critical news about the regime (as had been practiced in the past), the round-up of editors and the closure of sites in aggregate created a vacuum of domestic news reporting online.

As previously mentioned, IRIB initially refrained from covering the Green Movement protests. But when the demonstrations could no longer be ignored due to international coverage as well as domestic criticism from voices within the ruling establishment, IRIB changed course. The state broadcaster began to carry reportage of opposition demonstrations, but only in tandem with pro-government rallies, however small by comparison.[40] Still, barring a few exceptions, the national news media and the state broadcaster largely ignored the violence. For example, IRIB news programs largely overlooked the violent clashes between the government and the opposition activists on December 27, despite international media coverage. As one Reformist newspaper editorial complained:

> Most government controlled newspapers and news agencies run by those in power avoided any mention of the *Ashura* incidents and the blood that was shed in the month of Moharram. Instead, they covered the other important (!) news in the country. News such as the details of Mr. Ahmadinejad's future trips and his important remarks that "one can freely express opinions in Iran" and also "John Kerry's trip to Iran with ifs and buts" formed the headlines of the government-controlled media.[41]

The news agency affiliated with the IRGC, *Fars*, responded to international reports of multiple deaths during the December 27 protests with incredulity, accusing foreign media of exaggerating the totals. Citing the head of law enforcement for greater Tehran, Azizollah Rajabzadeh, *Fars* maintained that the police had received no reports of deaths or injury during the incidents.[42]

Another tactic the regime utilized during the post-election crisis related to short message service (SMS). Like Internet Service Providers (ISPs) in Iran, all mobile services were routed through the state-owned telecommunication giant Telecommunications Company of Iran (TCI). In 2005, Ahmadinejad's Principalists used this monopoly to send text messages to Basij members ordering them to vote for him. There is evidence to suggest that similar methods were used to mobilize the vote for Ahmadinejad in 2009.[43]

According to complaints filed with the Guardian Council following the election, SMS service was shut off entirely on election day. It is not clear how this would advantage one candidate over the other, besides the obvious impact on the ability of campaign committees to coordinate the monitoring of polls and the observation of the final counts.[44]

The Deterioration of Consensus

In the first days after the election, the establishment took a number of steps to convey unity of opinion within the establishment regarding the electoral results. The effort was headed by the Supreme Leader, who took the usual step of endorsing the election results the morning after the vote. Hailing the large turnout at the polls, the statement from the Office of the Supreme Leader deemed the election a victory for the Islamic Republic and urged the other candidates to concede defeat in the name of national unity. "The elected and honorable president is the president of the entire nation, and especially yesterday's rivals must support him in a unified manner," said Khamenei in the statement.[45]

While the Leader did not explicitly name Ahmadinejad the winner of the contest, consumers of state media products could be forgiven for thinking he did. The official television service, Vision of the Islamic Republic, for example, described the Leader's statement as congratulating the nation for their high turnout and the re-election of Ahmadinejad." A number of members of the ruling establishment followed Khamenei's example and issued statements of congratulations for distribution in the state and conservative press. On June 14, state television reported that both Majles Speaker, Ali Larijani, and the head of Iran's Judiciary, Ayatollah Mahmoud Hashemi Shahroudi, sent letters to the president-elect congratulating him on his victory. The same day, state media reported that more than 200 members of Majles signed a letter congratulating the president on his victory.[46]

Online and broadcast news media publicized a stream of congratulatory statements from foreign leaders as well. Palestinian Hamas, Pakistani prime minister Syed Yusuf Raza Gilani, Venezuelan president Hugo Chavez, Tajik president Emomali Rahmon, and Iraqi president Jalal Talabani were among those reported as endorsing Ahmadinejad.[47] It also appears that the Ahmadinejad administration actively sought recognition of his authority in the international community; he traveled to Russia to attend a meeting of the Shanghai Cooperation Organization even before the Guardian Council had deemed his re-election valid.[48] The image of Ahmadinejad shaking hands with Russian president Dmitry Medvedev signaled that Russia, an important global power and trade partner, accepted and embraced Ahmadinejad's authority.[49] The public support of foreign leaders signaled the endorsement of Iran's neighbors, important allies, and top trade partners of the election outcome and Ahmadinejad's authority to represent Iran.

In addition to foreign heads of state, some ayatollahs endorsed Ahmadinejad's claim. Ayatollah Tabataba'i, Imam Jomeh for Esfahan, for example, pronounced the election results valid and the winner clear: "Honestly, I have not seen a healthier or more extensive election than the tenth presidential election," Tabataba'i told congregants.[50] Barring this and a few other exceptions, however, the religious establishment was largely silent, neither congratulating the president nor decrying the results.[51] One editorial suggested that the establishment in Qom had been asked to refrain from issuing congratulations.[52]

While some officials worked hard to promote the appearance of regime consensus in support of Ahmadinejad, others made statements that drew attention to the growing cleavages within the ruling establishment. Indeed, one can argue that problem was not the existence of a formidable opposition to the president, but rather, the public airing of dissent from within the establishment about the establishments handling of the election results.[53]

The situation was an outlier in Iranian electoral politics to this point. In previous presidential elections, such as that of 2005, the losing contenders would make their objections known to the Guardian Council and the public, only to drop their complaints later in the name of national unity. The tradition in which the losing candidates accepted the results of the election, regardless of evidence of fraud, was not followed by the opponents of Ahmadinejad in 2009. On the contrary, Mousavi publicized the detailed complaint his campaign filed with the Guardian Council, while the conservative candidate Rezaei used a television appearance to express his dissatisfaction with the election process and also filed a complaint with the Council.[54] Later, it was announced that the Rezaei campaign had formally withdrawn his complaint, a move which is more indicative of the political pressure he felt from his conservative base, rather than any objective problem with his dispute filed with the Council.[55] But the damage was done. By openly questioning the legality of the election process and outcome, Mousavi and Rezaei's voices helped to pierce the facade of regime consensus.

Other voices, both lay and clerical, undermined the picture of unity that the Supreme Leader sought to convey. In a letter published on the Ghalam website, Ayatollah Yusef Sane'i urged the public to continue peaceful protests against the regime.[56] Despite having issued a formal letter of congratulations to the president-elect soon after the results were announced, Speaker Ali Larijani criticized the Guardian Council for its failure to serve as an impartial arbiter of the election disputes. He publicly reprimanded the council for its partisanship and suggested that the protesters' complaints had substance and should be respected.[57] Others expressed dissent through symbolic acts. The inauguration ceremony was nationally televised and an important demonstration of regime unity. Following the disputed 2009 election, however, a number of senior clerics and politicians chose not to attend. Khomeini's grandson, Hassan Khomeini, the keeper of his tomb and an unofficial, but symbolically important, member of the ruling elite, was also notably absent.[58]

Such hyper-mediated verbal and symbolic acts revealed significant fissures within the ruling establishment about the power of the president, Supreme Leader, and Guardian Council and the sanctity of elections. Khamenei invited this situation in part by striking out forcefully and publicly on the side of Ahmadinejad. Addressing the nation on June 19, Khamenei demanded that the nation accept Ahmadinejad as their president; to refuse to abide by the outcome of the election was to deny the sovereignty of the Supreme Leader and the legitimacy of the system he represented. But this is precisely what occurred.

The public dissent of regime insiders revealed deep cracks in the foundation of legitimacy from which the establishment derived hegemonic power.[59]

Manufacturing Consent

For years, the public ritual of popular suffrage worked to support the illusion of popular consent. The 2009 presidential election was no different. The fact that Iranians of all classes, ethnicities, and creeds had the ability to vote for president and the fact that a record 85 percent of the population participated served as a shining indicator of the system's popular legitimacy.[60] For those who wanted to see it, the Iran's near universal suffrage was further evidence of the democratic nature of the Islamic Republic.

Over the eighteen days of Iran's legally permitted campaign season, people all over the world watched the candidates face off in the nation's first live televised presidential debates. The campaign teams of Ahmadinejad, Karroubi, Mousavi, and Rezaei worked to rally supporters through the internet and other formal and informal organizing methods. The country opened its doors to foreign news reporters, who came to Tehran in droves to cover the election. Images of pre-election gatherings revealed an eager and engaged populace.[61] Enthusiastic public engagement during the days leading up to the election and on election day combined to lend the process legitimacy based on popular acclamation. It sent the message that most Iranians considered the act of voting a meaningful exercise with the potential to affect the election outcome. The impression of a competitive contest, complete with enthusiastic public participation, vigorous political debate, and foreign media coverage signaled that elections in Iran were a meaningful exercise of electoral choice. Although people expected a degree of manipulation, they could not have anticipated such blatant voting fraud. Ali Ansari explains the fury generated with the election results:

> Months of building anticipation, excitement and anxiety exploded into anger as people poured into the streets. The fury was generated not simply because Ahmadinejad had been re-anointed president, but because many people believed they had been duped into participating in a political charade.[62]

It is understandable, then, that regime leaders and spokespeople sought to minimize the protests, framing them as unexceptional and a natural and predictable reaction to the news that their avowed candidate had not won.[63] The fact that the opposition was able to organize and demonstrate at all served as evidence of the democratic process at work, suggesting a degree of official toleration, and even encouragement of, political conflict.

The promise of a legal pathway to rectifying the disagreement over the election results supported the facade of legal legitimacy and blunted the ire of the losing campaigns, at least a bit.[64] Indeed it may be argued that the strategy was successful for a time in mollifying public anger over the election's lawlessness by doubling down on their support for law and order. For a time, officials were able to avoid recognizing the public unrest or engaging with claims of fraud by deferring to legal process. The Minister of the Interior, for instance, told reporters that the constitution allowed candidates to file a protest with the Guardian Council within three days and then an investigation would take place; in the meantime, the public should stay calm and refrain from protesting.[65] Thus, the early demonstrations against the election results served the image of pluralist political process and its associated implication of popular consent and legalistic legitimate authority.[66]

9 Dey

As the seriousness of the opposition movement grew more difficult to ignore, the regime tried to use pro-goverment rallies as a way to reclaim the mantle of protest and revolutionary struggle that increasingly came to define the Green Movement. The rallies were unlikely to have changed the opinions of opposition supporters, but that was not their intention. The mass-mediated demonstrations spoke to an audience sympathetic to the Iranian government but suffering a crisis of confidence due to the ongoing Green Movement protests and retaliatory state-sponsored violence. It may be argued the IRIB served the regime well in this capacity, with each news report about the pro-government rallies creating the impression of popular consent to the system and its rulers.

One example of such news creation, or political spectacle, was the pro-government rallies held on Ashura, the holiday commemorating the battle of Karbala, December 30, 2009 and referred to as "9 Dey" for the date on the Iranian calendar. The event was held up as the beginning of the end for the Green Movement, the moment in which the "people" took back the streets and expressed the popular will.

Government supporters used 9 Dey as evidence of popular consent to the system, the Supreme Leader, and the Ahmadinejad presidency. In their characterization, the event signaled the reconciling of internal dissenters to the hegemony of the system and the uniting of the Iranian people behind its elected leaders. IRIB Director Zarghami described the event as a collective rebuttal to the enticements of foreign and internal conspirators. In his telling, it was the people who led and organized the rally, not the government. The protests during the weeks before were the last straw, Zarghami said in an interview in 2013. "The nation sensed the danger, took a firm decision and came on the stage." He continued:

> First, they rose up in provincial towns on 8th Dey and the following day on 9th Dey they rose up in Tehran. In fact, the officials of the country and the organizations that were in charge, such as us, walked behind the people and followed them. People themselves took charge of the events.[67]

Hamid Mowlana, an advisor to Ahmadinejad, similarly described 9 Dey as signaling the victory of the regime and the end of the opposition movement. "The atmosphere after 9 Dey shows that some of the opposition leaders, who realized that the situation was bad, decided to return to the system's fold."[68]

Overshadowing the consent-signaling tactics of the government were the powerful expressions of opposition to the election outcome and the system that allowed such a transgression to occur. The protests against the election process, against Ahmadinejad, and, later, against the Supreme Leader were among the largest in the history of the Islamic Republic. Iranians from all walks of life in urban centers across the country took part in the demonstrations. That the protests continued for almost a year after the election spoke of the depth of public anger and dissent. Any benefit the populist regime might have derived in the highly mediated election ritual was rendered null by the overtness of the election fraud and the accommodation of such blatant injustice by the Supreme Leader and his ruling circle.

Along the course of the crisis, the internet emerged as a powerful tool for the opposition to undermine the illusion of public consent and regime consensus. International observers and opposition sympathizers used it to record the antidemocratic acts and violations of electoral rights and so provide a real, uncensored history of events. One of the more ingenious tactics used by Green Movement activists was the appropriation of visual and audio material that accompanied state-sponsored cultural products aimed at bolstering allegiance to the state. I will discuss such tactics now.

A Challenge to the State's Monopoly on Shi'ite Nationalism

Green Movement opposition discourse embraced and re-appropriated symbols and themes of Twelver Islam and the Islamic Republic. Activists used patriotic music and images from the Iran-Iraq war to mobilize protestors against the state, ironically the original sources of such cultural products. In visual montages posted on YouTube, Green Movement digital activists paired photos of government brutality and the faces and names of those who died during the unrest with well-known anthems from the Iran-Iraq War. Supporters even repurposed Gholam Koveitipur's popular song lamenting the loss of comrades, *Chang-e Del* (Heart's Harp), which is best known for its use in Iran-Iraq War films, in a video tribute to those slain during the 2009 protests.[69] Similarly, digital activists drew from the Quran and Shi'ite narratives and iconography to generate and enthuse followers while remaining within the confines of acceptable speech by not criticizing the regime directly (Figure 4 and 5). One poster (Figure 4) reads:

> *Our politics is like our religion and in our religion, slander is a crime. In our religion lies are forbidden. In our religion stealing peoples' votes is a sin. In our religion protecting the sanctity of people is obligatory. In our religion killing people and rape is forbidden. In our religion God is great; God is greater than any idol and any master. God is great, death to the dictator, this is the sound of God erupting from the throats of our nation. Friday, 4 Dey [25 December] and Saturday, 5 Dey [26 December] at 10 pm, everywhere we are, we will become the voice of God.*[70]

Such digital posters, what Mona Kasra calls "digital-networked images" appropriated religious and cultural products traditionally associated with the

Figure 4 A digital poster from Green Movement website calling on Iranians to shout, "God is great" and "death to the dictator" from their rooftops at 10 pm on December 25th and 26th in a show of collective protest deliberately reminiscent of similar expressions of dissent by the revolutionary opposition movement protesting the Shah in 1978–79.

nation-state.[71] The Green Movement discourse seized upon the state's favored nationalist dichotomy of "us versus them"—a dichotomy that had been used with some success to generate patriotism during and after the Iran-Iraq war and later to describe and explain the US-Iran nuclear stand-off—and applied it to an online narrative of the unrest as the "people versus the state." In short, the opposition used the very communicative strategies previously employed to legitimize the state to challenge that legitimacy, casting the state and the regime in the role of oppressive "other" and the Iranian people and the opposition movement as the heroic martyr, in the tradition of Hossein and Yazid at Karbala.

Figure 5 Digital poster from a Green Movement website featuring the artistic appropriation of the Hand of Fatima with two fingers, a sign of peace, hope, and resistance.
Source: Author screenshot of a Green Movement website Facebook page. The image can be traced to the now defunct sabzlink.com via the Internet Archive.

Why Not Turn It Off?

By 2009, all the pieces needed for the regime to "turn off the internet" were in place. Given this institutional and legal control, what prevented the regime from flipping the off switch? What prevented it from exercising its autonomy over online communication?[72]

It was not for lack of technology. Thanks to a number of policies and institutional changes made during the Khatami administration, all ISPs in Iran, whether state or commercial, were routed through the state telecommunication monopoly, TCI. The routing of ISPs to TCI created a central choke point through which the entire country's access to the internet could be terminated. At the height of opposition organizing via the internet and the international dissemination of news that undermined the credibility and legitimacy of the political system, the regime possessed an internet "off switch" that could shut down all communication going out of or into the country.

It was not for lack of precedent. The option of turning off the internet to stifle popular unrest was exercised in similar times of crisis by governments in the

Middle East and Asia. The internet was cut off by authorities in the Maldives in 2004, Nepal in 2005, and Burma in 2007, for example. Amid similarly serious citizen protests in 2011–12, known as the Arab Spring, the regimes of Egypt, Libya, and Syria cut off their nations' connection to the internet.[73]

And it was not for lack of power. Ahmadinejad had the political influence necessary to execute the maneuver from a government and bureaucratic standpoint. He had the endorsement of the Supreme Leader. The head of the Ministry of the Interior, the body that managed the elections, was an Ahmadinejad supporter.[74] Seven out of the twelve members of Guardian Council, including its secretary, Ayatollah Jannati, had publicly endorsed Ahmadinejad as their favored candidate.[75] Ahmadinejad also enjoyed control over the major levers of cultural output through the allegiance of the IRIB director and a number of online and print news outlets and was heavily favored by the state news agency, IRNA.[76]

In the months following the 2009 election, Ahmadinejad's handle on the means of communication grew with the majority acquisition of the Telecommunication Company of Iran by an IRGC subsidiary. The IRGC group bought a 51 percent stake in the company through a $7.5 billion privatization deal aimed at making TCI, which controlled the national telephone, mobile, and internet infrastructure and dominated the electronics manufacturing industry, a public-private venture. Although conducted under the auspices of a long-awaited privatization program, it was far from privatization, as control over the state telecommunication monopoly would have been simply transferred from one government group to another.[77]

To answer the question of why the regime did not shut down the internet, one must consider the very nature of regime power and legitimation. Maintaining the superficial trappings of democracy, both through elections and the press, was advantageous to a regime that sought a chair at international table alongside other world powers. It also imparted a degree of legitimacy in the eyes of the Iranian people and the international community.

Several components of democracy were already baked into the system. Iranians enjoyed, at least on the surface, popular suffrage through parliamentary and presidential elections. Such freedom to choose one's elected representative was on full display in the 2009 presidential election. Depending on one's interpretation of Iran's founding documents and subsequent law, the system also allowed for a robust newspaper industry with the ability to express preference for elected leaders and policies online and in print. During the election, activity on the internet, both activism and reporting, supported the impression of free speech and a free press.

But the reality is that neither popular elections nor the news media in Iran are what they seem. The Majles lacks any meaningful legal, budgetary, or oversight authority over the unelected clerical leadership. The candidates allowed to compete for the presidency are not chosen by their base but are instead selected by the Guardian Council. Print and online newspapers must be granted a license to operate and are subject to closure and loss of license at the whim of the authorities, with very little transparency or procedure. Newspaper editors routinely practice self-censorship in order to stay in operation and protect their staff. These are but two examples of edifices of popular consent seemingly manufactured for the purpose of public consumption and populist legitimacy rather than for functional democracy. Thus, the choice to keep the internet online may be understood as a logical extension of this strategy.

But while the Iranian leadership sought to preserve some semblance of political diversity and democratic process in the eyes of the international community and its domestic supporters, they also wanted to limit the danger to regime hegemony. Perhaps sensing the opportunity and the risk, the Iranian security services sought to manipulate fact and opinion on the internet while concomitantly reducing Green Movement leader's and activist's ability to harness the power of the medium. Internet connection speeds were reduced to a crawl, filtering was increased, bloggers and website owners were arrested or held for questioning, but Iran's internet remained online.

To sum up, I have argued that the regime's response to the mass mediation of the 2009–10 protests demonstrated a somewhat perspicacious understanding of the communicative power of the internet and the dynamics of the global communication environment. While the option was there, it is likely that at some point the regime chose *not* to turn off access to the internet entirely. This decision, or lack of decision, is illustrative of a larger philosophy of communication held by the Ahmadinejad administration and, arguably, the ruling regime as embodied by the Supreme Leader. It is an ideology *about* media—what it is, what it does, and what it means—and it is key to understanding regime decision making and threat perception during the election crisis. Such an understanding is also critical for deciphering elite discourse and government action concerning information communication technology and the countries that make it—the purpose of this book.

+++

8

AFTER THE CRISIS: SOFT WAR AND THE '88 FETNEH

In the context of the 2009–10 election protests, the internet—a medium once hailed as harbinger of the "third wave" of democracy—paradoxically worked to undermine the democracy movement. Ultimately the nezam was able to co-opt the techniques and apparatus of this emerging "liberation technology" in service of its illiberal ends. In the years following the crisis, the government sought to rewrite the historical record by reframing events and flooding the internet with alternative narratives. Authority figures authored "in-depth" analyses and editorials aimed at minimizing the breadth and severity of the unrest. These voices did not deny that the crisis had transpired; there was too much information in circulation to credibly do so. Instead, they sought to reframe the protests as part of a foreign conspiracy aimed at overthrowing the regime and an opening salvo in the "soft war" (*jang-e narm*).[1]

Soft war, as a revisionist narrative, posited the Green Movement as a failed attempt by foreign powers to bring about a "velvet revolution" through mass communication media such as satellite television and the web. Thanks to the misinformation disseminated by foreign broadcasters such as BBC Persian and Voice of America and by online think tanks, the argument went, many otherwise loyal Iranians were tricked into demonstrating against the government; the foreign influence campaign was so advanced that even regime insiders and loyalists such as former Speaker of Parliament (Majles) and former Prime Minister Mehdi Karroubi and Mir Hossein Mousavi (respectively), were swept up in the plot.[2]

For the government and nezam, the appeal of the soft war narrative was that it played upon preexisting prejudices and paranoia to explain the protest while also serving to deflect scrutiny of domestic events by focusing on the external threat. Foreign media coverage of the post-election violence and Western condemnation of the Iranian government's actions buttressed that thesis. Reprimands by European and American leaders against the Iranian government for its violent suppression of the largely peaceful protests were spun as evidence of foreign meddling and motivated not by genuine concern, but by consternation that their plans for velvet revolution had been foiled.[3] With that logic, the state was able to identify dissidents as agents of sedition, mete out punishment, and intimidate others into silence, while simultaneously keeping open the possibility of forgiveness and national reconciliation.

The public face of the effort was the show trials and televised confessions of over 100 intellectuals and activist leaders of the Green Movement.[4] While justifying the punishment of the movement's most egregious offenders, the frame allowed the establishment to label hundreds of journalists, human rights workers, and academics who had been apprehended and/or found guilty of sedition during the protests as unwitting victims of soft war, and thus, not fully responsible for their actions. To put it another way, the conspiracy frame enabled the government to play the nationalist card, and argue that protesters had been misled by outsiders, and therefore not entirely at fault for their actions. This meant that their transgressions could now be forgiven in the name of national unity against a foreign enemy.[5]

In sum, the narrative of soft war served regime power by generating a consensus in support of the establishment line within and among Iran's ruling elite. As an explanatory discourse, it functioned to streamline the messages of the nezam by establishing a story to which everyone could subscribe and that enabled dissident members of the establishment a path toward salvation. The experience of the post-election and the trauma of widely publicized cyber-attack against its nuclear facilities jettisoned the evolution of the concept from its original, limited role as an explanatory device and mode of irregular warfare against Iran by its enemies, to an affirmative rhetoric, offensive strategy of the state against its enemies, and enabler of the regime's multipronged campaign of domestic surveillance, persecution, repression, and extraterritorial war.

The Crisis, Reframed

A major tactic of the regime's new soft war offensive was altering the historical record through the creation of new online content and narratives. State-sponsored actors enlisted the help of journalists, bloggers, and news outlets aligned with the government to rewrite the story of the election unrest. These digital actors also took aim at the Green Movement, which they characterized as a fringe minority whose opinions and antics had succeeded in temporarily drowning out the sentiment of the majority of the population.

Bolstering this reframing, the pro-establishment narratives concomitantly identified the rallies of 22 Bahman and 9 Dey as evidence of the "real" sentiments of Iranian society. These outlets echoed the official state media discourse, which presented 22 Bahman and 9 Dey as a revelatory moment in which Iranians reasserted the popular will. "The 22 Bahman indicated which side the people are standing on," Khamenei said.[6] Variously described as the "third revolution," "historic," and "amazing," the pro-regime rallies were held up as an affirmation of regime legitimacy through popular consent and a testament to the enduring allegiance of the Iranian people.[7] In an editorial entitled "Beginning of the End," Morteza Ghamari-Vafa hailed 22 Bahman as auguring the victory of the Iranian people over the foreign-backed "sedition":

The country-wide rallies on 22 Bahman with the participation of millions of Iranian nationals became a historic event as it was organized with the utmost glory, respect, greatness, and insight. The absolute majority of Iranians made it a historic referendum and showed the public opinion from the core of their hearts. Their reverberating presence and slogans in the streets put the seal of cessation on the groundless and immature imagination of the enemies of the Revolution and our beloved Iran. The dignity and sobriety of people in this great and amazing rally was clear proof of dismissal of all kinds of seditions against the system and the government of Islamic Republic of Iran. They demanded an end to the post-poll seditions and a decisive encounter with the chief plotters and rioters.[8]

In blogs, websites, and online news aggregates reference to 22 Bahman and 9 Dey became a leading re-telling of the otherwise jarring period. It framed events as part of a continuum of revolutionary struggle against foreign repression. It told a story about the unrest being manufactured by Iran's enemies where the people rose up to shatter the false facade of internal dissent to emerge victorious and united behind their leaders.

An editorial in *Kayhan* exemplified another approach to reframing the historical record. In it, the period was celebrated for exposing the Western conspiracy and for enabling the large-scale purge of seditionists and Western agents who had been operating under the guise of the Reformist faction.

Had it not been for this sedition, it could in truth never be said with certainty how much time the Iranian authorities would have needed to expose and neutralize the massive number of networks which Western intelligence agencies had set up in diverse and legitimate locations. And, more importantly, had it not been for this sedition the Western-leaning faction in Iran would continue to carry out its overt and covert acts of treason in the guise of labels such as reformism or any other labels, and continue to claim that it was a legitimate movement which had no objectives other than the aim of engaging in a political battle for the sake of achieving political power in Iran.[9]

The editorial praised the period as exposing Reformists as the "executive arm of Western intelligence agencies and the step-by-step enforcer of their orders and instructions in Iran."

According to the editorial's author, the sedition should be celebrated for providing "sufficient justification" for the elimination of the Reformist faction as a legitimate and tolerated political force: "So much so that it could now be said that an entity by the name of [the] Reformist faction no longer exists in the political society of Iran."[10]

The Operationalization of Soft War

The period following the election unrest featured a marked growth in the state's internet presence and a concomitant effort to develop the concept of soft war. As part of this intellectual work, the Supreme Leader commissioned a series of six essays on theoretical and applied aspects of soft war, thus official inducting the term into the national security lexicon.[11] In this process soft war as a Western strategy against Iran was transformed into an Iranian strategy against the West.

The theoretical basis apparently established, Iran's military and security apparatus set to work operationalizing soft war as a defensive and offensive strategy.[12] New institutions and agencies were created with the mandate of defending against soft war, including a National Conference on Soft War and an Institute for (the study of) Soft War.[13] Soft war, as an offensive strategy, was integrated into institutions traditionally dedicated to conventional warfare. In December 2012, for example, the armed forces announced the formation of a "Permanent Bureau for Soft War." Other new military organizations with a soft war mandate included the Center for Soft War and Psychological Operations and the Center for Information Dominance and Strategic Insight.[14] Media reports linked these institutions to hacking, denial-of-service attacks, sabotage, interception and other cybernetic activity. Iran launched a number of comparatively more sophisticated cyber operations also, including the (alleged) hacking of US-based ISPs and the stealing of security certificates from some of the internet's biggest websites such as Google, Yahoo, Microsoft, and Skype.[15]

The online presence of the country's intelligence, police, and military agencies notably increased in the last years of the Ahmadinejad administration. A new police force was created to monitor Iranian's online activity.[16] The Supreme National Security Council (SNSC) was designated the governing authority and was responsible for creating and overseeing intelligence-security policies and measures to counter the post-election unrest.[17] Tehran announced the creation of a "cyber army" of 10,000 Basij bloggers tasked with boosting pro-regime internet chatter and developing websites as alternatives to Western sites.[18] The government also announced the establishment of the first of a number of national cyber camps to fight the "culture war."

A bevy of new government websites came into operation aligned with the IRGC and the hardline faction. Their purpose appears to have been to recirculate information and decrees issued by the Supreme Leader as well as news stories consistent with the hardline conservative position. A prime example was Arnet.ir, a site "dedicated to the study of psychological operations" and exposing how "world imperialism" and "Zionists" use psychological operations to "dominate third world countries, especially Muslim countries." The site hosted more than 2,000 pages of articles and books on psychological operations and offered free registration, although it was not apparent what benefits came with membership. The website was well organized and fully functional. The center of the home page featured recent news items concerning what Arnet.ir perceived as foreign psychological operations against Iran and other Muslim countries; there was a heavy focus on Facebook's alleged role in Middle East unrest and remarks by Iranian officials concerning alleged psychological operations.[19] While the site was not outwardly affiliated with the Iranian government, the state's control of domain licensing and ability to shut down unfavorable sites suggested that at the very least the government was complicit in the site's creation and operation. More likely, however, is that the site was a direct beneficiary of the Iranian government.[20]

Cyberwar

It was June 2009 and Iranians were gearing for the presidential election when Iran's Natanz nuclear facility erupted in flames. Wikileaks founder Julian Assange broke the story and linked it to the mysterious resignation of the head of the Iranian Atomic Energy Agency.[21] Officials from the International Atomic Energy Agency (IAEA) later confirmed that a large number of centrifuges at Natanz had ceased to function. It ultimately linked the Natanz incident to the work of the Stuxnet worm.[22]

Stuxnet was at the time the most sophisticated malware ever deployed, with more than 15,000 lines of code that allowed it to self-replicate and yet remain essentially invisible.[23] It damaged the plant's infrastructure and equipment and was blamed for the deaths of ten people caught in the explosion. It was the closest to cyberwar the world had witnessed. In the words of one cyber security expert, "the Rubicon was crossed. There was no going back."[24]

The mission of Stuxnet, a combined effort of the US and Israeli governments, was to curtail the progress of Iran's nuclear program. Called Operation Olympic Games within the US government, the cyber weapon achieved this objective by disrupting, destroying, and disabling equipment involved in uranium enrichment. The Stuxnet malware was originally introduced to the network via a USB storage device. Once it was plugged into the host computer, the malware surreptitiously installed itself (using stolen digital signatures) and replicated autonomously in other computers connected to the network.[25] The virus infected the software Iran used at its nuclear plants and then used its access to disrupt the behavior of key machinery. Operational capacity at Natanz dropped by 30 percent as the virus forced electric motors to accelerate to damaging speeds, making their aluminum centrifugal tubes alternately expand and contract and straining the instruments to the point of failure. Roughly 1,000 out of 9,000 tubes were caused to self-destruct in this way, keeping large parts of the plant idle for months, delaying its expansion, and stopping or at least setting back the pace of enrichment.[26] By the time the malware was identified and neutralized by Iranian software engineers, it had set the nuclear program back by anywhere from eighteen months to two years.[27]

When Iranian officials finally publicly acknowledged the existence of Stuxnet, they described it as foreign espionage weapon, designed to spy on Iran's nuclear program. This explanation was deliberately misleading. While spying—the surreptitious collection and transfer of information—was one of its capabilities, Stuxnet was primarily designed for industrial sabotage. Officials also sought to downplay the impact on the nation's nuclear infrastructure, labeling reports of the malfunctions at Natanz as a propaganda and misinformation campaign.[28] As time wore on, and the evidence of the setbacks could not be ignored, Stuxnet was folded into the soft war narrative as part of a growing list of communications-technology-linked attacks by Iran's enemies.

It may be argued that Stuxnet was successful in that it set back the enrichment process by several months. This provided diplomats more time to do their job—which was an agreement to end Iran's nuclear program in exchange for sanctions relief and other concessions, ultimately called the Joint Comprehensive Plan of Action (JCPOA). It simultaneously allowed for the coercive bite of multinational sanctions to sink in thus increasing the Iranian leadership's motivation to reach a deal. A contrary argument can be made, however. One could argue that Stuxnet made a diplomatic resolution less likely, in part by heightening distrust between the United States and Iran and making it politically difficult for Iranian leaders to justify a deal with the "Great Satan" or make any move seen as buckling under duress.[29]

Cybernetic blowback and fallout was inevitable. Iran launched retaliatory cyber assaults on US banks and military computer networks, while government officials spoke of plans to improve Iran's cyber war capabilities. Eventually, Stuxnet escaped Iran, infiltrating more than 45,000 computers in Indonesia, Pakistan, India, Russia, Germany, Canada, China, and even the United States, although concerted efforts by Siemens led to its control and neutralization. More broadly, the incident formed the normative basis against which future cyberwar attacks are likely to be judged.

One of the more obvious lessons Iranian leaders took from the Stuxnet attack was the need for better network defenses and operating software. Officials announced a number of new software and networking solutions, such as the Padvish anti-malware program—a domestically engineered cyber-threat recognition and identification system. It also announced the creation of a dedicated network security operations center and the introduction of high-speed and high-capacity firewalls.[30]

Stuxnet had a less obvious but still profound effect on the establishment's thinking about internal security. For many in the nezam, the revelation of the Stuxnet malware virus made real the Iranian regime's largely notional claims of a communications-based conspiracy. Whereas the '88 conspiracy used media to undermine the intra-regime consensus and co-opt key leaders within the ruling establishment into "sedition," Stuxnet undermined Iran's national prestige by striking at its monument to technological development, its nuclear research program.

One Iranian military strategist framed the attack as evidence of the continued soft war against the homeland— the latest in a list of US-sponsored attacks on the

Islamic Republic that included Hillary Clinton's pronouncement of the election protests as a "Twitter Revolution," the US State Department Democracy Fund's purported aid to Iranian civil society and exile group working to overthrow the government, and the US Defense Department-originated Tor browser, which allowed Iranians to access the web without fear of surveillance. At the same time, Stuxnet represented a seismic shift in the "arena of confrontation," as another commentator described it.[31]

The Stuxnet attack doubtless motivated the Iranian government to develop and expand its offensive cyber operations. Cyber war became a new priority. But Iran's progress in developing reciprocal cybernetic warfare capacity was surprisingly slow in the years that followed.[32] This may partly be the result of Iran's limited access to international markets and the challenges of circumventing US and international sanctions. Or it may be due to the dearth of talent, as many would-be patriotic hackers were joining the exodus of people to and the Americas in pursuit of jobs and education. Or it may be the case that Iran did in fact invest in major complex operations on par with Stuxnet and the world had yet to see the fruits of that labor. Or it may be that, after Stuxnet, a strategic decision was made to focus on the development of asymmetric capabilities and actions, which I will discuss now.

Defacement, Hacking, and Digital Revisionism

While Iran's comparative cyber power was limited but growing in the 2010s, it nevertheless had an extraordinarily active defacement community.[33] Defacement is an attack on a website that changes its content, functioning, or visual appearance. Politically motivated attacks and website defacements became a common occurrence in Iran beginning in the summer of 2009.[34] A random sampling of defacements between 2010 and 2015 points to the public and symbolic nature of this practice. The operations were a primitive, low-level intrusion and only affect the html code and the outward face of a website, akin to digital graffiti.

In a defacement, the website targeted is no longer accessible to the general public. Instead of the landing page, the user will find an error message or more often a declaration by the hacker. Thus the hacked website is essentially pirated: stolen space upon which the hacktivist can directly communicate to a targeted website and the audience or interest group to which it caters. Such an interruption—or denial of the exchange of information and access—is in itself steeped in symbolism. It becomes a demonstration of the power of the hacker over both the targeted website and the individual consumer or client wishing to access the site. This message of dominance is rendered explicit when the hacker includes text, imagery, sound, GIF, or a combination thereof.

Groups like Ashiyaneh, Shabgard, and Simorgh used this tactic, infiltrating foreign government websites for the sake of symbolism and notoriety as well as, competition, and occasionally, profit.[35] The hacking tracking website Zone-H credited Ashiyane Digital Security Team and other groups linked to Iran with 4,372 mass defacements as of July 2017.[36]

Surveillance was another component of hacking. In a period of five years, 2010–15, nearly half of all intrusion and surveillance operations were directed inward, at the Iranian people.[37] Victims included dissident groups, minority ethnic and religious populations, and LGBT and women's rights activists. At politically sensitive times such as elections, the campaigns and personal accounts of members of the ruling establishment were targeted. Journalists and those active on social media were particularly attractive targets.

A report by Claudio Guarnieri and Collin Anderson provides insight into the methods and targets of four operations Infy, Rocket Kitten, Sima, and Operation Cleaver. Pointing to the distinct overlap in the personnel and tactics used, whether the target was internal dissidents or Iranians in the diaspora, the authors concluded that such attacks were likely the work of a single entity, the Iranian Cyber Army (ICA).[38]

ICA is a group within the Islamic Revolutionary Guards Corps, which is an extremely powerful intelligence and security force tasked with protecting regime ideology and answerable only to the Supreme Leader. In the wake of the election crisis, ICA launched a series of cyber defacements. ICA hackers defaced the homepages of popular websites like Twitter, Voice of America, Baidu, and Radio Zamaneh, often emblazoning pages with the Iranian flag and leaving pro-government messages.

For example, when it hacked Twitter, the ICA posted a poem declaring its obedience. "If the Leader orders, we will rush forward. If he asks us, we will offer our heads, If he wants us to be patient, we will tolerate and bear it." The message was clearly meant to signal that ICA was under the command of Khamenei and that his dominion included the realm of cyberspace. Similar messages were posted on dissident domestic and diaspora websites.[39]

Yet digital historical revisionism, one- offensive cyber operations, and largely superficial and symbolic hacking only went so far. What was needed, establishment insiders avered, was a more cohesive, long-term solution to the problem of cyberspace. The regime had to have the ability to control what people said and did on the internet while preventing the medium from becoming so popular and powerful that it posed a threat to the state's monopoly on mass communication. What was needed, these voices argued, was a national internet.

9

THE NATIONAL INTERNET

Why are we letting the internet roam free? Nobody is trying to shut down cyberspace. That would not make sense. But other countries are setting boundaries to protect their culture. So why aren't we?
—Ali Khamenei, 2 May 2016[1]

All of you saw the fire and catastrophe that cyberspace brought.
—Ahmad Khatami, 5 January 2018[2]

The twin challenges of the 2009 election unrest and the Stuxnet cyber-attack gave new life to the project of building a national internet. Drawing from primary source documents and digital artifacts, this chapter offers a history of the national internet and the political context in which it was conceived. It considers the objectives and network architecture that informed the design of the network, giving particular focus on its role in the decision to block the social networking and communication platform Telegram.[3]

Origin and Development

The idea of building an Iran-only internet dates back to at least 2005, with the launch of a pilot program connecting the networks of thousands of public schools and offices of the Ministry of Education. In 2008 the government allocated $1 billion for infrastructure development related to the project, then called the "National Internet."[4] The events of 2009 and 2010 gave the project for a national internet new urgency. Re-anointed the National Information Network (NIN, or *Shoma*), the national internet became a way for the regime to insulate itself from further internet-enabled protests.

Siavash Shahshahani was long-time director of IRNIC, the .ir Top Level Domain (TLD) Registry for Iran. He helped bring email to Iran and is credited for helping establish NIN.[5] In an interview with an Iranian newspaper in 2012, Shahshahani sought to allay public fears and misconceptions about the surveillance and filtering potential of the national internet:

> What is called the national internet implies better and more extensive domestic links. But it also means that all our international connections go through

completely controllable channels. Today, perhaps 95 percent of Iran's links and connections are through telecommunications or through fiber optics, so most of the time whenever you access a site, filtering is already in place. In fact, this is what national internet means. So it should not be the center of much focus.[6]

Indeed, a core deliverable of the project for a national internet was more extensive domestic links between networks, information intermediaries, and upgraded infrastructure. Together, such improvements created a more efficient and reliable domestic network, or intranet. When engineers and policy planners were thinking about the network in 2012, they understood that centralized state control would be key.[7] This could be achieved in large part through the architecture of the network (Figure 6). Through both design and infrastructural control over critical exchange points in the system, the national internet would provide the state with greater autonomy over the traffic which passed through and within its borders.[8]

Under Rouhani, the project for a national internet was presented as a means to stimulate the economy and push the country closer to its longer-term goal of leading the world in science and technology. However, Sepah and other security services that embraced NIN saw it differently. For them, NIN was important to

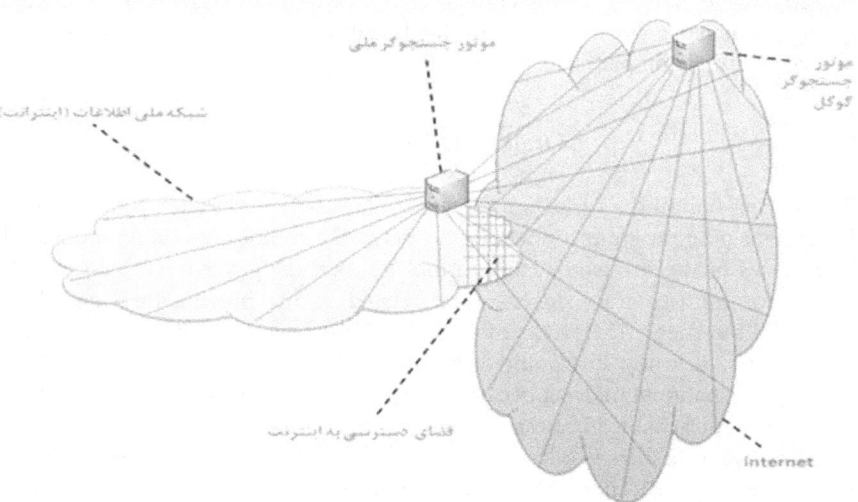

Figure 6 Infographic of the "Internet-Intranet Cohesion Model" featured on the website of the Ministry of Information Communication Technology in 2012. Translation clockwise from top: national search engine; foreign search engine Google; internet [technically, this is the World Wide Web, referred to in this book as the international internet for clarity]; access to the internet; National Information Network intranet.

regime security; it provided the infrastructure needed to censor, surveil, and in a crisis "turn off" the internet.

When the new project was unveiled to the public in March 2016, the Information Technology Administration, one of the bodies within the ministry charged with establishing the network, described NIN as an "aggregate of dedicated local and national networks," comprised of "state-of-the-art governmental and non-governmental data centers" and "software infrastructures distributed throughout the country." According to the Administration's website, NIN had six constituent objectives. Not insignificantly, "suppression of monopoly" was first on the list. They were:

- Establishing an appropriate state infrastructure for governance and suppression of monopoly while reducing ownership of unnecessary information technology
- Maximizing the power of the private sector by creating a fair competitive environment
- Establishing a secure advanced communication platform for the development of information and communication technology in the country
- Establishing the necessary platforms for informing and delivering the optimal electronic service to the public
- Setting the grounds for the transformation of Iran as a regional traffic and transit hub
- Reducing the cost of connecting to the internet[9]

Building NIN was no small task. It required major upgrades to the country's telecommunications infrastructure, more coverage and connectivity, and faster and cheaper internet and mobile internet service. These transmission-level improvements had the dual advantage of advancing NIN and fulfilling the president's campaign promise of greater information access and connectivity. Indeed, tech sector growth was especially important to the president, as it was concrete evidence of the improved lifestyle and increased opportunities intended to come from the opening of the Iranian economy to foreign investment as a result of signing the Joint Plan of Action (JCPOA) in 2015.[10]

The information communications technology sector was one of the first to reap the benefits of the nuclear accord. An energetic tech start-up sector emerged, and news sources such as TechRasa and the International Financial Tribune set to the task of spreading the word about Iran's emerging digital market.[11] The promise and potential of this controlled opening of the Iranian market was met with enthusiasm by foreign corporations and governments alike. A minister of trade for the United Kingdom went so far as to deem it "the largest economy to re-enter international markets since the fall of the Soviet Union."[12] The attractiveness of Iran for foreign investment was predicated, in part, on the existence of modern, high-speed, high-bandwidth telecommunications infrastructure. Increased speed, bandwidth, and reliability required the near-universal improvement of domestic communications infrastructure. It also required the expansion of

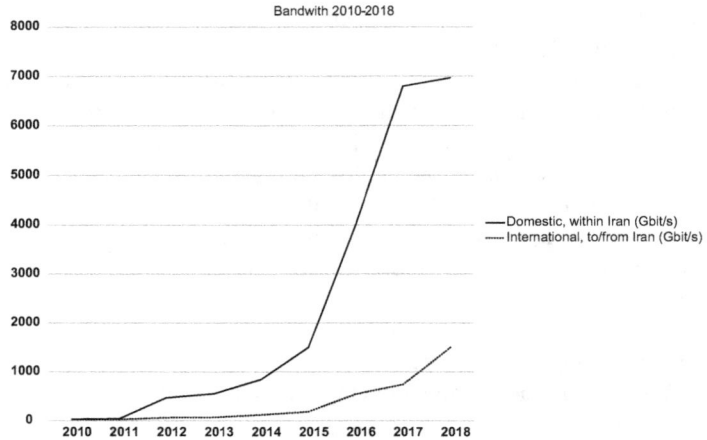

Figure 7 Changes to domestic (intranet) bandwidth relative to bandwidth for international traffic connecting to and from the World Wide Web, 2010–18.
Source: Data from M-Lab and TechRasa.

coverage nationwide and the integration of less developed, rural areas of the country via broadband and mobile.

Iran made significant advancements in both areas. Thanks to a combination of growth in domestic data centers; laying of fiber optic cable; and lifting the state-imposed, artificial restriction on upload and download speed, domestic bandwidth increased exponentially. A special project to improve the transmission layer of the internet, *Talash*, was reported to have laid 30,000 kilometers of fiber optic cable across thirty-one provinces.[13]

Along with bandwidth, domestic internet speed also increased. Metrics from M-Lab, which collects and analyzes more than 200 million tests of internet speeds worldwide, reflected an increase in international connection speed from 0.3 Mbps in 2013 to 1.0 Mbps in 2017.[14] Data from the online newspaper Tech Rasa and the Ministry of ITC data showed an increase in domestic speed as well, from a low of 127 Kbps to an average speed of 1.2 GB (Figure 6). Much of this increase was related to Rouhani's successful raising of the cap on internet speed imposed in 2006 as a means of censorship by making searching for information and uploading and downloading large files such as a video or a photograph.[15]

Another requisite of the national internet project was national routing. In the past, poor infrastructure meant that much of Iran's domestic traffic was by necessity routed through international servers before reaching its intended endpoint inside Iran. National routing meant that traffic to and within Iran remained inside Iranian boarders. This had the benefit of increasing connection speed by reducing the number of intermediaries that packets (essentially bundles of information) must traverse before reaching their destination. It also increased the state's ability to use the internet to serve regime security objectives, be it through filtering content and reducing internet speed; policing social media, digital news outlets and blogs; or surveilling citizens by collecting and intercepting email and other communications. National routing was achieved through the introduction of seven Internet Exchange Points (IXPs), which served as high-capacity data hand-off points connecting ISPs inside and outside the country, thus reducing the possibility of foreign interception and making it easier for the state to surveil and censor Iranian internet users.[16]

In the wake of the election unrest, the project's champions and architects laid out an ambitious five-year plan in which 80 percent of all internet traffic would travel through servers within NIN. Another argument in favor of the network was that it would make the exchange of data more secure by limiting data mobility both within the domestic net and vis-a-vi the outside world. This component of NIN architecture, proponents averred, would protect domestic data and networks from foreign surveillance and cyber-attacks and was therefore essential to national security. While the argument made sense in theory, in practice, limiting data mobility through routing did not make transmissions more secure. In fact, it made them more vulnerable to viruses while giving the regime the ability to force ISPs to filter, block, and throttle transmissions.[17]

Finally, an essential component to the success of NIN was the migration of users to the domestic network and the expansion of services and content that were housed there. To achieve the former, the state strongly encouraged Iranian users to use NIN websites and services such as the national email service and messaging apps. Success also required Iranian websites that were hosted by international servers to migrate to the domestic hosting service. The government set a goal of increasing the number of Iranian sites hosted on NIN to 80 percent by 2025. In 2013, 20 percent of Iranian-owned sites were hosted in Iran under the ".ir" domain. Two years into the relaunch of the national internet, that number doubled to 40 percent. By 2018, Iran's domestic email service and search engine ranked among the twenty most popular software applications in Iran.[18]

In March 2017, the state announced a new regulation which required foreign social networking apps to host their servers inside Iran. This requirement necessitated the creation of high-quality data centers. Previous efforts to build such infrastructure had been stymied by international sanctions on information-communications equipment such as routers and switches and the accompanying technical support that such purchases normally entail. That changed after the US Treasury and State Department lifted sanctions on the export of information telecommunication technology and equipment in 2014.[19]

Other imperatives of NIN were harder to meet. Consider the problem of content. When one used a search engine on NIN, one might get a page of results rather than hundreds of thousands of hits that the same search would retrieve on Google. To address this problem, the state purportedly commissioned and deployed "battalions" of people tasked with creating and promoting new, original content. The media-monitoring group Article 19 compiled a list of more than thirty new websites that appeared to be active in this way.[20]

But in the discussion of the technical and infrastructural requirements of NIN one should not lose sight of NIN's deeper purpose. NIN is a way to place boundaries on cyberspace, with the goal of more effective repression. Modeled in part on the "great firewall" of China, the project lets the regime implement filtering and surveillance more efficiently and at less cost. It also provides the infrastructure and capability to block, throttle, or cut off traffic within Iran or between Iran and the international community.

In NIN, filtering is done through ISPs, which provide users with last-mile network connectivity. Whether private, commercial, or government-owned, all Iranian ISPs are subject to strict licensing requirements and communications laws. These regulations hold ISP companies liable for the activities of their customers. They require an ISP to filter data content according to a vague and expansive definition of subjects deemed haram and criminal. ISPs are also required to block SSL protocols for services like Facebook and Twitter, which means that without a VPN, a user would not be able to access the social media sites. ISPs are also compelled to participate in surveillance. Under NIN, they are required to retain records of all data uploaded or downloaded by users for a three-month period (cyber cafes are required to hold user data for six months).[21]

The Protests of 2018 as a Testing Ground and Catalyst

In 2018, protests erupted across the country over spiraling inflation and the high price of basic foodstuffs like chicken and bread. Unlike in 2009, when the protests were largely centered in urban areas, the 2017–2018 protests were in all parts of the country. People normally aligned with regime hardliners now criticized their leaders and demanded they take action to address the economic crisis. As the days went on, the demonstrations appeared to become more violent. Images spread of people setting fire to cars and government buildings, defacing banners of the Supreme Leader, and even attacking the government forces. Many Iranians turned to the messaging platform Telegram to organize and publicize the public protests.

This section considers the politics and progress of NIN under the Rouhani administration, with particular focus on the multi-day, country-spanning demonstrations that rocked Iran in 2018. As part of this analysis, I look at government policy concerning the mobile messaging application, Telegram, and the technical aspects that make the medium unique. Before delving into those issues, however, we must begin with a chronology of events.

Chronology of the 2017–8 Protests

On 28 December 28, 2017 the people of Mashhad took to the street in protest over food prices and discontent with government officials. Mashhad, a city of 2 million in Khorasan Province, was the stronghold of Rouhani's hardline presidential campaign rival Ebrahim Raesi. The ire of the demonstrators was largely aimed at the president, with chants of "Death to Rouhani" and "Death to the Dictator" reverberating through the streets[22] Smaller demonstrations were reported in the northeastern cities of Neyshabour and Kashmar.[23] Mohammad Norouzian, governor of Mashhad, told state media that the protests were organized via social media by "counter-revolutionary elements."[24] Telegram was one such media, where the channel "Invitation to Protest" played a role in early mobilization efforts.

Many cities where people demonstrated had high unemployment and were struggling to attract the foreign investment that had been opened up by the JCPOA (such as Nahavand, Tuyserkan, and Izeh). As one observer noted, "Izeh has one of the highest rates of suicide in Iran. These statistics show that social ills and unemployment have come together to create an atmosphere of despair."[25] The early footage of the demonstrations certainly reflects this. They had an air of desperation: driven by anger and having nothing left to lose, protesters set fire to Basij office buildings and ripped down huge banners baring the face of the Supreme Leader.

Like a brush fire during a drought, the protests spread across Iran. Journalists and Telegram feeds reported demonstrations of various sizes (anywhere from 100 to over 1000 people) in several cities on December 29, including Rasht, Qom, Esfahan, Zahedan, and Kermanshah.

In the largely Kurdish city of Kermanshah, approximately 300 people gathered at Freedom Square and chanted, "care for us and leave Palestine," "political prisoners should be freed," "death or freedom," and "leave Syria, think about us!" In Sabzevar, a smaller group of people chanted, "No to Gaza. No to Lebanon. I give my life for Iran." A group of approximately fifty protesters gathered in Tehran. Video from Rasht showed a crowd chanting, "We don't want to be ruled by the clerics anymore."[26]

The following day, December 30, 2017, anti-government protests were held in at least nine cities, including Tehran, Shiraz, Khorramabad, Zanjan, Ahvaz, and Najafabad.[27] Two protestors were killed in Doroud.[28] In Tehran, protestors gathered outside of government buildings; students at Tehran University lobbed rocks at security forces and chanted, "death to the dictator."

Momentarily outshining the protesters that day, hundreds of thousands of people gathered in (reportedly) 1,200 cities and towns in state-sanctioned, pro-government celebrations in commemoration of 9 Dey, the anniversary of the martyrdom of Hussein at Karbala. The date took on new significance in the wake of the 2009 protests. It was celebrated by Khamenei and many within the ruling establishment as a turning point in the crisis, marking the triumph of "the people" over "seditionists."[29] "Nine Dey is a date that will be registered in history. This is what has preserved your revolution. This is why the arrogant powers…are afraid to attack the Iranian nation," declared Khamenei in a speech to the nation in 2010.[30] He continued:

> So, what kind of state can mobilize such a national rally across the country? Which country or state has the power to do so? Even if they do their best, the strongest and wealthiest states of the world that spend extravagantly to train

spies, terrorists, and to carry out acts of sabotage cannot gather 100,000 people on streets within just two days. Dozens of millions of people gathered across the country[Iran]…The fact is that in our country, the state and people are not separate, all of them are united. Officials, from me to other officials, are just a drop in the great ocean that is this nation.[31]

In short, Khamenei argued that foreign powers seek to drive a wedge between the ruling establishment and their Iranian subjects. Such efforts are doomed to fail, however, because the Iranian state and the Iranian people are so closely bound. It was a populist argument that establishment figures embraced and perpetuated throughout the crisis and after.

But we arrive at another finding also, that the state-organized and subsidized street demonstrations on 9 Dey were essentially legitimacy signaling exercises. As the mediation of protests against the nezam increased, so too did the establishment's reliance on such mass demonstrations to affirm its popular legitimacy. The rallies of December 2017 were particularly well publicized for this reason. Images of impassioned black shrouded female demonstrators and blocks-long throngs of people circulated in high rotation on state television.[32]

A New Phase of Soft War

While the reactions of public officials were mixed at the beginning of the protests, as the demonstrations went on, the establishment discourse coalesced into a summary condemnation of the violence and of social media as the cause and enabler of the unrest. But when the government blocked Telegram and Instagram and the demonstrations continued, hardliners began to push a different argument. The new narrative offered an alternative, more expansive explanation for the unrest using the all too familiar frame of foreign conspiracy. Perhaps unsurprisingly, it was the Judiciary, which is overseen by the Supreme Leader and not the president and dominated by hardliners and Khamenei loyalists, which originated the conspiracy story. Prosecutor General Mohammad Ja'afar Montazeri blamed the unrest on a trifecta of American, Israeli, and Saudi Arabian conspirators:

> The mastermind of the project was an American named Michael D'Andrea, former Chief of the CIA's Counter Terrorism Center, and an operations room composed of three sides, namely, the United States, the Zionist regime [in reference to Israel] and Saudi Arabia, was formed for leading the unrest. The project was funded by Saudi Arabia and mainly planned by D'Andrea and an intelligence officer affiliated with Mossad.[33]

Secretary of the Expediency Council, Mohsen Rezaei, joined his voice to the emergent narrative. Holding a press conference on January 6, he echoed the claim that the demonstrations were the result of a foreign conspiracy. Rezaei also identified D'Andrea as the mastermind, while adding new details to the story.

He said that D'Andrea traveled to Erbil two months earlier to meet Iraqi Kurdish independence leaders and the Iranian Mujahedin-e-Khalq (MEK) to plot the unrest.[34] While Rezaei and Montazeri's stories diverged on some details—such as which one of Iran's foreign enemies was behind the protests—they agreed on the underlying frame of an American-led conspiracy to undermine the Islamic Republic through faux protests and propaganda. When *Mehr News* ran a lengthy analysis of the protests on January 26, the soft war political myth was made explicit: "We are now entering a new phase in the soft war."[35]

Throughout the crisis, the state sought to prevent images, footage, and reportage from circulating within the country and to the outside world. It did this through ISPs by means of bandwidth throttling, targeted content and platform blocking, and blocking of circumvention tools, with much of the activity targeted at the provinces where the unrest was occurring. On December 31, however, there was a far more expansive disruption of traffic. Observers reported a short period in which all international traffic ceased. The period lasted thirty minutes. The full scale blocking of Telegram began the next day. While the measure was posited as "temporary" and was rescinded within two weeks, it presaged the imposition of a more indefinite ban on Telegram few months later.[36] To understand the significance of these developments however, we must begin at the beginning, with a very public complaint about Telegram by a key member of the Rouhani administration.

The Temporary Telegram Ban

On December 30, Minister for Information and Communications Technology, Mohammad-Javad Azari Jahromi, took to Twitter to blame the persistent, and in places destructive, unrest on the Telegram channel *Amad News*. The channel, which at the time boasted more than 1 million followers, had been posting videos and information about the demonstrations continuously for days.[37] Jahromi appealed directly to Telegram CEO Pavel Durov to shut down the channel. Jahromi wrote, "@Durov: A Telegram channel is encouraging hateful conduct, use of Molotov cocktails, armed uprising, and social unrest. NOW is the time to stop such encouragements via Telegram."[38] The minister's charge against the channel was not without merit. The channel did contain content promoting violent resistance.[39] Durov responded to the minister within hours, also via Twitter, vowing to investigate. He announced the suspension of the channel soon after.[40]

Jahromi's tweet to Durov may have been a publicity stunt aimed at signaling that the Rouhani administration was taking a strong stance against the growing unrest. It can equally be interpreted as a last-ditch effort to appease hardliners and slow the reactionary momentum toward imposing the wholesale blocking of Telegram. If the latter were true, then Jahromi's move appeared to have had the opposite effect; the sins of one Telegram channel became fodder for those calling for sweeping action against the entire platform.

What is clear is that Jahromi's gesture had little productive impact. Although Amad News was shut down, the service immediately returned to operation on

Telegram under another name. If anything, Jahromi's Twitter appeal laid bare the disconnect between the public remit of the Ministry of the ITC and its actual power of enforcement via the machinery of state. The same day that Jahromi made his appeal to Durov, state television began announcing the immediate imposition of a "temporary" block on Telegram and Instagram nationwide.[41] While the regime's action against Telegram may seem trivial (after all, the Iranian people weathered a similar ban on satellite dishes, among other communications technology), it was, in reality, relatively serious. In the following section, I explore the unique attributes of Telegram and its role in Iranian society at the time. This information contextualizes the protests of 2017–18 as well as the concomitant and subsequent government policies aimed at propelling the national internet project into a new stage.

The Unique Attributes of Telegram

At the time, the free messaging app Telegram was the platform of choice for commercial, personal, and public communication and even government business; according to one estimate in 2017, 40 million people—nearly half the population—used the platform.[42] As the popularity of Telegram grew, both in Iran and elsewhere around the word, people began to talk about Telegram as they would social media. Doing so is both erroneous and problematic, as it obscures important differences between Telegram and most social media platforms. One difference relates to data security and privacy. Unlike Twitter or Instagram, traffic on Telegram is encrypted end to end and one must have a Telegram account to see content. Such information exchange is not "social" and "public" in the way it might be on Twitter or Facebook. Indeed, these features remove Telegram from the surface web (the layer of the World Wide Web that can be scraped web crawlers and found with a quick search on Google). These features, and encryption in particular, make it harder for corporations and governments to surveil users.

Another difference between Telegram and most social media platforms relates to structure. In Telegram, the "channel" is the major organizing unit. Each channel has an administrator and subscribers. In theory, Telegram gives any user the ability to mass communicate. He or she need only create a new channel (thus becoming an administrator) and recruit a large number of subscribers. In practice, however, mass communication on Telegram is the province of a select few—namely, those with the public status, time, media savvy required for developing and maintaining numerous subscribers while withstanding the scrutiny of the Iranian state.

Given these differences, it is perhaps more accurate to label Telegram a medium for digitally networked mass communication. Whereas the social media user is an active participant in the communicative exchange—sending out messages and receiving feedback—the Telegram user is relegated to the role of spectator and audience—the end recipient in a one-way transmission of meanings and symbolic forms. When a user joins a popular Telegram channel, he or she must consume the content and messages produced by or referred through the channel administrator. There is no reciprocal feedback loop or independent capacity to communicate publicly with one or all followers of a popular Telegram channel, as would be the case in traditional social networking apps. The Telegram user is passive in this way; he or she can do little but consume the content provided. While the channel follower is demoted to that of receiver, the administrator takes on the role of sender-broadcaster, with autonomy over content, distribution, and even recipients. As Small Media explains:

> Channels with close to a million members have no arrangements for users to express their views, and members have no way of interacting with each other. The power of what is disseminated, when and to whom, lies with admins, and most Telegram users have been reduced to mere consumers.[43]

Short-Term Benefits and Blowback

The blocking of Telegram and Instagram had a number of short-term benefits for the ruling establishment. The blocking of Telegram served regime security by cutting off the circulation of videos and images of the protests within the country, thus eliminating the possibility that such images would instigate additional protests. It may have also been an attempt to stem the plummeting support for the conservatives and Khamenei among people who were both major participants in the unrest and traditional conservative constituencies. It also had the benefit, its proponents likely reasoned, of preventing or at least slowing the flow of images and news to the international media so as to preserve Iran's image as a stable power in the region.

Another practical benefit was compelling the Iranian people to migrate from Telegram (which was now blocked) to Iranian-made and -operated messaging apps. Records show a surge in downloads and users of alternative, government-sponsored platforms during the first weeks of the ban. Downloads of Sorush, which had flatlined at 200,000 in October 2017, surged to 500,000 by February 2018.[44] Another boost came with the Supreme Leader's closure of his own Telegram account in March. In a farewell message, he encouraged his 1 million-plus followers to follow him on the Iran-based Telegram alternatives, Sorush and IGap. In the wake of the announcement, both platforms enjoyed a surge of new users. Downloads of the Sorush app on Cafe Bazaar doubled, reaching over 1 million.

Yet the blocking of Telegram also had an immediate, negative consequence that the state could not ignore. Telegram was highly integrated into everyday life; businesses used the platform for client communication, financial transactions, and marketing, and many government agencies used the platform to communicate with contractors and share files and information. By blocking Telegram the authorities shut down a major commercial market. The secretary of Internet Businesses Crafts Union, Reza Olfat Nasab, predicted that 100,000 licensed online sellers would lose their jobs across the country if Telegram were to remain blocked.[45]

Figure 8 "The Big Migration from Telegram." Cartoon by Bozorgmehr Hosseinpur featured in the Iranian daily newspaper, Sazandegi.
Source: Author screen shot.

The Temporary Telegram Ban Becomes Permanent

Hardliners and conservatives seized on the experience of the protests to argue for a permanent ban on Telegram. On January 18, 170 members of the Majles signed a letter demanding the ban.[46] On April 18, the Supreme Leader issued a statement on his Telegram channel announcing closure of his account. Public institutions and government agencies and politicians were ordered to do the same and to create replacement accounts on domestic applications.[47] On April 26, the secretary of Supreme Cyberspace Council (SCC) annulled Telegram's content delivery network (CDN) license, signed in 2016. CDNs are servers for multimedia content and, when based in Iran, made the delivery of content faster for the Iranian end user.

With all official government representatives off Telegram and with the speed of its service downgraded for Iranian end users, the wholesale blocking of Telegram was all but assured. On April 30, the ban was extended to all members of the populace. The technical and political action was complimented by new legal measures to stop the use of circumvention tools.

The previously unheard-of Branch Two of the Culture and Media Prosecutor's Office in Tehran (most likely under the direction of the Supreme National Security Council) ordered ISPs and Ministry of ITC to clamp down on VPNs, which were being used to access Facebook, Twitter, and Telegram, as well as thousands of officially filtered websites. Those in violation of the ban could be prosecuted.[48]

The action was presented as a response to "complaints against the social networking app by Iranian citizens" and the "demand of security organizations." The Judiciary identified a host malign activity being committed by Iranians on Telegram. They were:

- Disruption of national security and unity, in particular by inciting racial and ethnic disputes;
- Collecting information from the Iranian public and providing it to foreign bodies;
- Publishing and distribution of pornography;
- Insulting Islamic sanctities and values;
- Publishing lies to shape public opinion;
- E-trading of goods and currencies;
- Use by terrorist groups;
- Violations of intellectual property and fraud;
- Publishing of propaganda against the Islamic Republic;
- Causing individual harm.[49]

While many of the transgressions identified were prohibited by existing press law, the list also included additional transgressions, including the use of cryptocurrency to mitigate skyrocketing inflation and devaluation of the national currency and high-profile scandals concerning the collection of user data by corporations and states.[50]

Forced Migration and Protectionism

The ostensible reason for the Telegram ban was to prevent the proliferation of foreign-originated moral and cultural corruption. The argument was not new, nor was the tactic of barring public access to a popular communication medium via legal and technical intervention. The Iranian government has, for example, blocked Facebook and YouTube since 2009. A similar decision was made with Viber in 2014.[51] What was new, however, was the state's coterminous promotion of similar Iranian made messaging platforms. Indeed, evidence suggests that the ban on Telegram was more than a political move or a religious or ideological imperative. It was, arguably, whether by happenstance or design, an important component in the state's campaign to more fully integrate Iranians into the national internet through a strategy of forced migration and protectionism.

The host of disincentives and incentives proffered by the state to Iranian users after and around the time of the ban lend credence to this argument. Disincentives for using Telegram included reduced connection speed, intermittent service (via throttling during and after the temporary ban), and higher costs for data usage through home internet and mobile providers. Soon after the ban was announced, the Judiciary ordered ISPs to clamp down on VPN traffic. As a result, the common filter circumvention tactic, always an inconvenience because of the slower speed and need to switch VPNs constantly, became even more tiresome.

Amid these disincentives for using foreign messengers and accessing the global internet, the state proffered an increasing number of incentives to court users into deepening their voluntary participation in NIN. This was largely done through subsidies and regulatory measures. In March 2017, the Communication Regulatory Authority issued a mandate requiring ISPs to offer a 50 percent discount to subscribers using the domestic NIN.[52] Government price setting rendered data rates for domestic messengers 60 percent cheaper than their foreign counterparts. Connections on NIN were faster and less likely to be disrupted due to international politics.

The Telegram ban can also be understood as a strategy of protectionism in which domestic messengers are "protected" from having to compete with more popular and established foreign apps. In the lead-up to the formal announcement of the ban, Khamenei ordered that all public agencies and officials close their social media accounts and create and promote accounts on domestic apps (Figure 8). This provided domestic apps with hundreds of thousands of captive users. This development is consistent with a pattern of government action to protect state-run media institutions from competition, be it domestic or otherwise. It fits a more general model of economic development and the ideological and practical motive of "self-reliance," where state intervention aims to buoy the development of domestic industry and foster self-sufficiency by protecting it from foreign competition. This protectionist bent can also be seen in earlier efforts to protect the state's communication monopoly. In the 1990s, for example, the government took action to block Voice Over IP on the basis that it was violating the constitutionally protected state monopoly on telecommunications. More recently, a court ruling found the quasi-private domestic internet company *Aparat* in breach of the state broadcast television and radio monopoly because it was creating and streaming multimedia content.[53]

To sum up, when we look at events in their context and implication, it becomes clear that the protests presented the opportunity to test-run NIN, both in terms of infrastructure and governmental action. NIN provided the government with the ability to "turn off" the internet, which it did for thirty minutes. But unlike in the past, the state was able to block traffic to and from the global internet while maintaining domestic connectivity. The episode also showed that through NIN, Iran had the capability of selectively blocking and then unblocking Telegram and Instagram traffic and that banning Telegram helped advance the national internet project by forcing many Iranians to use domestic messengers and other state regulated or sponsored information intermediaries on the domestic network.

If the protests of 2017–18 were a dress rehearsal for NIN, the protests of 2019 were the main event. The protests, which began in November were arguably the most extensive and violent demonstrations of dissent in the history of the Islamic Republic.[54] They were also the first time that a government had so comprehensively severed the international communities' access to Iranians reporting information on the ground so comprehensively.

Afterward: The Protests of 2019

On November 16, 2019, protests once again erupted across the country, this time in response to the announcement that National Iranian Oil Company had raised gas prices by 300 percent. Less than twenty-four hours after news of the price hike and large-scale protests hit the international press, the Iranian government commenced what would become a six-day internet blackout across Iran—and up to sixteen days in areas of the country were the protests continued. It was a complex technical feat that was deemed at the time the most advanced and comprehensive internet shut down recorded.[55]

The shutdown was done mainly through ISPs, which were ordered to stop transmissions of certain kinds of data. The measures prevented domestic traffic from going out of Iran. This meant that international press and human rights monitoring groups could not get information about was happening inside the country. This is turn meant that Iranian security forces could murder and maim with impunity—which they did, killing from 304 to upward of 1,500 people, including nearly two dozen children. The brutality came in a number of forms, including killing civilians via sniper shots to the head and torso and the torture and rape of protesters apprehended by security forces. An estimated 4,800 people were imprisoned as part of the crackdown.[56] Unfortunately, with no ability to publicize evidence of police brutality and government repression via foreign reporters and blogs, protesters and human rights defenders could not generate the kind of international scrutiny that might force the government to moderate its behavior.

Internet traffic was also prevented from coming into Iran or circulating within Iran via foreign information intermediaries. This meant, among other things, that Iranians did not have the ability to coordinate protests on apps such as Twitter and Telegram. In the absence of these externally hosted platforms, people had to use Iranian-made, state-sponsored apps that could be easily surveilled. This made it difficult for protesters to organize safely. It also made it difficult for Iranians to get reliable information about what was happening elsewhere in the country, as news and information published on NIN could be manipulated by the state.

Although there was an international internet blackout, Iran's domestic internet, NIN, remained online and functioning throughout.[57] This is a significant accomplishment. Indeed, as the reader will recall from the previous chapter, in the 2009 crisis, Iran's leaders likely had the ability to "turn off" the internet, but did not, in part, for fear of what it would do to the economy and government systems. Here, a decade later, the government had the ability to do what security and intelligence forces only dreamed of in 2009: to "turn off" the Iranian people's access to the World Wide Web while maintaining a functioning intranet with minimal impact to the economy and government.

The protests of 2017–18 provided a testing ground for the national internet. In the protests of 2019, we see the NIN censorship machine in full force. Both episodes demonstrated the complexity and capability of the national internet. They revealed NIN's unspoken reasons for existence—repression, censorship, and the maintenance of regime hegemony—as well as its utility, that it could be selectively turned off, turned down, or disconnected from the world at the behest of the faqih.

"Why are we letting the internet roam free?" Khamenei asked a group of government officials in 2016. "Other countries are setting boundaries to protect their culture. So why aren't we?"[58] The Supreme Leader's remarks reflect a conceptualization of media and society in which it is incumbent on the faqih to protect national "culture" and "identity" from the perversion of foreign information and ideas. This chapter has shown how this impulse to place boundaries on digitally networked communication, combined with pragmatic and strategic calculations concerning regime security and self-preservation, informed the discourse and actions of the ruling establishment across more than a decade. Viewing events through the prism of history and the protests of 2017–18 and 2019, it has offered insight into what may well prove to be the crowning achievement of the Rouhani era—the NIN.

+++

CONCLUSION

توانا بود هر که دانا بود
Tavana bovad har keh dana bovad

—Abolqasem Ferdowsi[1]

The past causes the present, and so the future.

—Peter Sterns[2]

This book has examined the process and politics of mass communication in late modern and contemporary Iran and its role in political power construction and legitimation. We observe, through the progress of eight decades, two different political regimes struggle with the same dual problems of how to adapt to rapidly changing media landscapes and how to use media to advance and protect its ideological hegemony. From the crucible of political, ideological, and technological conflict, several critical insights emerge. In this concluding chapter, I discuss thematic findings at the heart of the book.

Strategies for Managing Change

In contemporary history, we observe two major strategies for managing communicative-technological change. One approach can be described as *dominance through proscription and passive tolerance*. The satellite dish prohibition law is emblematic of this approach. The ruling establishment sought to protect its monopoly on broadcast television through the passage of a law prohibiting ownership of satellite television reception equipment. The law was crafted to provide the impression of consistency with, and safeguarding of, Islamic law and moral strictures while also providing the state television monopoly an opportunity to showcase new and improved programs and win back lost viewers. In the face of improving technology and rising demand, the state gradually settled for a symbiotic relationship with the black market for satellite dishes. At irregular intervals, such passive tolerance has been punctuated by highly publicized, largely symbolic episodes of police enforcement.

Another regime strategy may be described as *dominance through co-option and managed access*. This strategy is exemplified by the state's approach to the internet in 2009. The establishment sought to mitigate the de-legitimating impact of news and images of large public protests domestically and internationally by throttling connection speeds, staging mass street demonstrations in support of the regime, and ultimately cracking down on protesters systematically and decisively. It did so through the IRGC and Basij forces. The state's methods consisted of indiscriminate, at times murderous, violence against protesters and the coerced false confessions of movement leaders and high profile sympathizers on national television. Seemly undeterred, activists sent videos, photos, and written accounts of the violent crackdown to international news media via email, social media, and blogs. Major outlets such as BBC and CNN carried the footage and eye witness accounts of the crackdown, which were then broadcast into Iran through DBS and circulated over the internet.

The Iranian government's strategy to mitigate the de-legitimating impact of hyper-mediated symbolic expressions of popular dissent by managing access to the internet through throttling and filtering rather than taking the entire network offline reflects a communication acumen arguably atypical of governments in the Middle East at the time. It allowed the establishment to maintain the facade of pluralistic politics and relative freedom of expression, at least notionally. This, it was hoped, would create the impression of popular legitimacy in the eyes of foreign populations and world powers.

While these two strategies informed the policies of the ruling establishment at critical inflection points in recent history, there was a third, alternative vision for media and mass communication articulated by a leading member of that establishment. The philosophy was communicated at length by President Khatami, but only partly realized during his tenure. Far from calling for the regime to abdicate its authority over the cultural sphere, the Reformist leader advocated for the privatization of the mass communication sector. Putting the production of television, film, and other digital media content in the hands of businesses and artists, would, Khatami argued, enrich the culture industry as a whole and render regime ideology more potent and relevant to both the Iranian population and foreign publics.

The Reformist-led Majles passed a law for the privatization of television and radio in 2004. Yet, despite superficial actions such as issuing a "public offering" of the Telecommunication Company of Iran, the media industry has continued to be under the grip of the state, and particularly of the Supreme Leader via the IRGC. The military and intelligence force has considerable investment in, and command of, the Iranian economy and government and is answerable only to the Supreme Leader. Its continued participation in the media industry augurs poorly for any future efforts to change the paradigm of state control over mass communication, which would surely require the dismantlement, or at least reform, of a system supported by IRGC investment, carried out by entrenched institutions, and informed by an ideology about media that is nearly a century old. And yet the participation and, indeed, the dominance, of the IRGC in the media and cultural production industry may also be understood as a legacy of the original security context in which the modern mass communication industry was founded.

Military and Propaganda Legacy

One can understand the establishment's distinctly militarized, securitized view of mass communication as the product of history. In the 1930s and 1940s, Iran's British, Russian, and later American occupiers used radio to propagandize rival troops and their host populations. Nazi Germany also used radio for this purpose. Later, in the 1960s, the Shah's growing perception of threat posed by the influx of foreign, anti-regime propaganda and the worrying example of nationalist upheavals in Iraq and Turkey drove him to expand and improve the national radio network. It also informed his decision to create an international radio service which he envisioned as an offensive arm of the state. When his appeals to his American military benefactors for help on the project were rebuffed, the Shah settled for the large-scale purchase of equipment and expertise on the commercial market. While this was happening, a new media for mass communication was entering the scene: television. Television was not, as many histories of the period suggest, brought to Iran exclusively by "an enterprising young gentleman," but concomitantly by Habbibulah and Iraj Sabet (Pasal) and the US military.

As America's greatest ally in the region and the largest recipient of US arms sales, Iran hosted a large population of American troops, diplomats, intelligence agents, and business people and their families. But for the American troops stationed there, Iran was a career backwater, far from the battlefront. The Army established an Iran based branch of US Armed Forces Radio and Television as a way to retain servicemembers by making their deployment more comfortable. It was only because of the appeals of Sabet and a modicum of diplomatic sensibility that America agreed to forestall the unveiling of the service by a few weeks so that the powerful businessman and by extension, the Iranian people, could claim the historical prize of having established the first television service in Iran. But this small concession did little to disguise the message of militarized hegemony that AFRT sent to Tehranis, who received its signal just as surely as they did Televizion-e Iran's.

The military broadcaster out-competed Sabet's commercial service from the start. Without the need for advertising revenue, the US station aired popular Hollywood television productions commercial free, straight from the States. When the commercial enterprise began to flounder, the Shah's government swept in and took over Televizion-e Iran, renaming it National Iranian Radio and Television (NIRT) and building television infrastructure and programming that blanketed the nation. Later, as the Shah faced mounting internal pressure coupled with clear communication from Washington that it would no longer support him because of human rights violations, the Shah ordered the US army television and radio stations to close its doors, ending twenty years of operation in Iran. The Shah took over those assets also, thus eliminating the last domestic competitor for television and radio airspace. The nationalization of radio and television was finally complete. Pahlavi's NIRT was king of the land, a territory where no competitors, be it domestic or foreign origin, were allowed to operate.

But the Shah's dominion over the industry of mass communication proved short-lived. The Shah was soon forced to surrender NIRT to a martial government in a last bid to stave off popular revolt. Even the military stewardship proved transitory, as revolutionaries cast their sights on the national broadcaster. Khomeini loyalists breached the walls of NIRT headquarters and took the Tehran station for its own, proclaiming victory of the revolution airwaves across the nation.

The early history of mass communication has served to cement, or at least validate, the contemporary establishment's media ideology, encompassed by the conviction that control over the apparatus of mass communication is necessary for hegemonic power. This neo-Gramscian view holds ideology—in this case, the regime's Islamic revolutionary ideology—as the key to the palace, so important that any other competing ideology is a threat to the regime itself.

Thus, for the founders of the Islamic Republic and their contemporaries, the seizure of NIRT becomes cautionary tale. Just as revolutionaries eroded the legitimacy of the monarchy through the mediated spectacle of popular dissent and the circulation of an alternative vision for Iran, so too could a rival group overthrow the present regime by commandeering its hold on mass communication, a primary means of ensuring its ideological dominance. It is understandable, then, that media is a soft spot in the regime psyche—a source of vulnerability and anxiety. Technological developments that undermine or weaken the ruling establishment's real or aspirational mass communication monopoly are seen as a threat, not just to the continued relevance of its main institution of mass communication, IRIB, but to its hold on power.

Internet Nationalism and Nationalism on the Internet

This book has followed the course of nationalism in Iran, from a expression of pride and identity under the Shah, to a narrative of resistance and belonging in the final years of the monarchy, to a message of strength and exceptionalism in the early days of the Islamic Republic and the decades that followed. In each juncture, the power of nationalism lay in its ability to unite people behind a single idea—a vision of an Iranian state that charts its own destiny, and of an Iranian people free from the bondage and manipulation of foreign powers. In keeping with Benedict Anderson's "imagined community," Iranian nationalism was, and continues to be, both an ideation and performance of belonging and exclusion.[3]

Nationalism, the discursive strategy, proved an equal opportunity political device, available for appropriation by factions and political movements within and without the ruling establishment. In the fall-out from the election of 2009, we saw nationalism powerfully wielded by young activists. The Green Movement grew out of the outrage and dismay of supporters of the moderate presidential candidates, Mousavi and Karroubi, over the blatant and pervasive voting fraud. It appropriated deep rooted religious and historic symbols and myths to powerful effect. Digital activists circulated Shi'ite symbols and narratives such as the bloody hand of Fatima and the martyrdom of Hussein at Karbala and co-opted the language and tactics of the 1979 revolution, such as shouting "God is great" from rooftops. These speech-acts were powerful expressions of unity and defiance.

The Green Movement was not the only entity using this discursive strategy. Iran's ruling establishment, the target of Green Movement protests, called upon nationalism to motivate pro-government activists and stage large-scale spectacles of public support for the nezam and the Supreme Leader, essential for popular legitimacy. But such public displays of unity of people and state did not sway the loosing presidential candidates. Mousavi and other Reformist leaders refused to accept the election commission's dismissal of complaints of election fraud and choose not attend President Ahmadinijad's inauguration ceremony, a key unity signaling exercise. Yet ultimately, Mousavi and Karroubi, who were, after all, part of the ruling establishment, did what was in the interest of that establishment and stood down.

Soon after its violent suppression of Green Movement demonstrations, the state began disseminating a revisionist history of the election protests online. The unrest was not the result of popular discontent, these new histories insisted, but instead was the work of Iran's enemies. Conventional government security services joined a new class of online agents as two knives against the cutting board of history. They used online reportage and images of the unrest to support a synthetic story of events, one in which the protests were the work of Iran's foreign enemies, thus conforming to a long running myth about Iran and the West dubbed "soft war."

We can draw a line between the experience of 2009 and the drive to create a national internet. In 2009, the internet allowed digital artists and political organizers to distribute images and first-hand accounts of regime brutality en masse. Such acts implicitly questioned the moral and religious authority of the Supreme Leader and the political-ideological system in which he derived his power. At the time, the network structure of the Iranian internet was such that connections within the country and with the outside world depended on a limited number of exchange points. This gave the state the technical capability to "turn off" the internet during the crisis. The regime did not take this step, however. Instead, it began building a national internet.

Called the National Information Network (NIN), the Iranian internet (more accurately, the intranet) must be understood as an economic project beneficial to the entire country. But it must also be understood as an effort to stave off the perceived impending legitimacy crisis brought on by the massification of new communication technologies and forums such as Facebook, Twitter, and Telegram which give one person the ability to communicate to many.

Today's NIN puts cybernetic walls around the national internet, ostensibly protecting the country from outside threats such as cyber-attacks and morally corrupt ideas and images originating from the West. It also creates an architecture by which the Iranian regime can cut off Iran's contact with the international community. This is immensely beneficial to Iran's rulers. It provides the state the flexibility to repress dissent and punish those who offer internal resistance or ideological competition with comparatively little disruption to the economy and government.

But when stripped of its nationalist and economic dressing, NIN is an admission of ontological insecurity. It says that the sway of the state is uncertain at best, and that protectionism is needed to out compete the alternative technologies, cultural products, and accompanying ideologies available to Iranians through the World Wide Web. The ruling establishment, in other words, is concerned about its ability to maintain hegemony when its ideas and dictates are exposed to open, informed interrogation in the global digital public square.

Media, Culture, and Human (In)Security

At times, the state has used the national television and radio service to justify violence, to intimidate citizens, and to preempt and repress political organizing while simultaneously affirming the Leader's spiritual and corporal power. Other times, the government has used state sponsored media to clarify or make sense of the ubiquitous, intangible "redlines" within press law and actions by the Judiciary and Ershad. Despite the utility of a national television and radio service as interpreter of politics (a role like that of its precursor, NIRT, which was also viewed as a proxy for government communication), the mandate of the state-sponsored press and broadcast media has clear downsides. Failure to explain regime actions, or more powerfully, the failure of multiple officials from different parts of government to speak with the same voice, suggests that the state, and the Supreme Leader in particular, is indecisive or hypocritical. Indeed, much of public life in the Islamic Republic of Iran requires navigating the contradictions and inconsistancies of the applied governing system of velayat-e faqih.

But the problem for regular Iranians is more than that. The absence of rationalized, routinized bureaucratic institutions and laws is a major source of human insecurity. Anyone remotely connected to the media is impacted. Reporters working on seemingly a-political beats are at risk of persecution. Journalists have been jailed and worse because of conduct they did not consider to be crossing the boundary between what is acceptable and unacceptable–the so-called "redline." Indeed, often it seems to be political happenstance or perhaps gender or socio-economic status, as much as content, that lands a journalist, blogger, documentarian, or film director in a prison cell. Worse yet is the fact that who or what establishes and enforces such redlines is obscure and changeable. As Oscar Award winning film director, Asghar Farhadi explains:

> Exactly what makes it unpredictable is that you don't know who it is that decides. You can't look behind the curtain. Sometimes the person at the top decides, sometimes the one who's at the bottom. And you don't know who's at the top and who's at the bottom.[4]

The opacity and unpredictability of the state in its interpretation and enforcement of media laws and standards undermines the creation of compelling cultural products, even among those tasked with cultural production on behalf of the regime. It also leads to self-censorship and the exodus of generations of talented journalists, artists, and intellectuals. The perilous position that uncertainty, unpredictability, and censorship create for such people is made all the more acute when the media that the state seeks to control is ubiquitous, constantly changing, and part of the "electronic elsewhere" of cyberspace.[5]

Factionalism and Consensus

In the debates around each mass communication media, we see clear delineations between ideological factions within the ruling establishment. These divisions have been on full display during elections and Majles debates as politicians lock horns over how best to preserve power and advance the interests of the regime. We have seen also various constellations of power and in-built competition within state agencies and governing bodies themselves. In the course of this study, it becomes clear that for Khamenei and his ruling circle, it is not the public debate and internal politicking of political and governmental factions that is of concern. Indeed, the public airing of disagreement has been accepted even encouraged. But while such cleavages and debate may be tolerated within the machinations of government, such is not true with regard to the system itself. Narges Bajoghli observed this dynamic between the media, the regime, and the government. Her account of an interview with a journalist from Raja News is telling.

> This journalist, like other regime cultural producers made the distinction between the government (dowlat), which is made up of the president, the parliament, and the ministers who can be voted in and out of office, and the nezam, which embodies the framework of the Islamic Republic and the belief in the velayat-e faqih. The government can come under criticism, but the regime, in the eyes of the regime cultural producers, cannot be challenged.[6]

Thus, it is consensus within the nezam *about* the nezam that becomes critical to regime longevity. Mass communication serves this consensus signaling imperative. Even on occasions in this book where demonstrative consent and consensus was absent, subservience to the regime through the writ of Supreme Leader was all but assured.

Experience and the lessons of history, it seems, have produced a ruling establishment hardened around the idea that ideological dominance is key to sustained power, and that media is an ideological battlefield on which power is won and lost. It is a view that fails to recognize the deeply entwined, symbiotic nature of media, culture, and society today—to the detriment of us all.

+++

It is an oft quoted couplet of the late 10th century poet Abolqasem Ferdowsi, "tavana bovad har keh dana bovad," one who has knowledge is powerful, and it was one of the first lines of verse I learned as a young poet in college. In it is the key to the historian's universe—the deep conviction that truth is power, and history is where truth resides. It is an argument that has been proved and disproved since the dawn of the discipline. It is on this foundation that I began my journey into the history and politics of mass communication in Iran. I suffer no illusions about the success of this journey in the pages you see here. And yet, in this historical investigation, we begin to understand one key truth-- that Iran's media history is critical to understanding Iran's media present and so, perhaps, the future.

NOTES

Introduction

1. M. Khatami, trans. A. Mafinezam, "Observations on the Information World," in *Hope and Challenge: The Iranian President Speaks*. (Binghamton: Institute of Global Cultural Studies, Binghamton University Press, 1997), p. 61.
2. Ali Khamenei, "Speech to Islamic Republic of Iran Broadcasting officials," Voice of the Islamic Republic of Iran Radio, December 1, 2004.
3. Taylor Owen, *Disruptive Power: The Crisis of the State in the Digital Age* (Oxford: Oxford University Press, 2015). Monroe Price, Free *Expression, Globalism, and the New Strategic Communication*. (New York: Cambridge University Press, 2015).
4. David Karpf. *The Move on Effect: The Unexpected Transformation of American Political Advocacy*. (New York: Oxford University Press, 2012).
5. From here on, "Shah" will be used to refer to Mohammad Reza Pahlavi, and not to his father and precursor, Reza Pahlavi. General terms such as "regime," "state," etc., shall be presumed to refer to conditions under Mohammad Reza exclusively, unless otherwise indicated.
6. Owen, *Disruptive Power*. Manuel Castells, "Communication, Power and Counter-power in the Network Society," International Journal of Communication V1 (2007), 238–266.
7. B. Moore (1966). *Social Origins of Democracy and Dictatorship*. (Boston: Beacon, 1966). Theda Skocpol *States and Social Revolutions*. (Cambridge: Cambridge University Press, 1979, 1979); M. Herb, *All in the family: absolutism, revolution, and democracy in Middle Eastern Monarchies* (Albany: SUNY Press, 1999).
8. Guillermo O'Donnell and Phillippe Schmitter, *Transitions from Authoritarian Rule: Tentative Conclusions about Uncertain Democracies*. (Baltimore: Johns Hopkins University Press, 1986) p. 19.
9. Stephan Haggard and Robert Kaufman, *The Political Economy of Democratic Transitions* (Princeton: Princeton University Press, 1995); Arang Keshavarzian, "Contestation without democracy: elite fragmentation in Iran," in M Pripstein Posusney and M Penner Angrist (eds.), *Authoritarianism in the Middle East: Regimes and Resistance*. (Boulder: Lynne Rienne, 2005) p. 31.
10. H.E. Chehabi, "The Political Regime of the Islamic Republic in Comparative Perspective," Government and Opposition (36.1, 2001) pp. 48–70, Keshavarzian, (2005). P Abdolmohammadi. and G. Cama, "Iran as a Peculiar Hybrid Regime: Structure and Dynamics of the Islamic Republic. *British Journal of Middle Eastern Studies*, (42:4, 2015) pp. 558–578.
11. Keshavarzian, 2005, p 70. E. Chehabi and A. Schirazi, "The Islamic Republic of Iran," *Journal of Persianate Studies* (v5, 2012), p. 185.
12. Roozbeh Safshekan and Farzan Sabet, "The Source of Legitimacy in the Guardianship of the Jurist: Historical Genealogy & Political Implications," POMED Studies (v 27, 2017).

13 Babak Rahimi, Censorship and the Islamic Republic: Two Modes of Regulatory Measures for Media in Iran. *Middle East Journal, (69*: 3, 2015) pp. 358–378. Ervand Abrahamian, *Khomeinism: Essays on the Islamic Republic.* (Berkeley: University of California Press, 1993).
14 Weber identifies political force as unique to the modern state: "Ultimately one can define the modern state only in terms of the specific means peculiar to it, namely the use of political force." Max Weber and Talcot Parsons, *The Theory of Social and Economic Organization.* (New York: Free Press., 1964)., p. 77.
15 Ibid., pp. 130, 234. See: Jürgen Habermas, *Legitimation Crisis.* (Boston: Beacon Press, 1975).
16 David Beetham, *The Legitimation of Power.* (Hampshire: Macmillan, 1991).
17 Beetham, *The Legitimation of Power*, pp. 155–16.
18 Fred Halliday, "The Iranian Revolution: Uneven Development and Religious Populism," in *State and Ideology in the Middle East and Pakistan*, ed. Halliday and Hamza (Macmillan: Basingstoke, 1988), pp. 31–63; Fred Halliday, "The Iranian Revolution and Religious Populism," *Journal of International Affairs*, 36, /no. 2, (Fall/Winter 1982/83) pp. 187–207. Ervand Abrahamian, *Khomenism: Essays on the Islamic Republic.* (Berkeley: University of California Press, 1993); Mohsen Milani, *The Making of Iran's Islamic Revolution: From Monarchy to Islamic Republic.* (Boulder: Westview Press, 1994).
19 Mohammad Ayatollahi Tabaar, *Religious Statecraft: The Politics of Islam in Iran.* (New York: Columbia University Press, 2018); Shabnam Holliday, *Defining Iran: Politics of Resistance.* (London: Routledge, 2016).
20 Holliday, *Defining Iran*, p. 86.
21 For example: Ali Ansari, *The Politics of Nationalism in Modern Iran* (Cambridge: Cambridge University Press, 2012); Semati, 2008; Faris and Rahimi, 2015.
22 Said Amir Arjomand, *The Turban for the Crown: The Islamic Revolution in Iran* (New York: Oxford University Press, 1988).
23 See: Milani (1994) and Arjomand (1988).
24 It should be noted that the conjoining of religious mandate and reinterpretation of traditional role and mandate of clerics in society in the constitution of the Islamic Republic was not without opposition within the seminary at the time. For more on this see Chapter 2.
25 Steven H. Chafee and Miriam J. Metzger, "End of Mass Communication?" *Mass Communication & Society* 4, no. 4, (2001), pp. 369–70.
26 Ibid., p. 370.
27 J. Turow. "On Reconceptualizing 'Mass Communication,'" *Journal of Broadcasting and Electronic Media* 36. (1992), p. 107 as cited in Chafee, 2001.
28 *Constitution of the Islamic Republic of Iran*, translated and published by A. Tschentscher, u.d. www.servat.unibe.ch/icl/ir00t.html [May 18, 2015].
29 Raymond Williams, Robin Blackburn, and Robin Gable., *Resources of Hope: Culture, Democracy, Socialism.* (London: Verso, 2007).
30 Narges Bajoghli, *Iran Reframed: Anxieties of Power in the Islamic Republic.* (Stanford: Stanford University Press, 2019), p. 98.
31 John B. Thompson, *Ideology and Modern Culture: Critical Social Theory in the Era of Mass Communication* (Stanford, CA: Stanford University Press, 1990), pp. 218–19.
32 The fax machine and video cassettes were also communication technologies that drew debate and even government action. But these technologies quite simply did not present the kind of existential challenge to the state's mass communication monopoly.

33　Thompson, *Ideology and Modern Culture*, pp. 218–19.
34　Murray Edelman, *Constructing the Political Spectacle*, (Chicago: University of Chicago Press, 1988).
35　Carl Friedrich and Zbigniew Brzezinski *Totalitarian Dictatorship and Autocracy*. (New York: Praeger, 1961) p. 99.
36　George Sorel & J. Jennings, *Reflections on Violence*. (Cambridge: Cambridge University Press, 2009) p. 123; M. Tagor ""Myth and politics in the works of Sorel and Barthes" *Journal of the History of Ideas* (47:4 1986) pp. 625–626.
37　Roland Barthes, *Mythologies*, trans. Annette Lavers (New York, 1972) pp. 631–33. I would be remiss not to credit my dissertation supervisor, Ali Ansari at the University of St. Andrews for informing this component of my research. Both his PhD dissertation, "Shah Mohammad Reza Pahlavi & the Myth of Imperial Authority," as well as his book, Confronting Iran, discuss myth in some depth. See: Ali M. Ansari, "Shah Mohammad Reza Pahlavi & the Myth of Imperial Authority," (PhD dissertation, SOAS, University of London, 1998); Ali M. Ansari, *Confronting Iran: The Failure of American Foreign Policy and the Next Great Crisis in the Middle East* (New York: Basic Books, 2006).
38　Khamenei, "Speech to Islamic Republic of Iran Broadcasting" (2004).
39　Emily Blout, "Wired to Disconnect," Lecture at the University of Virginia, Department of Middle Eastern and South Asian Language and Cultures, 2016.
40　As summarized by Denis McQuail in *McQuail's Mass Communication Theory, 6th edition*. (London: Sage, 2010) p. 256.
41　Jalal Al-e-Ahmad, *Gharbzadegi* (Costa Mesa: Mazda, 1997). It should be noted that the phrase was first coined by Ahmad Fardid, a professor of philosophy at the University of Tehran, in the 1940s.
42　For an exceptionally thorough and insightful account of Al-e Ahmad's work and impact, see: Hamid Dabashi, *Theology of Discontent: The Ideological Foundations of the Islamic Revolution in Iran* (New York: New York University Press, 1993), pp. 39–102.
43　Joseph Nye, "Soft Power and American Foreign Policy," *Political Science Quarterly* (Summer 2003): 256–7.
44　This is an inversion of the meaning of the term, which Axworthy uses in reference to Iran. Michael Axworthy, *A History of Iran: Empire of the Mind* (New York: Basic Books, 2016).
45　Khatami was even successful in having the year 2001 named the "year of dialogue among civilizations" by the United Nations. See United Nations document A/55/100, available at http:// www.un.org/documents/ga/docs/55/chapter32-42.pdf
46　Monroe Price, "Iran and the Soft War," *International Journal of Communication* 6 (2012), pp. 2397–415; Annabelle Sreberny, "Too Soft on 'Soft War': Commentary on Monroe Price's "Iran and the Soft War," *International Journal of Communication* 7. pp. 801–4.
47　Seth Jones, "The United States' Soft War with Iran" *CSIS Briefs*, June 11, 2019, https:// www.csis.org/analysis/united-states-soft-war-iran
48　Babak Rahimi, "Censorship and the Islamic Republic: Two Modes of Regulatory Measures for Media in Iran," *The Middle East Journal* 69, no. 3.
49　Carl von Clausewitz, Michael Howard, Peter Paret, and Bernard Brodie (trans., ed.), *On War* (Princeton, NJ: Princeton University Press, 1984), Ch. 1, Section 24.
50　University of St. Andrews has one of the largest collection of Iranian literature and nonfiction in Western Europe. It also has a substantial archive of primary documents and film.
51　Much of the content is in Persian. A number include the audio of the interview and a transcript. Access is limited to scholars at the discretion of the project's leadership. https://fisiran.org/en/oralhistory.

52 "Iranian Calendar Converter," *Iran Chamber Society* website (copyright 2001–2022), accessible at: https://www.iranchamber.com/calendar/converter/iranian_calendar_converter.php
53 The Internet Archive can be accessed at: https://archive.org/web/

Chapter 1

1 Al-e-Ahmad, *Gharbzadegi*, 1997.
2 Archival material concerning US-Iran relations in 1973 can be found at the US National Archive in College Park, Maryland. Please see the bibliography for more information.
3 Peter Avery (ed.), *The Cambridge History of Iran: From Nadir Shah to the Islamic Republic* (Cambridge, 2007), pp. 808–14.
4 There is evidence of limited use of radio technology for military purposes before this date.
5 Avery, Cambridge History of Iran, p. 77. For example: UK National Archive, "Inauguration of Tehran broadcasting station," PZ 3506/40 OR/L/PS/12/397, June 22, 1940. Also see: UK National Archive, "Hostilities with Russia: Attitude of Iran," Report by L. Baggallay on behalf of the Joint Chiefs of Staff Committee to the War Cabinet, February 7, 1940.
6 BBC Persian, though in operation in Iran during this period, was not considered by US intelligence sources a formable source of propaganda.
7 US National Archive, "Propaganda in Iran," October 7, 1943.
8 Ibid. The procedures for Allied propaganda during the Russian-Anglo occupation in the First World War were similar, with the exception that Russia did not utilize its reserved broadcasting time on Radio Tehran. Russian propaganda operations were carried out through the embassy by press attaches and distributed country-wide through Russian consulates. British propaganda came from the "Public Relations Bureau" in the British embassy. However, it was directed from the British base in Cairo. Britain also maintained "close liaison" with the Publicity Office of the government of India.
9 Theories differ as to the underlying motivation for the Allied invasion, dubbed "Operation Countenance." Historians cite the country's strategic location and access to a vital waterway in the fight against Axis forces in North Africa. An official correspondence informed the Shah that Russia would "introduce Soviet troops into Iran in connection with the widespread anti-Soviet activity of German agents in that country." Alexander Werth, *Russia at War 1941–1945*. (New York: Simon and Schuster, 1964), p. 288.
10 Ibid. "Such freedom for the expression of new ideas in literature, with the zest which the novel sense of liberation from government guidance brought with it, has never been part of the Iranian intellectual and artistic experience since those years between 1941 and 1951."
11 Avery, The Cambridge History of Iran, pp. 810–14. On the other hand, one might argue that the shortcomings of the Iranian press are typical in the course of the development of independent media in societies with no tradition of "free" press. The superficiality of newspaper reports, for instance, can be partially attributed to editors' and reporters' lack of confidence in dealing with government authorities following

decades of operating under totalitarian rule. Restrictions consummate with wartime occupation may also provide partial explanation. It was not uncommon for occupying British and Soviet forces to restrict the flow of information and manipulate news for propaganda purposes.
12 That said, compared to the Reza Shah period, it was certainly more dynamic.
13 *Encyclopedia Iranica,* "Chronology," (u.d.), www.iranicaonline.org/pages/chronology-3 [December 10, 2015].
14 "Political consciousness was catapulted forward with the introduction of radio, which no longer required a literate public." Ansari, *The Politics of Nationalism in Modern Iran,* p. 127.
15 Stephen A. Tatham, "Strategic Communication: A Primer," Defence Academy of the United Kingdom, Advanced Research and Assessment Group, Special Series 08/28 (Shrivenham: Defence Academy of the United Kingdom, 2008), pp. 5–9. It is important to note that the American and Iranian notion of propaganda has since diverged significantly. Today, it is defined within the US military establishment and federal government as a US government activity directed at foreign audiences. US law prohibits the propagandizing of American citizens. In Iran, as in many other countries, the meaning of propaganda is more fungible. It is an activity done by the state and by non-state actors, and it can be directed to foreign and domestic audiences.
16 Avery, *Cambridge History of Iran,* p. 810. Special thanks to Niki Akhavan for her thoughtful feedback regarding this period.
17 Sandra Mackey, *The Iranians: Persia, Islam and Soul of a Nation.* (New York: Penguin Putnam, 1998), p. 194.
18 Ervand Abrahamian, *The Coup: 1953, the CIA, and the Roots of Modern U.S.-Iranian Relations.* (New York: The New Press, 2015), pp. 16–17.
19 US Government, "Appendix B," in Malcolm Byrne (ed.), *The Secret CIA History of the Iran Coup, 1953,* National Security Archive Electronic Briefing Book No. 28, Notes 163 (Washington, DC: George Washington University, 2000) http://nsarchive.gwu.edu/NSAEBB/NSAEBB28/appendix%20B.pdf.
20 US Government, "Appendix B," in *The Secret CIA History of the Iran Coup, 1953,* ed. Malcolm Byrne, National Security Archive Electronic Briefing Book No. 28, Washington, DC: George Washington University, 2000, http://nsarchive.gwu.edu/NSAEBB/NSAEBB28/appendix%20B.pdf. For more details see Abrahamian, *The Coup,* 2015. The book is arguably the most thorough examination of the event and it larger political and geopolitical context and aftermath.
21 One example is the choice to hold a commemoration ceremony of 30th Tir (July 21) by the Khomeini regime after just coming to power in 1979. It was on this date in 1951, with bazaars closed and many workers on strike, that hundreds of people took to the streets to demonstrate in support of Mossadegh and his drive to curtail the power of the monarch. In response, the Shah ordered his security forces to the streets to disperse the protesters and restore order and commerce to the city. Hundreds of protesters are said to have died at the hands of the Shah's security forces. Annabelle Sreberny Mohammadi and Ali Mohammadi, *Small Media, Big Revolution: Communication, Culture and the Iranian Revolution,* (Minnesota, 1994), p. 57. "Appendix B," National Security Archive, 2000.
22 Ibid.
23 This effort is reflected in the Khomeini's regime decision to hold a commemoration ceremony of 30th Tir (July 21) soon after coming to power in 1979. It was on that

date, in 1951, with bazaars closed and many workers on strike, that hundreds of people took to the streets to demonstrate in support of Mossadegh and his drive to curtail the power of the monarch. In response, the Shah ordered his security forces to the streets to disperse the protesters and restore order and commerce to the city. Hundreds of protesters were said to have died at the hands of the Shah's security forces.

24 US National Intelligence Survey, November 1958.
25 Records attest to USSR sponsorship of dissident radio broadcasts to Iran from Baku. History and Public Policy Program Digital Archive, "Message to CC CPSU G.M. Malenkov about obstacles in Iranian Azerbaijan," trans. Jamil Hasanli and Gary Goldberg, 1953, http://digitalarchive.wilsoncenter.org/document/120062 [November 21, 2015].
26 Abbas Milani, *The Shah* (New York, 2011), p. 231.
27 US National Archive, "Memo of Conversation with Iranian Ambassador," October 10, 1958.
28 US National Intelligence Survey, November 1958, p. 33.
29 Ibid.
30 Milani, *The Shah*, p. 205; Ansari, *Modern Iran*, p. 198.
31 "US National Intelligence Survey," November 1958.
32 Minutes of Country Team Meeting, September 17, 1958. A US embassy official noted that the Shah's position had changed from his previous insistence that all programming be presented in Persian. "The daily schedule now provides for one hour of Arabic and one hour of Kurdish service." The document explicitly notes the continued absence of Turkish-language content. Avery contradicts this and includes Turkish, along with Urdu and Pashtu in the menu of non-Persian-language radio programming. See: Avery, *Cambridge History of Iran*, p. 809.
33 Minutes of Country Team Meeting, September 17, 1958, p. 1. A US embassy official noted that the Shah's position had changed from his previous insistence that all programming be presented in Persian. "The daily schedule now provides for one hour of Arabic and one hour of Kurdish service." The document explicitly notes the continued absence of Turkish-language content. Avery contradicts this and includes Turkish, along with Urdu and Pashtu in the menu of non-Persian-language radio programming. See: Avery, *Cambridge History of Iran*, p. 809.
34 Ibid.
35 Ibid. Zolfaghari was undersecretary to the prime minister.
36 US Expenditure on Communication Projects, March 23, 1957.
37 Minutes of Country Team Meeting, September 17, 1958, p. 2.
38 Minutes of Country Team Meeting, December 3, 1958.
39 Ibid. "Colonel Yatsevitch said he believes on the basis of information he has had from Washington that Air Force planes can be used for this purpose if the CT so recommends. The cost to be borne in some manner yet undetermined would be $60,000."
40 For an example of Sabet being credited as the "founder" of television, see: "*Habibollah Sabet Pasal*," *Iran Nameh*, 14 Mehr 1389 / October 6, 2010, p. 16. "Moruri bar Tarikhcheh- ye Televizion-e Khosusi" [A Review of the History of Private Television], *Majaleh-ye Haftegi-ye Aseman* 1:1, Mehr 1390 / September 2011, www.asemanweekly.com/article/64 [February 26, 2014]. In a notable exception to the trend, *Faslname-ye Ettella'at* includes "[a] US Army Station" as among the three original stations. A Hossein Farajpahlu, "Moruri Bar Zir Sakht-e Technolozhiye Ettella'at Dar Iran,"

[Review of the Structure of Information Technology in Iran], *Faslnameh-ye Ettella'at* 10:4, Bahar 1373 / July 1992, p. 47 www.ensani.ir/storage/files/20101110081715-1.pdf [April 5, 2014].

41 Minutes of Country Team Meeting, 1957. RG059 1951–58 General Records of Department of State Mic Lot file, Subject Files Relating to Iran, 1952–1958, Lot File No. 60 D 533 (2 of 3) Box 10, US National Archive, College Park, MD, June 5, 1958. See bibliography for detailed index of archival documents.

42 Comptroller General of the United States, "Review of the Military Assistance Program for Iran B- 133134," US Government Accountability Office, Washington, D.C., January 9, 1959, http://www.gao.gov/assets/120/112121.pdf [December 10, 2013], p. 9.

43 The Iran Country Team was composed of the US ambassador, the chief of MAAG, the director of the Economic Aid Mission, and members of the intelligence community and their staff.

44 "History of AFRTVS: First 50 Years," US Department of Defense (1993), p. 79.

45 *Oral History Project*, interview with Gen. Hamilton Twitchell, Chief of Mission, US Military Assistance Advisory Mission in Iran, (1988). See also: Helen C. Metz, "*Iran: A Country Study*," US Government (Washington, DC, 1987).

46 Minutes of Country Team Meeting, May 20, 1958.

47 "History of AFRTVS: The First 50 Years," p. 78.

48 John Williams, "*After the Countercoup: Advising the Imperial Forces of Iran*" (MA monograph, US Army Staff College, 2010), p. 3.

49 By all indications, Television Iran remained a privately held commercial enterprise until its closure in 1969. "Television Iran was a purely private enterprise and its revenue was earned through broadcasting of commercials and advertising." "*Seda va Sima-ye Jomhuri- ye Eslami-ye Iran*" [Voice and Vision of the Islamic Republic of Iran: History of Radio and Television], *Secretariat of Supreme Council of Cultural Revolution*, November 17, 2010, www.iranculture.org/nahad/irib.php [March 13, 2014] via Internet Archive. As of March 2014, URL redirects to http://www.sccr.ir.

50 Minutes of Country Team Meeting, May 20, 1958. Identification of officials based on author's deductions from *Foreign Service List*, October 1959.

51 Ibid. The Air Force started development of the military's first television service in 1953 at Limestone Air Force Base in Northern Maine. It launched the first foreign television station in 1954 in Azores, Portugal and Tripoli, Libya, and in 1955 in Saudi Arabia. See, "History of AFRTVS," p. 79.

52 Minutes of Country Team Meeting, May 20, 1958.

53 Radio Corporation of America (RCA) was a leading developer and manufacturer of radio and television technology in the United States. RCA had a distribution agreement with Sabet's Firuz Trading Company. *Global History Network*, "RCA (Radio Corporation of America)," (u.d.), http://ieeeghn.org/wiki/index.php/RCA [November 4, 2013].

54 "Habib Sabet Is Dead: Iranian Altruist and Industrialist, 86," *New York Times*, February 24, 1990.

55 "Sabet Pasal," in *Daneshnameh-ye Jahan-e Eslami Eslam IX*. http://www.encyclopaediaislamica.com [April 20, 2018]; Mohammad Tavakkoli Ṭavak, "Baha'i-setizi va Eslam-gera'i dar Iran," *Iran Nameh* 19/, no. 1–2, pp. 79–124.

56 Ibid. Annabelle Sreberny-Mohammadi and Ali Mohammadi, *Small Media Big Revolution: Communication, Culture and the Iranian Revolution* (Minnesota, 1994), p. 21.

57 Minutes of Country Team Meeting, May 20, 1958.
58 Minutes of Country Team Meeting, June 5, 1958.
59 Ibid.
60 In an email to the author on May 19, 2014, the Harvard Business School registrar verified that Iraj Sabet attended Harvard Business School from September 1954 through June 1956 and graduated with a Masters in Business Administration on June 14, 1956. Iraj Sabet was also referenced in the university newsletter in 2002. *Harvard Business School Bulletin* 78 (Cambridge, 2002).
61 Sreberny refers to him as Firuz. This appears to be an error, although it may be that Firuz was a nickname. Sreberny-Mohammadi and Mohammadi, *Small Media*, p. 21.
62 There is no evidence that Iraj Sabet authored a paper or graduate thesis on television or any other subject while enrolled at Harvard. It is noteworthy that the scholarly works which include this detail directly or indirectly cite one particular source—the English translation of the 1961 memoir of Mohammad Reza Pahlavi. "One young man, the son of a prominent business man, studied at Harvard ... wrote a thesis on the possibility of adapting modern television broadcasting to Persia's particular needs. When he returned, he became a pioneer in establishing Iran's new television industry." Mohammed Reza Pahlavi, *Mission For My Country* (London, 1961), pp. 138–9.
63 Minutes, June 5, 1958. The Shah readily endorsed the project, going so far as to preside over the opening ceremony of the station later that year. "Iran Opens Commercial TV," *New York Times*, October 5, 1958, p. 82.
64 Minutes, June 5, 1958.
65 Ibid.
66 Ibid.
67 "Iran Opens Commercial TV," *New York Times*, October 5, 1958.
68 "The station was patterned somewhat after the American commercial television broadcasting system with a similar administrative structure and program offerings. The system operated on the American 525-line standard. The equipment was mostly Thompson and RCA." Bijan Kimiachi, "History and Development of Broadcasting in Iran," (Ph.D. dissertation, Bowling Green State University, 1978), p. 114. The Technical Cooperation Administration trained Iranian technicians in radio and film production. A letter by Paul Duncan, Director of Information and Reports at TCA, includes "audio-visual training" as necessary for achieving TCA's development goals. Letter from Paul Duncan, May 3, 1953.
69 Sreberny-Mohammadi and Mohammadi, *Small Media*, p. 62. Kimiachi, "History," p. 112.
70 Morteza Katebi, *Televizion Dar Tehran* (Tehran, 1968) as cited in Kimiachi, "History," p. 112.
71 "The History of AFRTS, Part 2," US Department of the Army (1993).
72 "Armed Forces Radio and Television Service 20th Anniversary Documentary with Glen Ford," (1962).
73 Minutes of Country Team Meeting, December 17, 1958.
74 Ibid.
75 Minutes of Country Team Meeting, June 22, 1958.
76 Abbas Milani, *Eminent Persians: The Men and Women Who Made Modern Iran, 1941–1979* (New York, 2008), p. 679. "Sabet tried to persuade the government to start a station of its own and to convince them that competition would be good for all sides."
77 Ibid. Quoted from Milani's interview with Iraj Sabet in 2002, p. 679.

78 "The government bought Iran Television from its owner called Sabet Pasal and by the merger of the station with National Iranian Television, the airing of two different programs from two different [frequencies] became possible." Secretariat of the Supreme Council of Cultural Revolution, "*Seda va Sima-ye Jomhuri- ye Eslami-ye Iran*" [*Voice and Vision of the Islamic Republic of Iran*] November 17, 2010, via Internet Archive [March 17, 2014]. Sreberny writes that Sabet was "forcibly bought out." Sreberny-Mohammadi and Mohammadi, *Small Media*, p. 66. Kimiachi writes that Sabet's television enterprise was "terminated by the Iranian government in order to expand the system and to establish a non-commercial television broadcasting system." Kimiachi, "History," p. 112.
79 Secretariat, "*Seda va Sima.*"
80 Sreberny-Mohammadi and Mohammadi, *Small Media*, p. 66.
81 Ibid.
82 "Habibollah Sabet Pasal," *Iran Nameh*, p. 16. Also: "Moruri bar Tarikhcheh," *Majaleh-ye Haftegi-ye Aseman*.
83 Sreberny-Mohammadi and Mohammadi, *Small Media*, p. 63.
84 Michael Fischer, *Iran: From Religious Dispute to Revolution* (Wisconsin, 2003), p. 187. 91
85 Secretariat, "*Seda va sima.*"
86 Sreberny-Mohammadi and Mohammadi, *Small Media*, p. 64.
87 Ibid.; Ervand Abrahamian, *Iran between Two Revolutions*, (Princeton, 1982), p. 439.
88 Majid Tehranian, "Communication and Revolution in Iran: The Passing of a Paradigm," *Iranian Studies* 13, no. 1–4 (1980), p. 15. Gholam Khiabani, "Religion and Media in Iran: The Imperative of the Market and the Straightjacket of Islamism," *Westminster Papers in Communication and Culture* 3, no. 2 (2006), p. 383.
89 Kimiachi, "History," p. 112.
90 Ibid.
91 "Iran TV Network," *The Wall Street Journal*, January 10, 1967, p. 9.
92 "Moruri bar Tarikhcheh" *Majaleh-ye Haftegi-ye Aseman*.
93 Avery, *Cambridge History of Iran*, p. 811.
94 Sreberny-Mohammadi and Mohammadi, *Small Media*, p. 66.
95 "Shah's Cancer Spreads," *Ottawa Citizen*, April 1, 1980, p. 77.
96 Oral History Project, "Interview of Iraj Gorgin by Mahnaz Afkhami," *Foundation for Iranian Studies*, (Los Angeles, 1985), pp. 15–16.
97 National Security Archive, "Interview with Mahnaz Afkhami," Confidential Cable, June 6, 1976, p. 1.
98 Majid Tehranian, "Communication and Revolution in Iran: The Passing of a Paradigm," *Iranian Studies* 13:1/4 (1980), p. 16.
99 It is interesting to note that one day before, on October 24, 1976, the US news program *60 Minutes* aired a somewhat scathing investigative report on the Shah. In it, Mike Wallace confronted the monarch with excerpts of a leaked CIA psychological profile describing him as a "dangerous megalomaniac" and an "uncertain ally." See: "Shah of Iran," Reported by Mike Wallace, *60 Minutes*, October 24, 1976, www.cbsnews.com/videos/102476-the-shah-of-iran/ [April 20, 2016].
100 Avery, *Cambridge History of Iran*, p. 813; Sreberny disputes this point, maintaining that both the television and radio channel broadcast content exclusively in English. Sreberny-Mohammadi and Mohammadi, *Small Media*, pp. 60–73.

Chapter 2

1. Richard Sennett, *Authority*. (New York: Knopf, 1980), p. 40.
2. William Sullivan, *Mission to Iran* (New York: WW Norton and Company, 1981) p. 212.
3. Arash Azizi, "How Did Iran Become an Islamic Republic?" *Iran Wire*, April 7, 2020, https://iranwire.com/en/features/66898/ [December 10 2020].
4. Peter Avery (ed.), *The Cambridge History of Iran: From Nadir Shah to the Islamic Republic*, (Cambridge, 2007), pp. 808–14.
5. Iranian Union of Journalists protests the closure of Iran's two biggest newspapers, Ettella'at and Kayhan by military government, Paris AFP in English, December 15, 1978 (FBIS). The decision of news organizations to stop publishing was convenient in light of the reporter strikes, which would have drastically reduced the content available for publication. "Tarikh-e Televizion-e Iran" [History of Iranian Television], "Howzeh Riasat-e Sazman-e Seda va Sima-ye Jomhuri-ye Eslami-ye Iran," 2010, www.hozeriasat.irib.ir/page.php?id=45 [April 5, 2014].
6. NIRT broadcast content that likely reinforced popular discontent with the government, which has since been credited with "awakening the people to victory in the achievement of the revolution." "Tarikh-e Televizion," 2010. *Hoze-ye Riasat, 2010*.
7. General's appointment as premier officially announced, *Paris AFP*, November 6, 1978 (FBIS).
8. "Tarikh-e Televizion," 2010. Clandestine radios on the Shah's departure, *Voice of Iran*, January 19, 1979 (BBC SWB).
9. National Security Archive, "Political/Security Report November 30," Confidential Cable Tehran 11754, November 30, 1978, p. 2.
10. National Security Archive, "Dispatch on Iranian labor unrest," Confidential Cable Tehran, December 5, 1978. Also see: Sayyedd Amir Arjomand, *The Turban for the Crown: The Islamic Revolution in Iran* (New York, 1988), p. 117.
11. National Security Archive, "NIRT organization in intense disarray; radio broadcasting stopped, restarted," Confidential Cable Tehran, January 17, 1979.
12. National Security Archive, "NIRT organization in intense disarray," Confidential Cable Tehran, January 17, 1979.
13. Most dailies fail to appear, journalists arrested, Tehran Domestic Service, November 6, 1978 (FBIS).
14. Shahriar Radpur, "65th Anniversary of the Persian Service," (BBC Persian Service, UK National Archive, (2006).
15. For an excellent example of this branding, see: Kamran Mashayekhi, "The Shah is Iran," *Washington Post*, July 29, 1978, p. 10.
16. The most memorable example was in 1977 when protesters gathered outside of the White House where the Shah was meeting with President Carter.
17. "Clandestine" is the term used in declassified US government reports and can be taken to mean sponsored by the intelligence agencies of a foreign state.
18. "Blood Flowing on Carter's Order," *National Voice of Iran*, December 14, 1978 (FBIS). Instability and mutiny within the ranks of the Army, *National Voice of Iran*, December 15, 1978 (FBIS). The clandestine station broadcast from 1959 through 1986 in Persian, Kurdish, and Azerbaijani. See: Richard Felix Staar, *Foreign Policies of the Soviet Union* (Stanford, 1991), p. 91.

19 "The Khomeini Era Begins," *Time Magazine* 113, no. 7 (1979), p. 32.
20 Ibid.
21 *Khabarnameh* [Bulletin], Newsletter of the National Front, Azar 22, 1357/December 13, 1978, pp. 1–2.
22 Ibid.
23 See: "Kainuri, First Secretary of the Tudeh Central Committee: The Tudeh Party of Iran Has Warned the Government about the Conspiracy of Imperialism," Bamdad, October 9, 1979, pp. 1, 2 (FBIS).
24 National Front denounces emergence of "religious clique," *Bamdad*, September 25, 1979, p. 8 (FBIS).
25 Ibid.
26 Kianuri, *Bamdad*, p. 12.
27 "National Front Denounces," *Bamdad*, September 25, 1979, (FBIS).
28 There is evidence that Khomeini's faction took action to remove all other voices and political competition within the bureaucracy, the military, and within the public sphere before the revolutionary victory. Indeed, Dabashi credits an extremely effective campaign of violence and populist maneuvering for the Islamist success. "What happened in Iran between 1977 and 1979 was not an 'Islamic' revolution but a revolution that was forcefully and violently 'Islamized.'" Hamid Dabashi, *Shi'ism: A Religion of Protest* (Cambridge, 2011), p. 310.
29 Muslim People's Republic Party resolution on the occasion of 17 Shahrivar, *Keyhan*, September 9, 1979, p. 2 (FBIS). Saeid Saffari, "The Legitimation of the Clergy's Right to Rule in the Iranian Constitution of 1979," *British Journal of Middle Eastern Studies* 20, no. 1 (1993), p. 77. Arjomand, *The Turban for the Crown*, p. 140.
30 Nicholas M. Nikazmerad, "A Chronological Survey of the Iranian Revolution," *Iranian Studies*, 13, no. 1 (1980), p. 366.
31 According to Nikazmerad, NIRT also broadcast a statement proclaiming Shari'atmadari the leader of all the world's Shi'ite Muslims. "A Chronological Survey," p. 366.
32 "Eighth December Communique of the Muslim People's Republic Party," *National Iran Radio* Tabriz, December 8, 1979 (BBC SWB).
33 Arjomand, *Turban for the Crown*, pp. 140–1.
34 "Eighth December Communique," December 8, 1979 (BBC SWB).
35 "Khomeini's [sic] 9th December Address to Radio and Television Council," *National Iran Radio* Tehran, December 9, 1979 (BBC SWB).
36 "Text of communique issued by Muslim People's Republic Party as Broadcast," *National Iran Radio*, Tabriz, December 8, 1979 (FBIS).
37 Saffari, "The Legitimation of the Clergy's Right to Rule," p. 77.
38 Mohsen Milani, *The Making of Iran's Islamic Revolution*, Second Edition Westview Press: Colorado 1994, pp. 172–5.
39 Saffari, "The Legitimation of the Clergy's Right to Rule," p. 77. Indeed, a number of books have been published to reinforce the branding. See, for example, Hamid Ruhani, *Shari'atmadari Dar Dadgah-e Tarikh* [Shari'atmadari in History's Court], Tehran, 1983. For a more recent publication, and perhaps an indication of his continued relevance as an ideological challenge to the state, see: Asghar Heidari, *Shari'atmadari be Revayat-e Sanad* [Shari'atmadari According to Documents], *Markaz-e Asnad Engelab-e Eslami* [Documentation Center of the Islamic Revolution], 2010. For an example of the historical revision on the internet, see: (unattributed) "*Naghsh-e Ayatollah*

Shariʿatmadari Dar Kudeta" [Ayatollah Shariʿatmadari Role in the Coup], *Teribun*, 22 Tir 1391/July 12, 2012, www.teribon.ir/archives/113918 [December 9, 2015].

40 "Text of announcement by the Rezaei family," Radio Iran, July 1, 1980 (BBC SWB).

41 Gordon Barthos, "Iran Hauled onto U.N. Carpet over Human Rights Violations," *Toronto Star*, December 8, 1985.

42 "Moruri Bar Tarikhcheh- ye Televizion-e Khosusi" [A Review of the History of Private Television], *Majaleh-ye haftegi-ye Aseman* 1, no.1 (Mehr 1390/September 2011), www. asemanweekly.com/article/64 [February 26, 2014]. According to this source, NIRT was taken over by the opposition on February 22, 1979 and the military occupation of the headquarters lasted less than a month. According to Sreberny, the opposition seized the headquarters on February 11 and the military occupation of NIRT lasted 99 days. See: Sreberny-Mohammadi and Mohammadi, *Small Media*, p. 169.

43 Iran Payanbakhsh, "*Radio va Televizion Cheguneh be Tasarrof-e Enqelabiyyun dar Amad*?" [How did the Revolutionaries Capture Radio and Television], *Tarikh-e Irani*, (u.d.), www.tarikhirani.ir/fa/files/10/listview [February 26, 2014].

44 For another account, see: "Video Commentary: Announcing the Revolution," Radio Free Europe / Radio Liberty, February 11, 2010. https://www.youtube.com/watch?app=desktop&v=PKtqIOHlGSg&ab_channel=RadioFreeEurope%2FRadioLiberty [December 10, 2021].

45 See, for example, Ayatollah Montazeri notes political nature of Islam, *Tehran Domestic Service*, 1 October 1, 1979 (FBIS).

46 Ruhollah Khomeini, "Remarks during Visit of Provincial Cabinet Ministers on the Occasion of the Iranian New Year, 20 March 1979," in *Seda va Sima dar Kalam-e Emam Khomeini* [Radio and Television in the Words of Imam Khomeini], (Tehran, 1984). My translation.

47 Ruhollah K. Ramazani,. "Constitution of the Islamic Republic of Iran.," *Middle East Journal*, vol. 34, no. 2, (1980), pp. 181–204. *JSTOR*, JSTOR, www.jstor.org/stable/4326018.

48 Specifically, Article 175. "The Articles of Association of Islamic Republic of Iran Broadcasting (IRIB)," www.iranculture.org/en/nahad/irib.php [August 22, 2009], See also: Asghar Shirazi, *The Constitution of Iran: Politics and the State in the Islamic Republic* (London, 1997).

49 The term "barefoot people" is ironic given that Mohammad Reza Pahlavi used similar language to persuade the public to support his modernization agenda in the 1960s. Pahlavi cast himself as champion of the barefoot millions against the avarice and greed of the "Thousand Families." UK National Archive, FO 371 133007, EP 1015/62 "Internal Political Situation in Iran," December 9, 1958.

50 Hamid Dabashi, *Iran, the Green Movement, and the USA: The Fox and the Paradox* (London, 2010), p. 105.

51 Homa Javedani, *Tarikh-e Televizion-e Iran* [History of Iranian Television] (Tehran:, 1384), p. 124.

52 The MEK and Tudeh were heavily targeted. See, for example, Text of announcement by the Rezaei family, *National Iran Radio*, July 1, 1980 (BBC SWB). Also see: *US Central Intelligence Agency FOIA Database*, "Execution of Shah's officials," National Intelligence Daily Report (May 8, 1979).

53 Payanbakhsh, *"Radio va Televizion," (u.d.)*. Also see: "Mashhad Teachers Plan Strike," *Tehran Domestic Service*, November 3, 1978 (FBIS). "Mahabad Judges Tender Resignations in Protest," *Tehran Domestic Service*, November 5, 1978 (FBIS).

"Weeklong Strike of Iran Air," *Paris* in English, November 7, 1978 (FBIS). Strikes in refineries, *Paris AFP* in English, December 27, 1978 (FBIS).
54 Sreberny-Mohammadi and Mohammadi, *Small Media*, p. 173.
55 Ibid.
56 "Interview of Iraj Gorgin by Mahnaz Afkhami," *Foundation for Iranian Studies*, p. 21.
57 Javedani, *Tarikh-e Televizion-e Iran*, p. 125.
58 NIRT organization in intense disarray; radio broadcasting stopped, restarted, January 17, 1979. 57 Sreberny-Mohammadi and Mohammadi, *Small Media*, p. 170.
59 Ibid.
60 Radio-Television Supervisor Ghotbzadeh [sic] discusses censorship, *Tehran Domestic Service*, August 5, 1979 (FBIS).
61 *Oral History Project*, "Interview of Iraj Gorgin," pp. 21, 26–9, 37–8.
62 Among the papers listed was *Omid-e Iran* [Hope of Iran] which was described as "Iran's *'Time'* magazine." One document seized during the US embassy occupation details a meeting of US embassy staff and the paper's editor, Ali Reza Nurizadeh. It describes Nurizadeh as a "liberal democrat" and "active member" of the Union for Freedom, a group established by a former member of the Majles who an outspoken critic of the regime. Among other things, Nurizadeh asked the official to provide material for placement in his paper to educate readers about Western democracy. "Visit with Ali Reza Nurizadeh, editor of *Omid-e Iran*," US Embassy Tehran, May 10, 1979, DFUSED 1–6, Center for the Publication of the US Espionage Den's Documents, Tehran, undated, p. 86.
63 Tehran paper lists forty-one publications earmarked for closure, *Ettella'at*, August 21, 1979 (FBIS).
64 Arjomand, *Turban for the Crown*, p. 144.
65 Javedani, *Tarikh-e Televizion-e Iran*, p. 123.
66 Ibid.
67 Mark Gasiorowski. "US Covert Operations toward Iran, February–November 1979: Was the CIA Trying to Overthrow the Islamic Regime?" *Middle Eastern Studies*, 2015. v. 51:1.
68 Ibid.
69 The Internet Archive has digital copies of many of them. See Internet Archive, "Documents from the US Espionage Den," (Tehran. 1979) https://archive.org/details/DocumentsFromTheU.s.EspionageDen
70 The English translation of these terms are approximations and differ or change according to context or intended meaning. All denote the unequal relationship between two socio-economic groups.
71 For footage, see: "Carter Iran Rescue Mission," Dan Rather website https://danratherjournalist.org/anchorman/breaking-news/iran-hostage-crisis/video-carter-iran-rescue-mission. [August 20, 2020].
72 Gary Sick. *All Fall Down: America's Fateful Encounter with Iran*. (London: I.B.Tauris & Co. Ltd, 1985).
73 Bernard Gwertzman. "Reagan Takes Oath as 40th President; Promises an 'era of national renewal'; Minutes Later, Fifty-two US Hostages in Iran Fly to Freedom after 444-Day Ordeal." *New York Times*, January 21, 1981.
74 Ibid.
75 Dilip Hiro, "Chronicle of the Gulf War," *Middle East Report* 126, (1984), pp. 3–14. According to Saskia M. Gieling, the Iranian government has published a fifty-seven-volume narrative history of the war. For an index, see: "*Sepah-e Pasdaran-e Enqelab-e*

Markaz-e Motale'at va Tahqiqat-e Zaman-e Jang." Ruzshomar-e Jang-e Iran va Iraq, 52, (Tehran, 2003), pp. 5–7. Saskia M. Gieling, "Iran-Iraq War," *Encyclopedia Iranica* 13, no. 6 (2006), pp. 572–81.

76 For an excellent, if dated, overview of the war, see Chubin and Tripp (1991). For an interesting examination of the collective memory of the war and its legacy for succeeding generations, see Varzi (2009). Shahram Chubin, and Charles Tripp., *Iran and Iraq at War*. (Boulder, CO: Westview Press, 1991); Roxanne Varzi., *Warring Souls: Youth, Media, and Martyrdom in Post-Revolution Iran*. (Durham: Duke University Press, 2009).

77 "The Articles of Association of Islamic Republic of Iran Broadcasting (IRIB)," www.iranculture.org/en/nahad/irib.php [August 22, 2009].

78 "In no other war in history has the art of persuasion been employed to the degree used by the Iranians in their eight-year long war against Iraq." Peter Chelkowski and Hamid Dabashi, *Staging a Revolution: The Art of Persuasion in the Islamic Republic of Iran* (New York, 1999), p. 262.

Chapter 3

1 "Banning Satellite Dishes an 'Appropriate, Necessary' Measure," *IRNA*, January 16, 1995 (BBC SWB).
2 "Hashemi Rafsanjani's Inaugural Speech," *Tehran Domestic Service*, August 17, 1989 (FBIS).
3 In particular, see Articles 4 and 5 of the Articles of Association of the Islamic Republic of Iran Broadcasting (*Asasname-ye Seda va Sima-ye Jomhuri- ye Eslami-ye Iran*), enacted December 28, 1980, November 17, 2010, http://www.iranculture.org/nahad/irib.php via Internet Archive [March 13, 2015]. "Khamenei Announces Changes," *Tehran Voice of the Islamic Republic Program Network*, February 13, 1994 (FBIS).
4 "Text of Khamenei Edict," *Tehran Domestic Service*, August 24, 1989 (FBIS).
5 Ibid.
6 "Mohammad Hashemi Reinstated as Broadcasting Chief," *Iran*, August 24, 1989 (FBIS).
7 The precise figure is 17.8 years old. *Statistical Centre of Iran* via Iran Data Portal, Princeton University, www.princeton.edu/irandataportal/socioecon/topics/population/ [February 23, 2015].
8 "Radio, -TV Chief on Goals of the Station," *Tehran Television Third Program Network*, December 5, 1993 (FBIS).
9 Radio, TV chief speaks on news reporting, *Tehran Television Service*, March 10, 1990 (FBIS).
10 As vividly demonstrated in the Majles report on IRIB (discussed in the next section).
11 "Meshkini Warns against Deviant Culture of the West," *Jomhuri-ye Eslami*, February 24, 1990 (FBIS).
12 Ibid.
13 Ibid.

14 "Ahmad Khomeini [sic] Espouses '"Resolute Policies,"' *Kayhan*, April 16, 1990 (FBIS). Also referred to as the "Inquiry and Investigation Group." The group was reported have held more than fifty meetings for a total of over 150 hours.
15 Majles members on the Commission for Cultural and Islamic Guidance Affairs included: Ali Movahedi Savoji (Chair), Hassan Kamran, Ali Akbar Parvaresh, Mohamad Reza Mavalizadeh, Mohsen Kuhkan, Ali Yusef Pur, and Lotfollah Zarei Ghanavati. See also: "Media Criticized for Western Influenced Programing," *IRNA* in English, November 3, 1993 (FBIS).
16 "President's Speech Inaugurates Third TV Channel," *Television Third Program Network*, December 5, 1993 (FBIS).
17 "External Media Broadcasts to be Increased," *Salam*, September 22, 1993 (FBIS).
18 "Radio, TV Officials on New Efforts in Broadcasting," *Voice of the Islamic Republic of Iran Program*, September 19, 1994 (FBIS).
19 It should be noted that the creation of Channel 3 was both in accordance with Hashemi's stated agenda upon his reappointment in 1989 and consistent with the directives of the Supreme Leader.
20 "Voice Vision Chiefs Interviewed," *Tehran Domestic Service*, March 23, 1990 (FBIS). In the interview, Hashemi discussed plans to bring high-definition television to Iran. The project would be unveiled in 1994, and if approved, would take five to six years to implement.
21 Ibid.
22 "Majles Inquiry and Investigation Report," *Resalat*, November 3, 4, 15, 1993 (FBIS). "The Voice and Vision organization, especially Vision, must use artistic and effective methods, such as films, serials, and recreational and attractive programs, in the best possible manner to convey its message and not be satisfied with the simple, primitive, low budget conveyance of the messages, such as speeches and direct statements. One of the bases of judgment is to see to what extent this important medium has made use of effective and attractive methods to transmit its message."
23 Ibid. "Among the programs related to Islam and the Revolution, 95 percent were in the form of direct messages, that is, speeches, news, call for prayers, and recitation of reports, and no programing in the form of films and serials."
24 Ibid. "The serials are made at high cost but have such internal problems that after production they are announced as unfit for broadcast."
25 Ibid.
26 "Voice, Vision Response to Majles Inquiry," *Jomhuri-ye Eslami*, November 8, 9, 11, 1993 (FBIS). 2 (BBC SWB).
27 "Majles Inquiry and Investigation Report," *Resalat*, November 3, 4, 15, 1993 (FBIS).
28 Ibid.
29 Ibid.
30 John Kifner, "Khomeini Bans Broadcast Music, Saying It Corrupts Iranian Youth," *The New York Times*, July 24, 1979. https://www.nytimes.com/1979/07/24/archives/khomeini-bans-broadcast-music-saying-it-corrupts-iranian-youth.html [May 1, 2019].
31 "Larijani Interviewed on Media, Cultural Issues," *Beirut Al-Safir* in Arabic, November 29, 1993 (FBIS).
32 "Voice, Vision Response to Majles Inquiry," *Jomhuri-ye Eslami*, November 8, 9, 11, 1993 (FBIS).
33 He also appointed Larijani to the High Council of the Cultural Revolution for a period of five years. See: "President's Brother Resigns Post Heading Radio, TV," *Paris AFP*, February 12, 1994 (FBIS). "Khamenei Announces Changes to IRIB," *Voice of the*

Islamic Republic First Program Network, February 13, 1994. "New Director General Appointed," *IRNA* in English, February 13, 1994 (FBIS). The president attempted to gloss over the forced removal of his brother by appointing him to the prestigious post of UN ambassador. "Proclamation by 170 Majles Deputies Congratulating the Exalted Leader on the New Appointment in the Voice and Vision Organization," *Resalat,* April 7, 1994 (FBIS).

34 "Critics Oppose the Cultural Invasion," *Resalat,* April 7, 1993 (FBIS). June 20, 1992 (BBC SWB).

35 "New Director General Appointed," *IRNA,* February 13, 1994; "Proclamation by 170 Majles Deputies Congratulating the Exalted Leader on the New Appointment in the Voice and Vision Organization," *Resalat,* April 7, 1994 (FBIS).

36 "Culture Minister Resigns," *APSR, APS Diplomatic Recorder Arab Press Service Organization,* July 18, 1992, 37:3.

37 "Khatami Cited on "Retrograde" Influences, Which Prompted his Resignation, *Paris AFP* in English, July 18, 1992 (BBC SWB).

38 FSS is discussed in the chapter that follows.

Chapter 4

1 "Meshkini Warns against Deviant Culture of the West," *Jomhuri-ye Eslami,* February 24, 1990.

2 Gholamreza Arjomandi, "Direct Broadcasting Satellite (DBS) Policy in the Islamic Republic of Iran: Popular, Religious and State Discourse" (PhD dissertation: University of Leicester, 1998), p. 131. https://citeseerx.ist.psu.edu/viewdoc/download?doi=10.1.1.933.1709&rep=rep1&type=pdf [December 10, 2021].

3 McLuhan, Marshall. *Understanding Media: The Extensions of Man* (Massachusetts: MIT Press), 2013

4 Bruce R. Elbert, *The Satellite Communications Applications Handbook* (Boston, 2004), p. 58.

5 Ibid., p. 248. Launched in April 1990, Asia Sat 1 was the first privately owned satellite communication network to cover all of the Asian continent.

6 Gholamreza Arjomandi, "Direct Broadcasting Satellite (DBS) Policy in the Islamic Republic of Iran: Popular, Religious and State Discourse." (1998). p. 129

7 Ibid., pp. 129–30. In 1992, Arab Sat C1 and Arab Sat D2 entered Asian air space. The former carried sixteen channels, including: Saudi Arabia, Egypt, Morocco, UAE, Mauritania, Kuwait, and Jordan, as well as CFI France, MBC, and CNN. The latter satellite carried ten channels geared toward art and entertainment (although these needed a decoder to receive). In 1995, additional channels, including two Israeli and a Turkish and a Russian channel, began broadcasting, and a menu of mostly American channels including TNT, CNN, ESPN, and Discovery became receivable in Iran via Pan Am Sat. In addition to foreign satellite channels, an estimated forty terrestrial channels were being broadcast from neighboring countries by means of terrestrial transmission.

8 *Gozaresh,* May 21, 1994, *Jahan-e Eslam,* December 26, 1994, *Resalat,* December 26, 1994, as cited by Arjomandi, "DBS Broadcasting in Iran". pp. 129–30.

9 Based on a 1994 black market exchange rate of 4000 rials to one US dollar.

10 *Bahar Weekly,* February 21, 1996, no. 1, as republished in Arjomandi, "DBS Broadcasting in Iran," Appendix.

11 Arjomandi, "DBS Broadcasting in Iran," p. 131 (Table 4).
12 Ibid.
13 *Kayhan,*, April 5, 1994 as cited by Arjomandi, "DBS Broadcasting in Iran," p. 131.
14 *Gozaresh-e Hafteh*, May 17, 1994 as cited in Arjomandi, "DBS Broadcasting in Iran," p. 132.
15 "Interior Minister Comments on Use of Satellite Dishes, *Tehran Times* in English, April 10, 1994, pp. 1, 14 (FBIS).
16 The multiple positions and viewpoints reflected in the discourse as well as technical and practical issues involving the government response are reviewed in detail in the next section.
17 "Outlines of Satellite Ban Approved," *IRNA* in English, September 20, 1994 (FBIS). "Majles Cultural Committee Adopts Draft Bill Banning Satellite Reception Equipment," *IRNA*, July 27, 1994, (BBC SWB). For a precursor, see: "Plan for the Prohibition of the Utilization of Satellite Reception Equipment," *Jomhuri-ye Eslami*, May 12, 1994 (FBIS).
18 "Outlines," *IRNA*, September 20, 1994 (FBIS). "Majles Cultural Committee," *IRNA*, July 27, 1994 (BBC SWB).
19 Ibid.
20 "Foreign Embassies and Research Centers Allowed to Keep Satellite Dishes," *Voice of the Islamic Republic of Iran Network 1*, April 21, 1995 (BBC SWB).
21 According to *IRNA*, the Guardian Council asked the Majles to amend two provisions,which it found in violation of the Constitution because of the cost to the government. However, comparison between the original bill and the final measure reveals additional changes, as discussed earlier.
22 "Majles Approves All Amendments Requested by Guardian Council to Ban Satellites," *Voice of the Islamic Republic of Iran Network 1*, January 21, 1995 (BBC SWB).
23 Majles Cultural Committee Adopts Draft Bill Banning Satellite Reception Equipment, *IRNA*, July 27, 1994 (BBC SWB). The language of Article 10 was also present in the May 1994 plan. However, that version placed the jurisdiction with the Foreign Ministry, rather than the Ministry of Post, Telegraph and Telephone. See: "Plan for the Prohibition of the Utilization of Satellite Reception Equipment," *Jomhuri-ye Eslami*, May 12, 1994 (FBIS).
24 "Opposition Radio Reports Clash in Tehran Over Satellite Dishes," *Voice of the Mojahed*, August 17, 1994 (BBC SWB).
25 "Majles Prepares for Debate on Foreign TV Broadcasts," *AFP* in English, July 30, 1994 (BBC SWB).
26 "Enforced Removal of Satellite Dishes from Rooftops to Begin on April 22," *IRNA*, April 19, 1995 (BBC SWB).
27 "Interior Ministry Statement on Dismantling of Satellite Dishes," *Voice of the Islamic Republic of Iran Network 1*, April 24, 1995 (BBC SWB).
28 Survey reportedly shows Tehran satellite dish owners removing them "voluntarily," *IRNA*, January 12, 1995 (BBC SWB).
29 Interior Minister Says Over 90 Percent of Satellite Dishes Dismantled Voluntarily, *Voice of the Islamic Republic of Iran Network 1*, April 24, 1995 (BBC SWB).
30 Arjomandi, "DBS Broadcasting in Iran," p. 133.
31 "Report on Majles Proceedings," *Resalat*, September 14, 1994 (FBIS).
32 *Mo'arefi-ye Namayendegan-e Dowreh-ye Chaharom* [Introduction to the Representatives of the Fourth Period], Government of the Islamic Republic of Iran, (1998), p. 448
33 Ibid. *Resalat*, May 9, September 19, 1994, as cited by Arjomandi, "DBS Broadcasting in Iran," p. 134.
34 "Report," *Resalat*, September 14, 1994 (FBIS).

35 See, for example, "Editorial: The Satellite Dish," *Tehran Times*, April 12, 1994, p. 2 (FBIS). West using satellite transmissions to "dilute" other cultures, *Tehran Times*, April 13, 1994 (BBC SWB).
36 Report, *Resalat*, September 14, 1994, p. 5 (FBIS).
37 The government banned video tapes, video clubs, and VCRs in 1983. In 1992, the minister of Culture and Islamic Guidance announced plans to end the ban and to establish 3,000 state-sponsored video clubs.
38 Abrar criticizes minister's remarks on satellite antennae, *Abrar*, 055 [05?] April 1994, p. 2, (FBIS).
39 Ibid.
40 "Kordestan Democratic Party Radio Comments on Recent 'Suppression' Government," Voice of Iranian Kordestan, April 13, 1994 (BBC SWB).
41 Ibid.
42 Editorial, *Tehran Times*, April 12, 1994 (FBIS).
43 Jannati Asks Saudis Not to Obstruct Iranian Pilgrims, Comments on Satellite, TV, *Voice of the Islamic Republic of Iran Network 1*, April 22, 1995 (BBC SWB)
44 Ibid.
45 "Ontological security" in the tradition of Jennifer Mitzen. "Ontological security is security not of the body but of the self, the subjective sense of who one is, which enables and motivates action and choice." Mitzen, Jennifer. "Ontological Security in World Politics: State Identity and the Security Dilemma." *European Journal of International Relations* 12.3 (2006): 341–70. p.344
46 Editorial, *Tehran Times*, April 22, 1995 (FBIS)
47 Report, *Resalat*, September 14, 1994, pp. 5, 15 (FBIS).
48 BBC reaction to ban on satellite dishes viewed, *Resalat*, September 1994, p. 2 (FBIS). 47 Jannati on West's influence, satellite dishes, *Voice of the Islamic Republic of Iran First Program Network*, July 29, 1994 (FBIS). See also: "Ayatollah Jannati Justifies Proposed Curbs on Satellite Dishes," July 29, 1994 (BBC SWB).
49 Ibid.
50 Yazdi on new human rights body, Eslamshahr, US prisoner, Roshdiye, other issues, *IRNA*, April 18, 1995 (BBC SWB).
51 Larijani comments on satellite broadcasting, *Voice of the Islamic Republic First Program Network*, April 26, 1994 (FBIS). He went on to say: "We are not opposed to the positive dimensions of satellite broadcasting; we must also strive toward improving the quantity and quality of our programs while adhering to our Islamic criteria."
52 Editorial, *Tehran Times*, April 22, 1995 (FBIS).
53 Outlines of satellite ban approved, *IRNA*, September 20, 1994 (FBIS).
54 Friday prayers: banning satellite dishes an "appropriate, necessary" measure, *Voice of the Islamic Republic of Iran Network 1*, January 16, 1995 (BBC SWB).
55 Report, *Resalat*, September 14, 1994, p. 5 (FBIS).
56 Candidate on Western onslaught, official corruption, *Voice of the Islamic Republic*, June 2, 1993 (FBIS).
57 Report, *Resalat*, September 14, 1994, p. 5 (FBIS).
58 Ibid.
59 Jannati on West's influence, satellite dishes, *Voice of the Islamic Republic of Iran First Program Network*, July 29, 1994 (FBIS).
60 Ruhollah Khomeini, *Islam and Revolution: Writings and Declarations of Imam Khomeini*, trans. Hamid Algar (Berkeley, 1981), p. 60. See also: "*Seda va Sima dar Kalam-e Emam Khomeini*" [Voice and Vision in the Words of Imam Khomeini], (Tehran, 1984).

61 *Mo'arefi-ye Namayandegan-e Dowreh-ye Chaharom* [Introduction to the Fourth Majles], (u.d.), p. 382.
62 Report, *Resalat*, September 14, 1994, p. 5 (FBIS).
63 Mohammad Javad Larijani commentary in *Resalat* on May 23, 1994, as quoted and translated by Arjomandi, "DBS Broadcasting in Iran," pp. 155–6.
64 Ibid.
65 It may be recalled that the conservative Society of the Militant Clergy enjoyed a majority of the seats in the Fourth Majles.
66 Ibid. The others were Azari Ghomi, Mo'men, and Amini.
67 *Kayhan*, May 22, 1994, as cited in Arjomandi, "DBS Broadcasting in Iran," p. 218.
68 Over ten *fatavi* on satellite dishes were issued. Ibid., p. 164.
69 Asghar Shirazi, *The Constitution of Iran: Politics and the State in the Islamic Republic*, trans. John O'Kane (London, 1997), p. 79. Shirazi cites a fax published by the Bureau of Public Relations for Radio and Television on May 25, 1994.
70 Ali Hosseini Khamenei, Practical Laws of Islam, "Satellite Television Equipment" (Questions 1205–9), Office of the Supreme Leader website, 1998, http://www.leader.ir/en/book/23?sn=5711 [May 1, 2015].
71 Majles prepares for debate on foreign TV broadcasts, *AFP* in English, July 30, 1994 (BBC SWB).
72 Over seventy members voted against the measure, according to Arjomandi. See: "Arjomandi," "DBS Broadcasting in Iran," p. 120.
73 The findings would necessarily be subjective, however. Satellite television is banned across the country, and therefore there is no one area free from the periodic raids of Basij and intelligence forces of homes and business on the basis of illegal satellite dish ownership, and therefore no control group for comparison.
74 "Emha-ye 800 Dastghah Mahvare- ke Mardom Davtalabaneh be Basij Tahvil Dadand" [People Voluntarily Hand-Over 800 Satellite Receiver Devices for Destruction by Basij] *Shiraze-ye Paygah-e Tahlil-e Khabari,*, 6 Mehr 1392/September 28, 2013, http://shiraze.ir/fa/news/44567 [April 18, 2016]. See my discussion of political spectacle in Chapter 1.

Chapter 5

1 Where "cultural transmission" is the exchange of symbolic forms between producers and receivers. John Thompson, *Ideology and Modern Culture*, (Stanford: Stanford University Press, 1991) pp. 164–5.
2 The term "traditional system" is used here and in future text to refer to the Iranian state television monopoly based on Fixed Satellite Service (FSS) broadcasting.
3 While Thompson names three aspects, I discuss two in particular. The third related to the possibility of bundling of data and technology services.
4 Thompson, *Ideology and Modern Culture*, p. 212.
5 Ibid., p. 213.
6 In the latter days, some local news programs were produced and broadcast from provincial networks from IRIB stations located in several provinces. In such cases, a transmission delay was similarly established in order to mitigate against messages considered immoral or threatening to the regime during live broadcasts. Nevertheless, some illicit content was relayed. See: "Head of Tehran TV Reportedly Fired, Arrested," *Kayhan*, April 19, 1990, p. 1 (FBIS).

7   According to Khomeini: "The true rulers are the *fuqaha* themselves, and rulership [*sic*] ought officially to be theirs." Khomeini, *Islam and Revolution*, p. 57.
8   "Article 5 states that during Occultation, the *velayat-e amr* and the Imamate of the *umma* is upon the just and pious … jurist." Arjomand, *The Turban for the Crown*, p. 179.
9   This relationship is abundantly clear when one reads the text of the Islamic Republic's founding documents. See: Constitution of the Islamic Republic of Iran, translated and published by A. Tschentscher, (Bern, 2010). www.servat.unibe.ch/icl/ir00t.html [May 18, 2015].
10 This is significant, given the system's inbuilt Gramscian conception of ideology as key to regime hegemony.
11 Mehdi Semati, *Media, Culture and Society in Iran: Living with Globalization and the Islamic State* (London, 2008), p. 8.
12 Ibid.
13 Ibid.
14 "Committee Set Up to Investigate Foreign-Based Persian Speaking TV Networks," *IRIN*, August 6, 2010 (WNC).
15 Ibid.
16 "Structure of Iran's State-un TV IRIB," December 16, 2009 (OSC).
17 *Nationmaster*, "Information and Communications Technology: Iran," UNESCO Institute for Statistics via Nationmaster Database (2011), www.nationmaster.com/time.php?stat=med_inf_and_com_tec_exp_cur_us&country=ir [July 21, 2011].
18 "Information and communications technology" includes communication services, computer hardware, software and support, and wired and wireless equipment.
19 *Nationmaster*, "Information and Communications Technology: Iran."
20 *Seda va Sima-ye Jomhuri-ye Eslami-ye Iran* [Voice and Vision of the Islamic Republic], "*Site-e Pakhsh-e Zendeh-ye Barname-ha-ye Seda va Sima*" [Site for Live Broadcast of Television and Radio], http://live.irib.ir [December 10, 2013].
21 Ibid.
22 *Seda va Sima*, "*Site Pakhsh*," 2013. Also,: Stephen Barraclough, "Satellite Television in Iran: Prohibition, Imitation and Reform," *Middle Eastern Studies*, 37, no. 3, pp. 25–48.
23 Audience Analysis and Market Profile, May 2005 (FBIS Media Survey).
24 For example, see: "Coalition Backed Iraqi Media Struggling Six Months On," November 19, 2003 (BBC Monitoring).
25 Arjomandi, "DBS Broadcasting in Iran," p. 180. Another example of intra-government cooperation is the utilization of broadcasting time by IRGC.
26 "Cable TV Operation Depends on Voice, Vision Approval," *Salam*, January 19, 1994, p. 1 (FBIS).
27 For a chilling, though dated, account of the practice see, Ervand Abrahamian, *Tortured Confessions: Prisons and Public Relations in Modern Iran*, University of California Press: Berkeley, 1999.
28 "Reformist Iranian Cleric to Launch TV Network on December 21," *Iranian Student News Agency* online, December 5, 2005 (WNC). "Plug Pulled on Moderate Satellite TV, *AKI* online, December 28, 2005 (WNC). Annabelle Sreberny, "Society, culture, and Media: Thinking Comparatively," in J. D. Downing, D. McQuail, P. Schlesinger (eds.), The SAGE Handbook of Media Studies, (Thousand Oaks, CA: SAGE, 2004), pp. 83–104.

29 "Karroubi Discusses Private TV Channel, New Party, *E'temad* online, December 29, 2006 (WNC).
30 Baran Zarrin-Ghalam, "And Now Satellite," *Farhang-e Ashti*, December 9, 2005 (WNC).
31 BBC Monitoring, "Iran Media Guide," March 27, 2007.
32 "Advisability of Private Satellite TV Broadcasts Debated, *Shargh*," September 20, 2005, p. 7 (WNC).
33 Untitled report, *Fars News Agency*, December 27, 2005 (BBC SWB). 37.
34 Zarrin-Ghalam, "And Now Satellite."
35 Larijani was reported to have written a letter to the Guardian Council arguing that the new channel was unconstitutional. See: "Plug Pulled on Moderate Satellite TV," *AKI*, December 28, 2005 (WNC).
36 Karroubi Discusses Private TV," *E'temad*, December 29, 2005 (WNC).
37 *Seda va Sima*, "Site Pakhsh," 2013.
38 "*Bashgah-e Persepolis Saheb-e Nakhostin Shabake-ye Khosusi-ye Iran Shod*" [Persepolis became the Owner of Iran's First Private Network], *Jam-e Jam* online, (1 Tir 1392/ June 22, 2013), http://sport.jamejamonline.ir/NewsPreview/1091505435551629085 [May 1, 2015].
39 Whether the satellite channel received full government approval is unclear.
40 "*Bashgah-e Persepolis*," *Jam-e Jam*, 2013.
41 This influence has been noted by both Fischer and Ansari. Michael M. J. Fischer, *Iran: From Religious Dispute to Revolution* (Madison, 2003). Ansari, *Modern Iran*, (London, 2007). According to Gilles Kepel, Shari'ati translated *Wretched of the Earth* into Persian in 1988. Giles Kepel, *Jihad: The Trail of Political Islam* (London, 2006), p. 39.
42 Ali Davani, "Moaze-ye Ulama Dar Barabar-e Hojum Farhang-e Gharb be Iran" [The Positions of Ulama on Western Cultural Invasion Against Iran], Ruyaruyi Farhangi-ye Iran va Gharb Dar Dowreh-ye Mo'aser [The Cultural Confrontation between Iran and the West in Modern Times], (Tehran, 1996), pp. 91, 104.
43 Website of IRIB in 2010, retrieved via Internet Archive [December 10, 2015].
44 "Campaign against modern fashion," *IRIB TV* (September 1, 2008), via *MEMRI Project* website, http://www.memritv.org/clip/en/1919.htm [December 10, 2013].
45 Ibid.

Chapter 6

1 Some scholars, including Sreberny and Khiabani, date the first connection to the internet to 1992. See: "Annabelle Sreberny and Gholam Khiabani," *Blogistan: The Internet Politics in Iran* (London, 2010), p. 11–13. I should note from the offset that I encountered some discrepancies between the global internet registries and the history of the Iranian internet as proffered by several scholars referenced here. I encourage the reader to consult ICANN and IANA records, and I am happy to discuss it further.
2 Sreberny and Khiabani, *Blogistan*, p. 11; Hamed Bayati, "The Value of using ICT on Private Iranian Companies," *Articlesbase*, November 1, 2011, www.articlesbase.com/

industrial-articles/the-value-of-using-ict-in-private-iranian-companies-5353650.html [October 1, 2015].

3 Azadeh Shafaei and Mehran Nejati (eds.) *Annals of Language and Learning: Proceedings of the 2009 International Online Language Conference* (Boca Raton, FL: Universal Publishers, 2009) p. 72. See also: Bayati, "The value of using ICT."

4 A. Abbasi, A Niaraki, and B. Dehkordi, "A Review of the ICT Status and Development Strategy Plan in Iran," *International Journal of Education and Development Using Information and Communication Technology* 4, no. 3 (2008), http://ijedict.dec.uwi.edu/viewarticle.php?id=506 [September 10, 2015].

5 Sreberny and Khiabani, *Blogistan*, p. 11.

6 Ibid.

7 Study by BBC Persian as cited by Sreberny and Khiabani, *Blogistan*, p. 26.

8 Guy Dinmore, "Iran Internet cafes closed in crackdown," *Financial Times*, May 14, 2001.

9 Babak Rahimi, "Internet and the State: The Rise of Cyberdemocracy in Revolutionary Iran," Paper delivered at the ISA Conference, Brisbane, Australia (January 2003). p. 5.

10 Rahimi attributes the policies to a decree by the Supreme Leader in 2000/1. His source, www.irjob.ir/rule/inc/1_01.pdf is no longer available online (the website has been taken down). An Internet Archive search revealed that the directory page with a link to the decree as well as other policies and findings by the Supreme Council on Information and Technology existed at one time, but the actual documentation was not recoverable. However, the author was able to find a similar collection of decrees dated November 2004. See: "Rules and Decrees," Aban 1383 / November 2004, www.Irjob.irvia Internet Archive [October 3, 2015]. Iran CSOs Training & Research Center, "A Report on the Status of the Internet in Iran," November 8, 2005, http://www.genderit.org/upload/ad6d215b74e2a8613f0cf5416c9f3865/A_Report_on_Internet_Access_in_Iran_2_.pdf [October 3, 2015].

11 Ibid.

12 Internet World Statistics, "Usage and Population Statistics," www.Internetworldstats.com/stats5.html [December 3, 2015].

13 Internet World Statistics, "Usage and Population Statistics," www.Internetworldstats.com/stats5.html [December 3, 2015].

14 Economist Intelligence Unit, "Country Profile," July 1, 2004.

15 Telecommunications Company of Iran, "Annual Report," July 2004, http://www.irantelecom.ir/press/intro8306/tci11.htm [October 15, 2014].

16 DCI was the subsidiary of TCI and operated under the Ministry of Information and Communication Technology. See: Telecommunications Company of Iran, "Annual Report," 2004.

17 Saeid Golkar, "The Internet, the Green Movement and the Regime in Iran," *International Journal of Emerging Technologies and Society* 9, no. 1 (2011), p. 57.

18 Ibid. According to Rahimi, the student demonstrations of 2 Khordad (May 23, the day Khatami was elected) were organized on the Internet. See also: Golkar, p. 57. The author's own investigation found the earliest archival record of the Khatami website was from December 5, 1998; the last record was August 16, 2000 and featured the email address president@khatami.com. Khatami website, "Welcome page," December 5, 1998, www.Khatami.comvia Internet Archive [September 28, 2015].

19 Akbar Ganji's "Republican Manifest" was published as an online journal. Rahimi, *Cyber Dissent*, p. 11.

20 The significance of the move and its resonance after the website was taken down is indicated by the coverage of, and reference to, the memoirs in the Iranian press several months after the event. See for example: "Policy of Laxness Paved Way for Montazeri Memoirs, *Resalat*, April 11, 2001. Also see: Hossein Shariatmadari, "Mr. Montazeri: Such Behaviour From You Is Not Far-Fetched!" *Kayhan*, January 16, 2001 (BBC Monitoring).
21 Ali Nourizadeh, "Iranian Authorities Said to be Jamming Dissident Ayatollahs Website," *Al-Sharq al-Awsar*, December 14, 2000 (BBC Monitoring). It is interesting that the language describing the technique, "jamming," was previously associated with the blocking of satellite television signals.
22 In an interview with press, Montazeri's son confirmed the website's closure, which he attributed to "certain problems." See: "Dissident Ayatollah's Website Said Closed Due to 'Certain Problems,'" *Tehran Times* online, December 26, 2000 (BBC Monitoring).
23 Niki Akhavan, *Electronic Iran: The Cultural Politics of an Online Evolution* (New York, 2013), p. 8; Sreberny and Khiabani, *Blogistan*, p. 40.
24 *Veblog-ha* [Weblogs] *Hamshahri*, (u.d.), [December 1, 2012]. My translation.
25 "*Mo'alem, Internet, Bank-ha Mo'tamed-tarin-ha-ye Jame'eh Hastand*" [Teachers, Internet, Banks are Most Trustworthy Community], *Iranian Students News Agency*, September 8, 2004, www.isna.co.ir/news/NewsCont.asp?id=427457&lang=P [December 11, 2010]. My translation.
26 "Birthday Party for Persian Blogs Scheduled for June 13," *Iranian Students News Agency*, June 12, 2006 (WNC).
27 Data from Blogcount.com as cited by Sreberny and Khiabani, *Blogistan*, p. 36.
28 Editorial views growing use of web logs, Internet in Iran, *Hemayat*, December 16, 2006 (WNC).
29 Ibid.
30 Ibid.
31 President Says Iran to Utilize IT to Promote Islamic Culture," *IRNA*, November 13, 2005 (WNC).
32 "Editorial Hails Qom Seminary Website, urges more Religious Sites," *Hezbollah*, August 12, 2007 (WNC).
33 Works published included the lessons of Grand Ayatollahs Khamenei, Shobeyri-Zanjani, Fazel-Lankarani, Tabrizi, Makarem-Shirazi, Khansari, Javadi-Amoli, and Mesbah-Yazdi.
34 Mehdi Ahmadi, "Cultural Activity by Means of Chat," *Siyasat-e Ruz*, January 3, 2006, p. 8 (WNC).
35 Ra'uf Pishdar, "Let's Not Persist in the Impossible" *E'temad*, April 4, 2007 (WNC).
36 Khamenei, "Speech to Religious Scholars of Kerman," (11 Ordibehesht 1384 / May 1, 2005) as reproduced in Mehdi Ahmadi, "Cultural Activity by Means of Chat," *Siyasat-e Ruz*, January 3, 2006, p. 8 (WNC).
37 "38,000 Websites and Blogs to Provoke Ethnic Minorities," *Ya Resalat ul -Hossin*, January 3, 2007 (WNC).
38 "Iranian Blogger Derakhshan Allegedly Confesses to Spying for Israel," *Tabnak*, November 18, 2008 (WNC). Derakhshan was sentenced to nineteen years in prison. At one point, he was reported to be slated for execution. In 2014, Derakhshan was released from prison after serving six years. See: "Iran Releases 'Blogfather' Hossein Derakhshan," *BBC News*, November 20, 2014.
39 "IRNA Chief Says Iran Seeking Soldiers of Soft War," *IRNA*, 1 February 1, 2006 (WNC), http://www.bbc.com/news/world-middle-east-30136003 [March 14, 2017].

40 Derakhshan was sentenced to nineteen years in prison. At one point, he was reported to be slated for execution. In 2014, Derakhshan was released from prison after serving six years. See: "Iran Releases 'Blogfather' Hossein Derakhshan," *BBC News*, November 20, 2014, http://www.bbc.com/news/world-middle-east-30136003 [March 14, 2017].
41 Mohammad Imani, "Beyond the Elections," *Kayhan*, January 21, 2008 (WNC). "The Battle Against Models" and "Cultural Infiltration" (n.a.), *IranWire*, March 10, 2017. https://iranwire.com/en/features/4489 [March 14, 2017].
42 "Iranian Culture Ministry Launches Scheme for Registration of Websites, Blogs," *Iranian Labor News Agency*, January 2, 2007 (WNC).
43 Iranian Official Explains Scheme to Regulate Websites, Blogs, *Voice of the Islamic Republic of Iran Radio 1*, January 3, 2007 (WNC).
44 Culture Minister ascribes Baztab's ban to "anonymity" of ownership, *Baztab*, February 19, 2007 (WNC).
45 Ibid.
46 See, for instance,: Iranian Communications Expert Comments on Plan to Regulate Blogs," *Iranian Labor News Agency*, May 31, 2006 (WNC).
47 Rahimi attributes the policies to a decree by the Supreme Leader in 2000/1. See footnote #10.
48 Ra'uf Pishdar, "Let's Not Persist in the Impossible," *E'temad*, April 4, 2007 (WNC). See also: "Iranian Communications Expert Comments on Plan to Regulate Blogs," *Iranian Labor News Agency*, May 31, 2006 (WNC).
49 "When Did Filtering of Sites and Blogs Begin?" *Ettella'at*, May 10, 2010 (WNC).
50 Open Net Initiative, "Filtering in Iran," 2009, p. 4.
51 "Khamenei Holds Question-and-Answer Session with Students," *Vision of the Islamic Republic of Iran Network 1*, May 15, 2003 (FBIS).
52 Stop Censoring Us website, "IRNA: Iran Government Uses American Filtering Software," January 24, 2005, via Internet Archive record for February 6, 2005, original source URL: http://stop.censoring.us/archives/013307.php [October 11, 2015].
53 Open Net Initiative, "Country Study: Internet Filtering in Iran in 2004–2005," 2005, p. 1, at http://opennet.net/studies/iran [October 8, 2015].
54 Open Net Initiative "Internet Filtering in Iran," p. 4.
55 Rauf Pishdar, "Let's not Persist in the Impossible" *E'temad*, April 4, 2007 (WNC).
56 Open Net Initiative, "Internet Filtering in Iran," p. 3
57 Saeid Golkar, "Liberation or Suppression Technologies? The Internet, the Green Movement and the Regime in Iran," *International Journal of Emerging Technologies and Society* 9, no. 1 (2011), p. 59.
58 Ward Carroll, "Iranian Cyber Warfare Threat Assessment," *Defense Tech*, September 23, 2008, http://defensetech.org/2008/09/23/iranian-cyber-warfare-threat-assessment/ [December 10, 2015].

Chapter 7

1 Ali Khamenei, "Speech by Iranian Supreme Leader Ayatollah Sayyed Ali Khamenei to Iranian Students, Representatives of Student Groups, and Elite," *Tehran Vision of the Islamic Republic of Iran Network 1*, August 26, 2009 (WNC).
2 For example see: Brad Stone and Noam Cohen, "Social Networks Spread Defiance Online," *New York Times*, June 15, 2009, http://nyti.ms/1VmYl6X; P. Quirk, "Iran's Twitter Revolution," *Foreign Policy In Focus*, June 17, 2009, http://www.fpif.org/

fpiftxt/6199; Lev Grossman, "Iran Protests: Twitter, the Medium of the Movement," *Time*, June 17, 2009, http://www.time.com/time/world/article/0,8599,1905125,00.htm; M. Landler and B. Stelter, "Washington Taps into a New Potent Force in Diplomacy," *New York Times*, June 16, 2009, http://www.nytimes.com/2009/06/17/world/middleeast/17media.html?_r=1.

3   For a good synopsis of the literature on the internet and globalized social movement theory see: Lauren Langman, "From Virtual Public Spheres to Global Justice: A Critical Theory of Internetworked Social Movements," *Sociological Theory* 23, no. 1 (2005), pp. 42–74.

4   Marwan Kraidy, Revisiting hypermedia space in the era of the Islamic State in Emily L. Blout & Bruce Williams. (ed.), Power and sovereignty in hypermedia space: Middle East case studies, The Communication Review, 20:3, 2017.

5   Ali Ansari, Crisis of Authority: Iran's 2009 Presidential Election (Chatham House: London, 2010), p. 7.

6   The scope of analysis is limited to the post-election crisis, which I define as the period spanning from June 12, 2009, the day of the presidential election, to February 11, 2010, the date both opposition and pro-regime commentators had deemed the last gasp of the Green Movement.

7   Full video of the debate was later made available on the IRIB website. "Debate," *IRIB online*, June 12, 2009, http://www.iribnews.ir/News/Video/192016_413987c0.wmv [June 14, 2009]. See also: "Mousavi Ahmadinejad June 3 Presidential Debate Transcript," *Iran Tracker*, June 9, 2009, http://www.irantracker.org/analysis/mousavi-ahmadinejad-june-3-presidential-debate-transcript [June 20, 2009].

8   According to a news bulletin on the Press TV website, more than 250 international reporters were in Tehran to cover the election. "Over 250 Foreign Journalists Cover Iran Election," *Press TV*, June 12, 2009 (BBCM).

9   Polling stations were originally scheduled to be open for ten hours; the hours were extended at the discretion of local officials. See: "Iran Extends Voting Time to 1630 gmt," *Vision of the Islamic Republic of Iran Network* 2, June 12, 2009 (BBCM). "Iran Governors-General Authorized to Extend Voting Time 'At Own Discretion,'" *Voice of the Islamic Republic of Iran*, June 12, 2009 (BBCM). "Iran Extends Voting Time for Another hour to 1730 gmt," *Vision of the Islamic Republic of Iran Network* 2, June 12, 2009 (BBCM). "Voting Extended by One Hour in Iran's Presidential Election," *IRNA* website in English, June 12, 2009 (BBCM).

10 BBC puts it at 70 percent of 50 million eligible.

11 Indeed, people were still waiting in lines at polling stations when the announcement was made.

12 Ali Ansari, Daniel Berman and Thomas Rintoul, "Preliminary Analysis of the Voting Figures in Iran's 2009 Presidential Election," (Chatham House: London, 2009), http://www.chathamhouse.org.uk/files/14234_iranelection0609.pdf [December 10, 2013]. The report compared the 2009 provincial tallies with those in the 2005 election and found Ahmadinejad's increase in votes in 2009 so sharp as to be implausible. Ansari, "Preliminary Analysis," 2009.

13 "Protests Erupt after Iran's Presidential Election," *Press TV* website, June 13, 2009 (BBCM).

14 Abbas Milani, "The Green Movement," *Iran Primer*, US Institute of Peace, (u.d.), http://iranprimer.usip.org/resource/green-movement [December 10, 2015].

15 Borozou Daragahi and Ramin Mostaghim, "Mousavi Forms New Political Front," *Los Angeles Times*, August 16, 2009, https://www.latimes.com/archives/la-xpm-2009-aug-16-fg-iran-mousavi16-story.html; For an overview, see: Abbas Milani, The Green

Movement, *Iran Primer*, October 6, 2010, https://iranprimer.usip.org/resource/green-movement [December 10, 2019].

16 Ibid.
17 "Khamenei Leads Tehran Friday Prayers," *Islamic Republic of Iran News Network*, June 19, 2009 (BBCM).
18 Among the unlikely victims was the son of conservative candidate Mohsen Rezaei's chief of staff, Abdolhossien Ruholamini. Ansari, *Crisis of Authority*, p. 69.
19 "Iran: Halt the Crackdown: End Violent Attacks on Protesters, Arrests of Critics," Human Rights Watch (June 19, 2009), https://www.hrw.org/news/2009/06/19/iran-halt-crackdown# [December 10, 2015].
20 For more on this subject, see: Masserat Amir-Ebrahimi, "Blogging from Qom: Behind Walls and Veils," *Comparative Studies of South Asia, Africa, and the Middle East* 28, no. 2 (2008).
21 Mohammad Hossein Adib, "The Third Wave and Digital Democracy," *Mardom Salari*, November 20, 2003 (BBCM).
22 "Iran begins trials of opposition activists after election protests," *The Guardian* (n.a.), August 1 2009. https://www.theguardian.com/world/2009/aug/01/iran-trials-election-protests [December 10, 2020].
23 Saeid Golkar, "Liberation or Suppression Technologies? The Internet, the Green Movement and the Regime in Iran," *International Journal of Emerging Technologies and Society* 9, no. 1 (2011), p. 55.
24 M. Hadi Sohrabi-Haghighat and Shohre Mansuri, "Where Is My Vote? ITC Politics in the Aftermath of Iran's Presidential Election," *International Journal of Emerging Technologies and Society* 8, no. 1 (2010), p. 28.
25 For a stream of consciousness record of the events surrounding the planned opposition protests 22 Bahman, see: "Live blogging the Iranian Protests," *The New Republic*, February 10–11, 2009, http://www.newrepublic.com/article/politics/live-blogging-the-iranian-protests [December 10, 2015]. Also see: Robert Worth, "Opposition in Iran meets a Crossroads on Strategy," *The New York Times*, February 14, 2010.
26 Iranians say how they'll mark anniversary of revolution," *BBC News*, February 9, 2009, http://news.bbc.co.uk/2/hi/middle_east/8504907.stm [October 27, 2015].
27 How much of a factor or how much restraint it actually imposed on officials in the treatment of citizens is a matter of debate, however.
28 "Zarghami's Untold Secrets About the Management of National Media During the Fitneh," *9 Dey* website, December 30, 2013, www.9day.ir [October 27, 2015].
29 Iranian TV downplays widely -publicized death of young woman in Tehran unrest, *Vision of the Islamic Republic of Iran Network 1*, June 26, 2009 (BBCM).
30 The HBO documentary "For Neda" vividly recounts the story through interviews and eyewitness footage. Antony Thomas (dir.), "For Neda," *HBO Documentary* (2010). Human Rights Watch, "The Islamic Republic at 31," February 11, 2010, www.hrw.org/sites/default/files/reports/iran0210web.pdf [October 27, 2015], pp. 3–4.
31 Human Rights Watch, "The Islamic Republic at 31," February 11, 2010, www.hrw.org/sites/default/files/reports/iran0210web.pdf [October 27, 2015], pp. 3–4.
32 Cameron Abadi, "Iran, Facebook and the Limits of Online Activism," *Foreign Policy* February 12, 2010, http://foreignpolicy.com/2010/02/12/iran-facebook-and-the-limits-of-online-activism [October 15, 2015].
33 See for example: "Iran Commander Vows to Deal Firmly with Protestors at 11 Feb Rally," *Iranian Students News Agency*, January 30, 2010 (BBCM).
34 On the latter: the information comes from the author's interviews with recipients of the text messages directing them to attend the pro-government demonstrations. In

one case, the author observed the text message on his/her cell phone. The names of the interviewees have withheld at their request, citing security concerns.

35 "Fifty Million People Took Part in 11 February Rallies," *Far News Agency*, February 11, 2010 (BBCM). See also: "East Azerbaijan Province Friday Prayer Sermons," *Vision of the Islamic Republic of Iran East Azerbaijan, Provincial TV Tabriz*, January 29, 2010 (BBCM).

36 "Fifty Million People Took Part in 11 February Rallies," *Far News Agency*, February 11, 2010 (BBCM). See also: "East Azerbaijan Province Friday Prayer Sermons," *Vision of the Islamic Republic of Iran East Azerbaijan, Provincial TV Tabriz*, January 29, 2010 (BBCM).

37 Post on website of *Gerdab* [IRGC Office for Investigating Organized and Cyber Crimes], June 22, 2009, www.Gerdab.ir [August 4, 2009]. Screen shot by the author.

38 Post on blog of *Gerdab-e Sabz* [Green Gerdab], August 4, 2009, http://gerdabsabz.blogspot.com [August 4, 2009]. Screen shot by the author.

39 Kamran Ashraf, "#iranelection: The Digital Media Response to the 2009 Iranian Election," remarks at Berkman Center for Internet & Society at Harvard University on November 24, 2009, https://cyber.law.harvard.edu/interactive/events/luncheons/2009/11/iranelection

40 "Statement Number Seven of Engineer Mir Hossein Mousavi about the Arrest of the Editorial Board of Kalame-ye Sabz and Restrictions Imposed on Non-governmental Media," *Kalameh* website, June 25, 2009.

41 See for example: "Iran TV Airs Footage of Demonstrations by Mousavi, Ahmadinejad Supporters," *Vision of the Islamic Republic of Iran Network 1*, June 17, 2009 (BBC Monitoring).

42 Mozhgan Modarres Olum, "Iran's Government Controlled Media Still in Denial" *Rah-e Sabz* online, December 29, 2009 (OSC with edits for clarity).

43 Ibid.

44 "Principalist" refers to Ahmadinejad's faction of conservative supporters of the Supreme Leader and advocates for protecting the ideological "principles" of the Islamic Revolution's early days. They are considered more hardline then traditional conservatives, with a distinct populist approach to politics.

45 "Electoral and Non-electoral Issues," *Aftab-e Yazd* online, June 13, 2009 (BBCM).

46 "Speaker, Head of Judiciary Congratulate Ahmadinejad,"Vision of the Islamic Republic of Iran Network 1, June 14, 2009 (BBC Monitoring).

47 Ibid. "220 Iranian MPs Congratulate Ahmadinejad on Re-election," *Mehr News Agency* (in English) June 14, 2009 (BBC Monitoring).

48 "Hamas: Iranian Elections Outcome Meets People's Aspirations for Safeguarding Its Interests and Confronting the Challenges," Palestinian Information Centre online, June 13, 2009 (BBC Monitoring); "Pakistani Premier Congratulates Iranian President on Poll Victory," *Associated Press of Pakistan*, June 14, 2009 (BBC Monitoring); "Chavez Congratulates Ahmadinejad on Victory in Iran Election," *Fars News Agency* website, June 13, 2009 (BBC Monitoring); "Tajik Leader Congratulates Iranian President on Re-election," *Tajik Television First Channel* on June 13, 2009 (BBC Monitoring); "Iraqi President Congratulates Ahmadinejad on Re-election," *IRNA* website, June 14, 2009 (BBC Monitoring).

49 The Guardian Council finished its investigation on June 30. "Watchdog Body Closes File on Iran Election," *Press TV* website, June 30, 2009 (BBC Monitoring).

50 Ali Ansari remarked on this publicity move in *Crisis of Authority*. See also: "President to Attend Regional Summit in Russia," *Islamic Republic of Iran News Network*, June 15, 2009 (BBC Monitoring).

51 Iran cleric says protesters linked to "BBC radio," *Vision of the Islamic Republic of Iran Esfahan Provincial TV*, Esfahan, June 16, 2009 (BBC Monitoring).
52 "All This for 'Dust'!" *Aftab-e Yazd* website, June 16, 2009 (BBC Monitoring).
53 "Pressures on Offices of Senior Clerics to Prevent Them from Sending Congratulation Messages" *Iran* website, June 15, 2009 (BBC Monitoring); Manal Lutfi, "Qom's religious leaders intervene and reports of 50 messages sent to the Guide about the crisis: Guardian Council members visited Qom to get Ayatollahs' support and Ayatollah Golpayegani urged them to be 'above politics,'" *Al-Sharq al-Awsat* online, June 24, 2009 (BBC Monitoring).
54 Ansari, *Crisis of Authority*, p. 75.
55 "Rezaei urges Authorities to Respect People, Take Complaints Seriously," *Islamic Republic of Iran News Network*, June 18, 2009 (BBC Monitoring). See also: "Candidate Questions Recount of Ballot Boxes, 'Lack of Cooperation,'" *Iranian Labour News Agency* website, June 25, 2009 (BBC Monitoring).
56 The statement accompanying the decision suggested his concerns remained. Aftab- e Yazd published an incisive editorial about the decision. See: "Higher than a Precipice" (unattributed) *Aftab-e Yazd online*, June 25, 2009 (BBC Monitoring).
57 In response to the letter by Khatami, Mousavi and Karroubi, Grand Ayatollah Sane'i wrote: "One Should Continue the Path of Achieving One's Rights without Violence and by Maintaining Security," *Ghalam News* online, July 28, 2009 (BBC Monitoring).
58 Specifically, Larijani criticized the Guardian Council for partiality and partisanship and suggested the protesters complaints had substance and should be respected. See:"Interview with Majles Speaker," *Vision of the Islamic Republic of Iran Network 2*, June 21, 2009 (BBC Monitoring).They included: Ayatollah Akbar Hashemi-Rafsanjani, the conservative cleric Ayatollah Mahdavi-Kani, the conservative cleric and former head of the Judiciary, Ayatollah Mohammad Yazdi, conservative cleric, Ayatollah Emami-Kashani, as well as Reformist leaders such as former President Sayyed Mohammad Khatami, former speaker and senior advisor to the Supreme Leader, Ali Akbar Nategh-Nuri, and 2009 presidential candidates Karroubi, Mousavi and Rezaei. See: "Report on Absentees at President's Inauguration," *Mehr News Agency*, August 5, 2009 (BBC Monitoring). It should be noted that the absence of Reformist leaning politicians such as Rafsanjani was predictable; it nevertheless rankled the ruling elite. Ansari, *Crisis of Authority*, p. 90.
59 Ansari, "Crisis of Authority," p.77.
60 Ibid., p. 54.
61 The Supreme Leader was among those who pointed to the high participation rate as proof of "Iran's religious democracy." "Western Intelligence Services, Zionists behind Post-Election Disturbances," *IRIN*, June 19, 2009 (BBCM).
62 Ansari, *Crisis of Authority*, p. 55.
63 Ibid., p. 71.
64 The Guardian Council extended the time it usually allocated to evaluate the complaints, thereby extending the period of uncertainly and opposition restraint in anticipation of judgment. "Morteza Nabavi: The Referendum Issue Is Mentioned to Continue the Unrest," (unattributed) *Resalat*, July 27, 2009 (BBCM).
65 See for example: "Iran Guardian Council urges candidates' fans to wait for 'final results,'" *Vision of the Islamic Republic of Iran Network 2*, June 15, 2009; "Weekly Political Analysis," *Jomhuri-ye Eslami* website, June 25, 2009; "Morteza Nabavi," *Resalat*, July 27, 2009 (BBCM).

66 "Zarghami's Untold Secrets about the Management of National Media during the Fitneh."
67 "President's Advisor: We Have Been Laying the Foundations of Democracy for Four Years Now," *Aftab-e Yazd*, March 15, 2010 (BBCM).
68 See for example: "Change Del Iranian Uprising 2009," YouTube video posted by *Gunagun*, November 15, 2009, https://www.youtube.com/watch?v=s_b-bTidhIk [November 13, 2015].
69 My translation of the text. See the image for the original Persian.
70 Mona Kasra (2015). "The Digital-Networked Image: Temporality and Post-National Sociopolitical Expression." University of Texas at Dallas.
71 Mona Kasra, Digital-Networked Images as Personal Acts of Political Expression: New Categories for Meaning Formation, Media and Communication 5(4):51 2017.
72 Special thanks to the Internet Governance Lab and Laura Denardis of American University, Camilla Fojas of University of Virginia, and the experts at ART19 and the Center for Human Rights in Iran for their feedback on this research.
73 Mark Hachman, "Syria and 7 Other Places the Internet Has Been Shut Off," *PC Magazine*, May 8, 2013, http://www.pcmag.com/slideshow/story/311237/syria-and-7-other-places-the-Internet-has-been-shut-off [Accessed October 27, 2015]. See also: Mathew Prince, "How Syria Turned off the Internet," Cloudflare Blog, November 29, 2012, https://blog.cloudflare.com/how-syria-turned-off-the-Internet [Accessed October 27, 2015].
74 Ansari, *Crisis of Authority*, pp. 34–5.
75 *Sadegh Mahsuli: sor'at-e Ahmadinejad manand-e yek jet-e fantom ast* (Sadegh Mahsuli praised Ahmadinejad as having the speed and power of a fighter jet), *Advar News*, August 21, 2007. See also: "The Detailed Report of the Committee in Charge of Protecting the votes of Mir Hossein Mousavi," *Ghalam News*, July 5, 2009 (BBC Monitoring).
76 Ansari, *Crisis of Authority*, p. 23.
77 Sadegh Dehghan, "TCI Privatization elaborated," *Iran Daily*, October 7, 2009, 5; "The General Policies Pertaining to Principle 44 of the Constitution of the Islamic Republic of Iran," Proclamation of Supreme Leader Sayyed Ali Khamenei, Khordad 1384/June 2005 via Iran Data Portal, Princeton University website, available at www.princeton.edu/irandataportal/laws/labor-civilsociety/principle-44-policies/ accessed [October 6, 2015]. While the IRGC repeatedly demonstrated its support for Ahmadinejad's Principalist faction during and after the election, it remains controlled by and answerable to the Supreme Leader. Thus both men benefited from the transaction.

Chapter 8

1 See, for example: "Bayanat Dar Jam'-e Kasiri az Basijiyan-e Keshvar" [Speech to a Large Crowd of the Nation's Basij], Center for Preserving and Publishing the Works of Grand Ayatollah Sayyed Ali Khamenei, November 25, 2009. The concepts of "third wave" democracy and "liberation technology," are addressed in previous chapters.
2 For more on this argument, see: Ali Ansari, *Crisis of Authority: Iran's 2009 Presidential Election* (Chatham House: London, 2010).
3 Ibid.
4 "Over 100 Iranians Face Grossly Unfair Trials," Amnesty International, August 4, 2009, https://www.amnesty.org/en/latest/news/2009/08/over-100-iranians-face-grossly-unfair-trials-20090804/ [December 10, 2019]. Indeed, over the next year, state

media televised numerous trials featuring prominent reformist figures, activists, and journalists making (obviously coerced) confessions about their role in the foreign conspiracy to depose the regime.
5   Ansari, *Crisis of Authority*, 2010.
6   Khamenei speech, *Voice of the Islamic Republic*, February 18, 2010 (BBCM).
7   For example, see: Mehdi Faza'eli, "The Iranian Nation has Answered the Questions," *Jam-e Jam*, February 14, 2010 (BBCM). "Sedition-mongers Received a Hard-Hitting Slap from People on 22 *Bahman*," *Iran*, February 18, 2010 (BBCM).
8   Morteza Ghamari-Vafa, "A Beginning and an End," *Iran*, February 14, 2010 (BBCM).
9   Mehdi Mohammadi, "When America Becomes Angry," *Kayhan*, February 18, 2010 (BBCM).
10 Ibid.
11 The website of the Supreme Leader hosts a six-part collection of essays on various aspects of "soft war." Morteza Amiri, "Jang-e Narm va Teheed Shenasi" (Soft War and Threat Recognition), October 18, 2009, http://farsi.Khamenei.ir/print-content?id=8239 [November 12, 2015].
12 Amiri applies a "levels of analysis" framework used in military science to present a strategic and operational theory of "soft war."
13 "*Mo'aven-e Parlemani-ye Ra'is-e Jomhur: Emruz Owlaviyyat-e Keshvar Moghabeleh ba Jang-e Narm-e Doshman ast*" [President's Representative to Parliament: Today, the Country's Top priority is to Fight against the Enemy's Soft War], *Rasa News*, October 12, 2010, http://www.rasanews.ir/TextVersion/Detail/?Id=87473&Serv=36 [December 10, 2013].
14 "*Tashkil-e Gharargah-e Jang-e Narm Dar Setad-e Koll-e Niruha-ye Mosallah*" [The Formation of a Soft War Headquarters in the Islamic Republic of Iran Armed Forces General Headquarters], *Fars News Agency*, December 1, 2012.
15 "Iranian Cyber Army Defaces Voice of America and 93 other Domains," *The Tech Herald* online, www.thetechherald.com/article.php/201108/6849 [July 3, 2013]. Christopher Williams, "Iranian Hacker Claims Revenge for Stuxnet," *Telegraph*, March 28, 2011, www.telegraph.co.uk/technology/news/8411252/Iranian-hacker-claims-revenge-for-Stuxnet.html [November 12, 2015].
16 "*FATA, Vahed-e Jadide Polic-e Iran Baray-e kontrol-e Faza-ye Internet*" [FATA, a New Iranian Police Unit for Controlling the Internet], *BBC Persian*, January 23, 2011, www.bbc.co.uk/persian/iran/2011/01/110123_l39_cyberpolice_iran_ahmadimoghadam.shtml [July 3, 2013].
17 "Internet Security Provision Rests with Intelligence Agency," *E'temad*, November 15, 2009 (BBCM).
18 "Plan for 10,000 Basij bloggers," *Sobh-e Sadegh* blog, (u.d.), www.sobhesadegh.ir/1387/0386/M08.HTM [July 3, 2013].
19 "Iran Security Virtual Presence," OSC Media Report (2011), p. 68.
20 Another example is the blog, *Afsaran-e Jang-e Narm*,, which includes posts such as "List of 60 years of criminal American (evil devil) acts against the great nation of Iran," which appears to be identical to a post on the Khamenei.ir Facebook page. See: "*Afsaran-e Jang-e Narm*" [Soldiers of Soft War], http://www.afsaranjnarm.ir/1394/06/18/1818 [September 18, 2015].
21 Julian Assange, "Serious Nuclear Accident May Lay behind Iranian Nuke Chief's Mystery Resignation," *Wikileaks*, July 17, 2009, https://wikileaks.org/wiki/Serious_nuclear_accident_may_lay_behind_Iranian_nuke_chief%27s_mystery_resignation [November 12, 2015].

22 A worm is a type of malware (malicious software) that is secretly planted on a computer. The name "Stuxnet" is an anagram of letters found in parts of its code.
23 Farwell, J. and, & Rohozinski, R. Rohozinski. "(2011). Stuxnet and the Future of Cyber War." Survival: Global Politics and Strategy, 53\(no. 1 (2011), 23–40.
24 Interview with Peter W. Singer, July 1 2018.
25 Although the virus also infected computers at Bushehr, the primary target, as of this writing, is believed to have been Natanz, which was suspected of housing a covert nuclear weapons program. Stuxnet's success in stymying Iran's nuclear progress remains a matter of dispute. While Iran hosted the largest concentration of systems infected, at 40 percent, the worm was found dormant in operating systems throughout Europe and Asia.
26 Michael Joseph Gross, "A Declaration of Cyber-War," *Vanity Fair*, March 2011, http://www.vanityfair.com/news/2011/03/stuxnet-201104 [November 12, 2015].
27 Ibid.
28 In a question and answer session with reporters, for example, Foreign Ministry spokesman Ramin Mehmanparast deemed the reports of the Stuxnet virus "propaganda" and a "new game of soft warfare." "Foreign Ministry Spokesman Comments on Stuxnet," *Islamic Republic of Iran News Network*, September 28, 2010 (BBCM). "Nine Types of Spyware in the Country's Industrial Systems," *Iran*, September 8, 2010 (BBCM).
29 Putting aside the violation of trust between the US government and the manufactures of operating systems and equipment.
30 "Iran Unveils 12 Cyber Products," *Fars News Agency*, December 14, 2013 (BBCM).
31 Interviews with two retired members of the national security establishment in 2012. Their names have been withheld as a condition to speaking with me.
32 For an interesting empirical analysis of cyber power among nations, see Aaron Franklin Brantley et al., The Decision to Attack: Military and Intelligence Cyber Decision-making, (University of Georgia, 2016).
33 Amir Bagherpour and Roya Soleimania, "Oppression 2.0: Iranian Discontent in Cyberspace," PBS Frontline, Tehran Bureau, July 22, 2011, http://www.pbs.org/wgbh/pages/frontline/tehranbureau/2011/07/oppression-20-iranian-discontent-in-cyberspace.html [October 24, 2012]. "Moje Sabz Website Has Been Hacked," [in Persian] Khabar Online, December 16, 2009, http://www.khabaronline.ir/news-30712.aspx [March 20, 2012]. Robert Mackey, "Twitter Attacked by 'Iranian Cyber Army,'" *New York Times*, December 18, 2009, http://thelede.blogs.nytimes.com/2009/12/18/twitter-hacked-by-iranian-cyber-army/ [July 1, 2018].
34 Authors deductions from data taken form ZoneH on July 1, 2017.
35 Claudio Guarnieri and Collin Anderson, "Iran and the Soft War for Internet Dominance," *Black Hat USA*, August 2016. Available at: https://iranthreats.github.io/us-16-Guarnieri-Anderson-Iran-And-The-Soft-War-For-InternetDominance-paper.pdf accessed [March 1, 2016].
36 Zone-h.org, "Ashiyane Digital Security Team," https://www.zone-h.org/archive/notifier=Ashiyane%20Digital%20Security%20Team?hz=1 [July 10, 2017]. By November 29, 2021, the total had grown to 60,364. [October 24, 2022].
37 Guarnieri and Anderson, "Iran and the Soft War," 2016.
38 Ibid.
39 Scott Peterson, "Twitter Hacked: 'Iranian Cyber Army Signs off with Poem to Khamenei," "*The Christian Science Monitor*, December 18, 2009, http://www.csmonitor.com/World/Middle-East/2009/1218/Twitter-hacked-Iranian-Cyber-Army-signs-off-with-poem-to-Khamenei [July 1, 2018].

Chapter 9

1. "Meeting with Teachers and Students," Website of the Supreme Leader Khamenei, May 2, 2016, http://farsi.khamenei.ir/news-content?id=32954 [January 31 2016].
2. Khatami's Friday Prayer speech. (January 5, 2018) Mehr News. https://tinyurl.com/y7xb8cvz
3. *I am indebted to the cyber-experts at the Center for Human Rights in Iran and Small Media for contributing their data and expertise to this chapter.*
4. Christopher Rhoads, Farnaz Fasshi and Andres Gonalez, "Iran Vows to Unplug Internet," *The Wall Street Journal*, May 28, 2011; Behrang Tajdin, "Will Iran's National Internet Mean no World Wide Web?" BBC Persian, April 27, 2013, www.bbc.com/news/world-middle-east-22281336 [November 12, 2015].
5. A Top-Level Domain (TLD) registry is an online database, that which contains information about the domain names associated with a specific TLD. There are 244 country-specific TLD registries (.uk for United Kingdom, .fr for France, and so on). The TLD for the Islamic Republic of Iran ois".ir." I found records that show that the TLD was registered on April 6, 1994 under Shahshahani and the Institute for Research in Fundamental Sciences. Cyrus Farivar, *The Internet of Elsewhere: The Emergent Effects of a Wired World*, New Jersey: Rutgers University Press, 2011.
6. Nazanin Kamdar, [in Persian] "42,000 Computers Will Be Isolated from the World: National Internet to Go Live Next Week," *Rooz Online*, September 13, 2012, www.roozonline.com/persian/news/newsitem/article/42000-computers-will-be-isolated-from-the-world.html [November 12, 2015].
7. For example, see: "Launching the Halal Internet in Iran," *Tabnak*, April 15, 2012 (BBCM).
8. "What Is the National Information Network," original website of the Ministry of Information Communications Technology, 2013. Accessed in Persian via the Internet Archive for March 28, 2013 which is the earliest recording of the webpage with that name, content, and url, See: https://web.archive.org/web/20130328092811/http://www.itc.ir/Default.aspx?tabid=420 [January 31, 2016].
9. Ibid.
10. Unfortunately, investment plummeted with the Trump administration's withdrawal from the agreement in 2018.
11. TechRasa is a business focused think tank. It decreased activities notably over the years, but still appears to be functioning as of 2021. It describes its work as thus: "TechRasa's task is to expose the activities of Iran's startup ecosystem with the vision of empowering and inspiring Iranian entrepreneurs. TechRasa also aims to give startups the international exposure they need and to help promote Iranian entrepreneurs to become global stakeholders. In addition to these activities, TechRasa also provides consultancy services and market research reports to companies that want to enter Iran." https://techrasa.com; The Financial Tribune is a online newspaper that (accurately) describes itself as "the first Iranian English economic daily." https://financialtribune.com/ Both outlets report from inside Iran from an Iranian viewpoint.
12. Hannah Murphy, "Iran Is Back in Business," *Financial Times*, January 29, 2016. https://www.ft.com/content/325fdf4a-bec6-11e5-846f-79b0e3d20eaf [July 3, 2018].
13. Islamic Republic of Iran, Ministry of Information Communication Technology (online) www.stats.tic.ir [July 1, 2018].
14. Measurement Lab, https://viz.measurementlab.net [July 1, 2018].

15 S. Hamed Jafari and Mohammad Reza Azali, "Ad Tech Overview 2018," *Tech Rasa*, http://techrasa.com/wp-content/uploads/2018/07/Iran-AdTech-Overview-2018.pdf [July 1, 2018].
16 Kyle Bowen and James Marchant, "Internet Censorship in Iran: Preventative, Interceptive, and Reactive," in *Revolution Decoded, Small Media*, (n.d.) pp. 19–20.
17 Ibid.
18 S. Hamed Jafari and Mohammad Reza Azali, "Ad Tech Overview 2018," *TechRasa*, http://techrasa.com/wp-content/uploads/2018/07/Iran-AdTech-Overview-2018.pdf [July 1, 2018].
19 "Iran Minister says Nuclear Deal Eased Access to Modern Technology," IRNA, July 14, 2016.
20 Article 19, "Tightening the Net Part 2: The Soft War and Cyber Tactics in Iran" (2017), p. 28–9.
21 Bowen and Marchant, "Internet Censorship in Iran," pp. 19–20.
22 Authors notes and screen shots.
23 Bozorgmehr Sharafedin, "Hundreds Protest Against High Prices in Iran," Reuters, December 28, 2017. https://www.reuters.com/article/us-iran-economy-protests/hundreds-protest-against-high-prices-in-iran-idUSKBN1EM19P.
24 Mohammad Norouzian, Governor of Mashhad, told state media the protests were organized via social media by "counter-revolutionary elements." http://www.bbc.com/news/world-middle-east-42506666.
25 Farhad Khosrokhavar "Iran: Revolt of the Deprived," *Open Democracy*, January 10, 2018, https://www.opendemocracy.net/author/farhad-khosrokhavar [July 10, 2018]; See also: Kaveh Ehsani and Arang Keshavarzian, "The Moral Economy of the Iranian Protests," *Jacobian Magazine*, January 2018, https://www.jacobinmag.com/2018/01/iranian-protests-revolution-rouhani-ahmadinejad [July 10, 2018].
26 *Author's notes and observations*, December 28, 29, 30, 2017. For example, see Potkin Azarmehr's Twitter post on December 29, 2017, pic.twitter. com/lzROiYyRss [July 10, 2018].
27 "Iran Protests Continue for a Third Day Despite Warnings," *BBC News*, December 30, 2017, http://www.bbc.com/news/world-middle-east-42521298 [July 10, 2018].
28 "At Least Two Protesters Shot in Western Iran, Social Media," *Reuters*, https://www.reuters.com/article/us-iran-rallies-shooting/at-least-two-protesters-shot-in-western-iran-social-media-idUSKBN1EO0JN [July 10, 2018].
29 For background on 9 Dey, see the previous chapters.
30 Speech, *Voice of the Islamic Republic of Iran*, January 9, 2010 (BBCM).
31 Ibid.
32 One woman (unnamed due to security concerns) showed me a number of text messages she had received from her employer instructing her to attend the government rally. This is not an uncommon practice. Personal communication with the author, January 10, 2018. See also: *Dideh Ban-e Iran*, u.d. https://tinyurl.com/ybkxne96; Rohollah Faghihi "Iranian Hard-liners Smell Blood as Rouhani Under Fire Over Economy" *Al Monitor*, (June 18, 2018), http://www.al-monitor.com/pulse/originals/2018/06/iran-rouhani-hardliners-impeachment-resignation-pressure.html#ixzz5NchZJtLH
33 He continued: "The US president immediately began to post several tweets in support of the unrest in Iran, and was soon followed by UK, the Zionist regime, and come European countries. This trend was calculated and pre-planned." See: U.a. "Attorney Gen. names Michael D'Andrea as mastermind of Iran's unrest," *Mehr News*, January

34 4, 2018. https://en.mehrnews.com/news/130920/Attorney-Gen-names-Micheal-D-Andrea-as-mastermind-of-Iran-s [July 10, 2018].
34 "Riots in Iran Were Engineered in Erbil: Rezaee," *Tehran Times*, January 6, 2018, http://www.tehrantimes.com/news/420080/Riots-in-Iran-were-engineered-in-Erbil-Rezaee. Later, in a speech to Majles leaders, President Rouhani denounced the United States, Israel, and Saudi Arabia for their role in fomenting the unrest.
35 Mohammad Mazhari, "Targeting Iran's Security, New Phase in Soft War," *Mehr News*, January 26, 2018. *Mehr News* https://en.mehrnews.com/news/131631/Targeting-Iran-s-security-new-phase-in-soft-war [May 5, 2018].
36 ONI research found that the blocking of Instagram during the protests was done via Deep Packet Inspection (DPI) https://ooni.torproject.org/post/2018-iran-protests-pt2/
37 Jahromi spent his career in the Ministry of Intelligence, where he was personally involved in building surveillance infrastructure. He took part in interrogations and abuse of individuals involved in the 2009 Green Movement protests.
38 Author's screen shot of tweet by MJ Azari Jahromi (@azarijahromi) on December 30, 2017. See also: Theodore Schleifer, "Telegram is Shutting Down a Channel that Called for Violent Protests Against Iran's Government," *Recode.*, December 30, 2017, www.recode.net/2017/12/30/16833542/telegram-iran-demostrations-messaging-protests-pavel-durov [July 10, 2018].
39 The author observed one particularly popular video of a man sitting in his car waving a gun and calling for blood.
40 For an excellent research report, see: "Guards at the Gate: The Expanding State Control over the Internet in Iran," Center for Human Rights in Iran (CHRI), January, 2018, https://iranhumanrights.org/wp-content/uploads/EN-Guards-at-the-gate-High-quality.pdf; See also: Bowen and Marchant, "Internet Censorship in Iran, Small Media, 2018. p. 19–21. [March 31, 2018].
41 The channel did include content worthy of the claim of incitement or at least violence.
42 TechRasa, "Telegram Usage Statistics," September 6, 2017. https://techrasa.com/2017/09/06/infographic-telegram-usage-statistics-in-iran/ [September 26, 2017].
43 Bowen and Marchant, "Internet Censorship in Iran, Small Media," 2018. p. 19–20. For an excellent research report, see: "Guards at the Gate: The Expanding State Control Over the Internet in Iran," Center for Human Rights in Iran (CHRI), January 2018, https://iranhumanrights.org/wp-content/uploads/EN-Guards-at-the-gate-High-quality.pdf [March 31, 2018].
44 The author tracked downloads of Sorush on Cafe Bazaar between October 2017 and February 2018, https://cafebazaar.ir/app/mobi.mmdt.ottplus?l=en
45 Some merchants launched an effort on Twitter to pressure the government to remove the block, citing damage to their business. Jahromi acknowledged the financial hardships associated with the blocking of Telegram soon after it was imposed. "I apologize to those businesses and for those who have been financially affected," Jahromi said on January 2. "When peace returns, those [restrictions] will be lifted." Melissa Etehad, "Iran Tried to Block the Internet to Disrupt Protests. It Wound Up Disrupting Daily Life," *The Los Angeles Times*, January 9, 2018. [December 10, 2019]; Maysam Bizaer, Al-Monitor, "Internet Censorship a Double-Edged Sword for Tehran," *Al-Monitor*, January 12, 2018, https://www.al-monitor.com/originals/2018/01/iran-protests-internet-filtering-online-business-telegram.html?amp [December 10, 2019].

46 "Letter of 170 MPs in Iran's Parliament Calling for a Ban on Foreign Social Media." IRNA. https://tinyurl.com/yc94w6k4; See also: "Majority of Iranian MPs Call For Ban on Foreign Social Media Apps," Center for Human Rights in Iran (January 18, 2018) https://tinyurl.com/y8fu9dsg

47 Small Media, "Khamenei's Dropping of Telegram Channel Lays Groundwork for Banning Messaging App in Iran," *Payvand*, April 18, 2018. http://www.payvand.com/news/18/apr/1083.html [May 5, 2018]. "Guards at the Gate: The Expanding State Control Over the Internet in Iran," Center for Human Rights in Iran (CHRI), January, 2018, https://iranhumanrights.org/wp-content/uploads/EN-Guards-at-the-gate-High-quality.pdf [March 31, 2018].

48 Asa Fitch and Aresu Eqbali, "Iran Clamps Down on Telegram App, Blaming It for Unrest," *The Wall Street Journal*, April 30, 2018, https://www.wsj.com/articles/iran-clamps-down-ontelegram-app-blaming-it-for-unrest-1525111301 [May 5, 2018].

49 Mizan News Twitter post. See also: "Iran's Judiciary Banned the Popular Telegram Messaging App," *Radio Zamaneh*, April 30, 2018, https://en.radiozamaneh.com/articles/irans-judiciary-banned-the-popular-telegrammessaging-app/ [May 5, 2018].

50 It should be noted that Iran blocked the use of the currency on Telegram prior to the protests.

51 Viber was a popular messaging app in Iran that also provided a cheap Voice over IP (VoIP) service for international calls. The CEO's "Zionist" affiliation was used to justify blocking the app.

52 "Iran's New Initiative Promotes Indigenous Messengers," *Financial Tribune*, November 18, 2017, https://financialtribune.com/articles/economy-sci-tech/76315/irans-new-initiative-promotes-indigenous-messengers

53 At the same time, the mass exodus from Telegram can be seen as a blow to Iranian foreign influence and public diplomacy. However, with the majority of Telegram users in non-Western locations (mostly Russia), the *nezam* may have judged this a necessary exchange.

54 Up to that point.

55 Netblocks, "Internet Disrupted in Iran Amid Fuel Protests in Multiple Cities," *Netblocks*, November 16, 2019. https://netblocks.org/reports/internet-disrupted-in-iran-amid-fuel-protests-in-multiple-cities-pA25L18b [November 23, 2020]."The ongoing disruption is the most severe recorded in Iran since President Rouhani came to power, and the most severe disconnection tracked by Netblocks in any country in terms of its technical complexity and breadth."

56 "Iran: Internet Deliberately Shut Down during November 2019 Killings, New Investigation," Amnesty International (November 16, 2020). https://www.amnesty.org/en/latest/news/2020/11/iran-internet-deliberately-shut-down-during-november-2019-killings-new-investigation/[November 24, 2020].

57 "Iran: Tightening the Net 2020: After Blood and Shutdowns," Article 19 (September 2020). https://www.article19.org/wp-content/uploads/2020/09/TTN-report-2020.pdf

58 Khamenei, "Speech to Iranian Students," August 26, 2009.

Conclusion

1. Abolqasem Ferdowsi and James Atkinson (trans.), *The Shahnameh*, (Durham: Duke Classics, 2012).
2. Peter N. Stearns, "Why Study History?" American Historical Association (1998). https://www.historians.org/about-aha-and-membership/aha-history-and-archives/historical-archives/why-study-history-(1998) [December 10 2019].
3. Benedict Anderson, *Imagined Communities*. (London: Verso Books, 1983), p. 5.
4. Gazelle Emami, "Asghar Farhadi, Golden Globe Winner For 'A Separation,' Talks Getting Past The Censors In Iran," *The Huffington Post*, (January 17, 2012). https://www.huffingtonpost.com/2012/01/17/asghar-farhadi-a-separation-iran-golden-globes_n_1209976.html [December 10, 2020].
5. Chris Berry, et al., *Electronic Elsewheres: Media, Technology, and the Experience of Social Space* (University of Minnesota Press, 2010).
6. Narges Bajoghli, Iran Reframed: Anxieties of Power in the Islamic Republic, (Stanford: Stanford University Press), 2019. pp. 72–3.

BIBLIOGRAPHY

(I) Archival Sources

US National Archives, College Park, Maryland

RG 59, DoS Decimal File, 1940–44, BOX 5818 891.00
42.05.22: Telegram reporting that the UK Foreign Office is prepared to urge Iranian government to submit a formal request to the US government for a US military mission
42.05.22: Letter from Undersecretary of State proposing US military mission to Iran (two pages)
42.04.25: Questionnaire from Office of Coordinator of Information to American Legion in Iran on Iranian media environment (six pages)
42.5.26: State Department memo relating to Iranian request for US military support
42.5.27: Memo from Secretary of War to Secretary of State on establishing a US military mission
42.5.29: Department of State memo expressing support for the establishment of a US military mission to Iran
42.11.04: Memo from US mission head, Dreyfus, suggesting that the British are forestalling a solution to the food crisis
42.11.07: Telegram from US Embassy in London concerning British charges of a German conspiracy to occupy Iran (three pages)
42.11.10: Telegram from Foreign Minister Eden concerning allegations of a German plot in Iran. (two pages)
42.11.01: US Embassy memo describing bread riots and currency crises in Tehran.

RG 165, Records of the War Department and Special Staff, Military Intelligence Division, Regional File, 1922–44, Iran 2910
22.07.12: Military attaché report entitled "Journalism in Persia"
42.02.03: Urgent memo from Dreyfus to Secretary of State on US propaganda in Iran
42.06.11: "Soviet Propaganda in Iran" (three pages)
42.12.09: War office Weekly Intelligence Summary No. 174, December 9, 1942, to December 16, 1942, on Allied food declaration
43.03.18: British War Office Weekly Intelligence Report Summary Number 187
43.03.27: Reports on a press item published on March 19
43.04.02: Press is vilifying British, inflaming fears, Persian Gulf Service Command, Weekly Intelligence Bulletin No. 6
43.04.03: Anti-Allied campaign in newspapers (two pages)
43.04.05: Enemy and Arabic broadcasts
43.05.02: USAFIME (Cairo) Periodic Reports May 1 to May 8, 1945
43.05.03: Press behavior, CICI Tribal and Intelligence Weekly Intelligence Report.
43.06.20: Office of Strategic Services notice that the Iranian Department of Press and Propaganda is to be reorganized
43.07.16: Hejavi appointed head of Iranian Department of Press and Propaganda

43.07.16: Department of Press and Propaganda to reduce budget
43.07.22: "Misconduct of American Troops in Iran Has Attracted the Notice of the Tehran Press" (two pages)
43.08.04: Office of Strategic Service press summary for the weeks of August 1 to August 15, 1943
43.10.07: "Enemy and Allied Propaganda in Iran: Enemy and Allied propaganda efforts in Iran, including our own; Methods, means and degree of success achieved," R&A No.1297 (twenty-six pages)
44.03.07: "Miscellaneous Developments in Iran since February 24th," State Department Dispatch No. 872.

RG 262, Entry 3, Transcripts of Monitored Foreign Broadcasts, 1940–6 IRAN
46.08.28: Transcription of Radio Tehran Persian domestic broadcast on August 28, 1946
46.09.30: Tehran Radio broadcast in Russian

RG 469, Records of US Foreign Assistance, Mission to Iran, Classified Subject Files 1951–50, Executive Offices, 1948–61
53.11.02: Details "Point Four" information program
51.12.04: Memo to John Evan from William Warnes about sharing of equipment and facilities in Iran with USIE
52.09.20: US technical cooperation for Iran General Order No. 31
53.00.00: Farsi document about "candidates"
53.01.13: Shiraz audiovisual operations report (three pages)
53.05.01: Point Four information guide, TCA (twelve pages)
53.06.02: Memo on audio visual equipment (six pages)
53.06.03: Memo by Warnes on the transfer of the Technical Cooperation Administration to the Department of Mutual Security (two pages)
53.06.12: On Technical Corporation Administration (two pages)
53.06.19: On Syracuse film contract (two pages)
53.09.19: Telegram relating to need for support staff for US information activities inside Iran (two pages)
53.10.22: On training grant and anti-Americanism
53.11.01: USIS report for November 1 to November 15, 1953 (seven pages)
53.11.02: US Ambassador to Iran comments on memo by Wells entitled "A Point Four Information Program"
53.11.02: Wells memo on USIS "A Point Four Information Program" (five pages)
53.11.02: Attachment with statistics for one-month period on "Point Four" information campaign. Indicates that newspapers were primary target (three pages)
53.11.15: USIS report for the weeks of November 15 to November 26. Details US regional information operations (four pages)
53.11.18: Foreign Service Circular No. 49 entitled "Substantive Relationships with USIA" (six pages plus transmission slip)
53.6.02: Film shipping list (five pages)
58.07.19: Minutes from Country Team meeting (two pages)
59.04.16: Budget justification for Iranian Ministry of War, FY1960 (two pages)
59.05.14: Report on ARMISH MAAG (six pages)
59.05.21: Telegram notes proposal for USAFE "skyblazers" acrobatic show

RG059 1951–8 General Records of Department of State, Mic Lot file Subject Files Relating to Iran, 1952–8 Lot File No. 60 D 533 (2 of 3) Box 10

58.10.10: Memo of conversation with Iranian ambassador (two pages)
58.07.03: Background paper drafted by Country Team for Shah of Iran visit
58.08.14: Memo of conversation with Israeli embassy
58.09.29: Ali Asqar Hekmat appointed Foreign Minister. (two pages)
58.09.29: Ali Asqar Hekmat biography
58.08.05: Memo of conversation on Middle East situation, American University in Shiraz (two pages)
58.07.27: Memo of conversation on Iranian membership to Baghdad Pact (three pages)
58.09.22: Doriel is Israel's unofficial ambassador in Tehran. (three pages)
58.01.25: Letter to Secretary Dulles sent through Iranian source in Shiraz (three pages)
58.10.15: ARMISH/GENMISH agreement to expire (two pages)
58.12.05: Regarding expiration of ARMISH/GENMISH agreement on March 20, 1958 (two pages)
57.03.23: US expenditure on communication projects
57.03.23: Background papers packet for Richard Mission
58.12.03: Minutes of "special" Country Team meeting
58.12.06: Minutes of Country Team meeting (two pages)
58.11.06: Minutes of Country Team meeting (three pages)
58.05.20: Minutes of Country Team meeting (three pages)
58.06.05: Minutes of Country Team meeting
58.10.21: Minutes of Country Team meeting
58.09.17: Minutes of Country Team meeting (three pages)
58.08.27: Minutes of Country Team meeting (three pages)
58.08.20: Minutes of Country Team meeting (five pages)
58.08.02: Minutes of Country Team meeting (three pages)
58.12.03: Minutes of Country Team meeting (two pages)
58.12.17: Minutes of Country Team meeting (two pages)

RG59 Bureau of Near Eastern and South Asian Affairs, Office of Iranian Affairs, Records Relating to Iran, 1963–75, Box 9–11

57.05.22: Defense Department letter to Department of State regarding "over-the-counter sale" of spare military parts (two pages)
57.10.12: Letter on US military aid to Iran
57.11.07: Regarding the revision of ARMISH MAAG agreement (two pages)
57.03.04: Memorandum on Military Construction budget (two pages)
57.06.28: Letter from General Motors Corporation on sale of diesel generators to Iran (two pages)
57.09.12: On military construction budget, FY1959
58.10.31: Draft memorandum on the renewal of military mission in Iran (three pages)
58.11.24: Memorandum on ARMISH renegotiations. Reference to GENMISH agreement of 1943, ARMISH agreement of 1947 (two pages)
69.10.16: Memorandum on Integrated National Telecommunication System negotiations
69.12.17: US Export Import Bank letter on Integrated National Telecommunication System project in Iran (two pages)
69.12.23: Letter to US Import Export Bank regarding financing of integrated electricity and telecommunication project commissioned by government of Iran (two pages)
73.01.27: Miklos letter on newspaper commentary by Amir Taheri (three pages)
73.02.03: Telegram from US consulate in Tebriz regarding the White Revolution (five pages)

73.12.6: Letter referencing Iran relations with Oman and Saudi Arabia, UK naval sales to Iran (two pages)
73.02.7: Memo on the Tenth Anniversary of the White Revolution (two pages)
73.3.30: Policy Planning Paper on Nixon Doctrine in the Middle East. Memo by Jack C Miklos NEA/IRN to NEA Mr Davies (two pages)
73.06.08: Record of trip by Government Accountability Office representatives Mr. Watson, Mr. Brady and Mr. Betts to Tehran on May 30 to June 6, 1973 to explore "US Persian Gulf Policy and Persian Gulf Realities" (three pages)
73.07.12: Comments on draft paper on Iran's foreign policy
73.07.09: Inquiring about Iranian "pro-Arab" stance

US Central Intelligence Agency Freedom of Information Act Archive
"Execution of Shah's officials," National Intelligence Daily Report, (May 8, 1979).

US National Security Archive, George Washington University
"NIRT organization in intense disarray; radio broadcasting stopped, restarted," Confidential Cable, January 17, 1979.
"Dispatch on Iranian labor unrest," Confidential Cable Tehran, December 5, 1978.
"Interview with Mahnaz Afkhami," Confidential Cable, June 6, 1976.
"NIRT organization in intense disarray; radio broadcasting stopped, restarted," Confidential Cable Tehran, January 17, 1979.
"Political/Security Report November 30," Confidential Cable Tehran 11754, November 30, 1978.

UK National Archive, Kew, United Kingdom
PZ 3506/40 "Inauguration of Tehran broadcasting station" IOR/L/PS/12/397 22 Jun 1940–2 Jun 1940.
FO 371 133007, EP 1015/62 "Internal political situation in Iran," December 9, 1958.
"65th Anniversary of the Persian Service." with Shahriar Radpour. BBC Persian Service, (2006).
"Hostilities with Russia: Attitude of Iran," Report by L. Baggallay on behalf of the Joint Chiefs of Staff Committee to the War Cabinet, February 7, 1940.
PZ 3506/40 IOR/L/PS/12/397 "Inauguration of Tehran broadcasting station", June 22, 1940.
FO 371 133007, EP 1015/62 "Internal political situation in Iran," December 9, 1958.

Documents from the US Espionage Den (DFUSED), Tehran, Iran
"Visit with Ali Reza Nurizadeh, editor of Omid-e Iran," US Embassy Tehran, (May 10, 1979).

History and Public Policy Program Digital Archive
"Message to CC CPSU G.M. Malenkov about obstacles in Iranian Azerbaijan," 1953, Jamil Hasanli and Gary Goldberg (trans.) http://digitalarchive.wilsoncenter.org/document/120062 [November 21, 2015].

Oral History Project, Foundation for Iranian Studies
"Interview with Gen. Hamilton Twitchell, Chief of Mission, U.S. Military Assistance Advisory Mission in Iran," Foundation for Iranian Studies. (1988).
"Interview of Iraj Gorgin by Mahnaz Afkhami," Foundation for Iranian Studies. (Los Angeles, 1985).
"Interview with Ahmad Ahrar by Sharin Semii," Foundation for Iranian Studies (Paris, 18, September 19, 1983).

(II) Additional Primary Sources and Reports

Asnadi Az Tarikhch Ah-i radiyu Dar Iran, 1318–45 [Documents on Radio in Iran, 1940–67] 1379/2000. Isc PN1991.3I8A87

Ansari, Ali, Daniel Berman and Thomas Rintoul. *Preliminary Analysis of the Voting Figures in Iran's 2009 Presidential Election*. Chatham House: London, 2009.

"Delegation record for. IR domain name." Internet Assigned Numbers Authority (IANA) website (April 6, 1994, updated March 24, 2015), www.iana.org/domains/root/db/ir.html [September 3, 2015].

Khamenei, Ali "*Bayanat Dar Jam'-e Kasiri az Basijiyan-e Keshvar*." [Speech to a Large Crowd of the Nation's Basij] Center for Preserving and Publishing the Works of Grand Ayatollah Sayyid Ali Khamenei, November 25, 2009.

Khamenei, Ali. "Speech to Students, Representatives of Student Groups, and Elite," Tehran Vision of the Islamic Republic of Iran Network 1, August 26, 2009 (WNC).

Khamenei, Ali. Untitled Speech, *Voice of the Islamic Republic*, February 18, 2010 (BBCM).

Khamenei, Ali, and Hamid Algar. *Islam and Revolution: Writings and Declarations of Imam Khomeini*. Berkeley, CA: Mizan Press, 1981.

Khamenei, Ali. *Khomeini va Junbish (Collection of Speeches and Declarations)*. (n.p.) 1394/2015.

Khamenei, Ali. "Satellite Television Equipment" (Questions 1205–9), Practical Laws of Islam, Office of the Supreme Leader (1998) http://www.leader.ir/en/book/23?sn=5711 [May 01, 2015].

Khomeini, Ruhollah. "Last Will and Testament." Interest Section of the Islamic Republic of Iran, Embassy of the Democratic and Popular Republic of Algeria, Washington, DC, 1989. http://www.alseraj.net/maktaba/kotob/english/Miscellaneousbooks/LastwillofImamKhomeini/occasion/ertehal/english/will/ [May 1, 2015].

Khomeini, Ruhollah. *Seda va Sima dar Kalam-e Emam Khomeini* [Voice and Vision in the Words of Imam Khomeini]. Tehran: Sorush, 1984.

Khomeini, Ruhollah, and Hamid Algar (trans.). *Islam and Revolution: Writings and Declarations of Imam Khomeini*. Berkeley: Mizan Press, 1981.

Internet World Statistics, "Usage and Population Statistics." (u.d.), www.internetworldstats.com/stats5.htm [December 3, 2015].

Islamic Republic of Iran, *Asasname-ye Seda va Sima-ye Jomhuri-ye Iran* [Statute of the Voice and Vision of the Islamic Republic of Iran], (December 28, 1980), http://www.iranculture.org/nahad/irib.php via Internet Archive [March 13, 2015].

Islamic Republic of Iran, and Ghulam Riza Salami and Rustayi, Muhsin. *Asnad-i matuʻat-i Iran*, 1320–32 [Iran Press Documents, 1941–53]. 1374/1995. Isc PN5449.I82A8

Islamic Republic of Iran, Asghar Shirazi, and John O'Kane, trans. *The Constitution of Iran: Politics and the State in the Islamic Republic*. London: I.B. Tauris and Co Ltd, 1997.

Islamic Republic of Iran, Constitution of the Islamic Republic of Iran, (as amended in 1989) P. Werth (trans), https://faculty.unlv.edu/pwerth/Const/Iran(abridge).pdf [May 1, 2015].

Islamic Republic of Iran, "*Seda va Sima-ye Jomhuri-ye Eslami-ye Iran: Radio va Televizion*" [Voice and Vision of the Islamic Republic of Iran: History of Radio and Television], Dabir Khaneh-ye ʻAli-ye Showra- ye Enqelab- e Farhangi [Secretariat of Supreme Council of Cultural Revolution], November 17, 2010, www.iranculture.org [March 13, 2013] via Internet Archive.

Islamic Republic of Iran, "*Sazman-e Moderiyat Barnamerizi Keshvar*" [State Management and Planning Organization], (1380/2010) www.iranculture.org [March 13, 2014] via Internet Archive.

Islamic Republic of Iran, *Morafiye Namyandegan Doreh Chaharam* [Introduction to the Representatives of the Fourth Period], (1998).
Islamic Republic of Iran, Statistical Centre, "Population." via Iran Data Portal, Princeton University, www.princeton.edu/irandataportal/socioecon/topics/population/ [February 23, 2015].
Islamic Republic of Iran, *Telecommunications Company of Iran*, "Annual Report." July 2004, http://www.irantelecom.ir/press/intro8306/tci11.htm [October 15, 2014].
Islamic Republic of Iran, "*Site-e Pakhsh-e Zendeh-ye Barnameha-ye Seda va Sima*" [Site for Live Broadcast of Television and Radio], http://live.irib.ir [December 10, 2013].
Nationmaster. "Information and Communications Technology: Iran." UNESCO Institute for Statistics via Nationmaster Database (2011), www.nationmaster.com/time.php?stat=med_inf_and_com_tec_exp_cur_us&country=ir [July 21, 2011].
Nationmaster. "Households with Television, Iran (historical)." UNESCO Institute for Statistics via NationMaster.com [December 10, 2015].
Open Net Initiative. "Country Study: Internet Filtering in Iran in 2004–2005." (2005), http://opennet.net/studies/iran [October 8, 2015].
Open Net Initiative. "Internet Filtering in Iran." 2009.
Pahlavi, Mohammed Reza. *Mission For My Country*. London: Hutchinson, 1961.
Tehranian, Majid. *Socio-Economic and Communication Indicators in Development Planning: A Case Study of Iran*. Communication and Society, 5. Paris: UNESCO, 1980.
United Kingdom, BBC Monitoring, "Iran Media Guide," March 27, 2007.
United States Department of Defense, "History of AFRTVS: First 50 Years." (1993).
United States Department of Defense. "The History of AFRTS, Part 2." (1993).
United States Department of State. "Foreign Service List." US Government, October 1958.
United States Foreign Broadcast Information Service, "Iran: Audience Analysis and Market Profile." May 2005.
United States government. "Review of the Military Assistance Program for Iran B-133134." US Government Accountability Office, Washington, DC (January 9, 1959), http://www.gao.gov/assets/120/112121.pdf [December 10, 2013], p. 9.
United States Government. "US National Intelligence Survey: Iran, Supplement VI." U.S. Joint Chiefs of Staff, Joint Doctrine for Psychological Operations, Joint Publication (1996).
United States Library of Congress, Federal Research Division. "Iran Country Study." 1989.
World Justice Project, "Rule of Law Index." 2015.

(III) Periodicals and Blogs

Afsaran-e Jang-e Narm (blog)
Aftab-e Yazd
Aseman Weekly
Associated Press
Bahar
Baztab
BBC Persian
Beh Kasi Nago (blog)
Derang
Donya-e Eqtesad
E'temad

Ettella'at
Farhang-e Ashti
Fars News Agency
Gerdab Sabz (blog)
Ghalam News
Global Digitial TV Magizine
Hamshahri
Harvard Business School Bulletin
Hemayat
Hezbollah
Iran
Iran Daily
Iran Nameh
Iranian Labor News Agency
Iranian Student News Agency
Islamic Republic of Iran Broadcasting News
Jam-e Jam
Jang-e Narm (blog)
Javan
Jomhuri-ye Eslami
Kalemeh
Keyhan
Mardom Salari
Mehr News Agency
PC Magazine
Press TV
Rah-e Sabz
Rasa News
Resalat
Rooz
Sazman-e Tudeh-ye Enghelabi
Siyasat-e Ruz
Tariki Irani
Tabnak
Tech Herald
Teribon
Time Magazine
The New Republic
The New York Times
The Wall Street Journal
The Washington Post

(VI) Broadcast Media Translations and Transcriptions

220 Iranian MPs congratulate Ahmadinejad on reelection, *Mehr News Agency* in English, June 14, 2009 (BBCM).

38,000 websites and blogs to provoke ethnic minorities, *Ya Lesarat ol-Hoseyn*, January 3, 2007 (WNC).
Abrar criticizes minister's remarks on satellite antennae, *Abrar,* April 05, 1994 (FBIS).
Adib, Mohammad Hossein. "The Third Wave and Digital Democracy." *Mardom Salari*, November 20, 2003 (BBCM).
Advisability of private satellite TV broadcasts debated, *Sharq*, September 20, 2005. (WNC).
Ahmad Khomeyni espouses "resolute policies," *Keyhan,* April 16, 1990 (FBIS).
All this for "dust," *Aftab-e Yazd* website, June 16, 2009 (BBCM).
America's think tanks in search of a new strategy for the sedition leaders, *Javan,* February 16, 2010 (BBCM).
Ayatollah Montazeri notes political nature of Islam, *Tehran Domestic Service*, October 1, 1979 (FBIS).
BBC reaction to ban on satellite dishes viewed, *Resalat*, September 1994 (FBIS).
Birthday party for Persian blogs scheduled for June 13, *Iranian Students News Agency*, June 12, 2006 (WNC).
Blood Flowing on Carter's Order, *National Voice of Iran*, December 14, 1978 (FBIS).
Cable TV operation depends on Voice, Vision approval, *Salam*, January 19, 1994 (FBIS).
Candidate on Western onslaught, official corruption, *Voice of the Islamic Republic*, June 02, 1993 (FBIS).
Candidate questions recount of ballot boxes, "lack of cooperation," *Iranian Labour News Agency* website, June 25, 2009 (BBCM).
Chavez congratulates Ahmadinejad on victory in Iran election, *Fars News Agency* website June 13, 2009 (BBCM).
Clandestine radio on resignation of Hashemi as IRIB head, *Voice of Iranian Kordestan,* February 14, 1994 (FBIS).
Clandestine radios on the Shah's departure, *Voice of Iran*, January 19, 1979 (BBC SWB).
Committee set up to investigate foreign-based Persian speaking TV networks. *IRIN.* August 06, 2010 (WNC).
Conservative watchdog to rule on lifting of satellite ban, *Iran Daily* in English, December 19, 2002 (BBC SWB).
Credits to oppose the cultural invasion, *Resalat,* April 07, 1993 (FBIS).
Culture Minister ascribes Baztab's ban to "anonymity" of ownership, *Baztab*, February 19, 2007 (WNC).
Dissident Ayatollah's website said closed due to "certain problems," *Tehran Times online*, December 26, 2000 (BBCM).
East Azarbayjan Province Friday prayer sermons, *Vision of the Islamic Republic of Iran East Azarbayjan, Provincial TV Tabriz*, January 29, 2010 (BBCM).
Editorial hails Qom Seminary website, urges more religious sites, *Hezbollah*, August 12, 2007 (WNC).
Editorial views growing use of web logs, internet in Iran, *Hemayat*, December 16, 2006 (WNC).
Editorial: The Satellite Dish, *Tehran Times*, April 12, 1994 (FBIS).
Eighth December Communique of the Muslim People's Republic Party, *National Iran Radio Tabriz*, December 8, 1979 (BBC SWB).
Electoral and non-electoral issues, *Aftab-e Yazd* online, June 13, 2009 (BBCM).
Enforced removal of satellite dishes from rooftops to begin on April 22, *IRNA*, April 19, 1995 (BBC SWB).
External media broadcasts to be increased, *Salam*, September 22, 1993 (FBIS).

Fifty million people took part in 11 February rallies, *Far News Agency*, February 11, 2010 (BBCM).
Foreign embassies and research centres allowed to keep satellite dishes, *Voice of the Islamic Republic of Iran Network 1*, April 21, 1995 (BBC SWB).
Foreign Ministry spokesman comments on Stuxnet, *Islamic Republic of Iran News Network*, September 28, 2010 (BBCM).
Friday prayers: banning satellite dishes an appropriate, necessary measure, *Voice of the Islamic Republic of Iran Network 1*, January 16, 1995 (BBC SWB).
General's appointment as premier officially announced, *Paris AFP*, November 6, 1978 (FBIS).
Hamas: Iranian elections outcome meets people's aspirations for safeguarding its interests and confronting the challenges, *Palestinian Information Centre* online, June 13, 2009 (BBCM);
Hashemi interviewed on Voice, Vision appointment, *Tehran Domestic Service*, September 07, 1989 (FBIS).
Hashemi-Rafsanjani's inaugural speech, *Tehran Domestic Service*, August 17, 1989 (FBIS).
Head of Tehran TV reportedly fired, arrested, *Keyhan*, April 19, 1990 (FBIS).
Higher than a precipice, *Aftab-e Yazd* online, June 25, 2009 (BBCM).
Instability and mutiny within the ranks of the Army, *National Voice of Iran*, December 15, 1978 (FBIS).
Interior minister comments on use of satellite dishes, *Tehran Times* in English, April 10, 1994 (FBIS).
Interior minister says over 90 percent of satellite dishes dismantled voluntarily, *Voice of the Islamic Republic of Iran Network 1*, April 24, 1995 (BBC SWB).
Interior Ministry statement on dismantling of satellite dishes, *Voice of the Islamic Republic of Iran Network 1*, April 24, 1995 (BBC SWB).
Internet security provision rests with intelligence agency, *E'temad*, November 15, 2009 (BBCM).
Interview with Majles Speaker, *Vision of the Islamic Republic of Iran Network 2*, June 21, 2009 (BBCM).
Iran cleric says protesters linked to BBC radio, *Vision of the Islamic Republic of Iran Esfahan Provincial TV*, June 16, 2009 (BBCM).
Iran commander vows to deal firmly with protestors at 11 Feb rally, *Iranian Students News Agency*, January 30, 2010 (BBCM).
Iran extends voting time for another hour to 1730 gmt, *Vision of the Islamic Republic of Iran Network 2*, June 12, 2009 (BBCM).
Iran extends voting time to 1630 gmt, *Vision of the Islamic Republic of Iran Network 2*, June 12, 2009, (BBCM).
Iran governors-general authorized to extend voting time "at own discretion," *Voice of the Islamic Republic of Iran*, June 12, 2009 (BBCM).
Iran Guardian Council urges candidates' fans to wait for final results, *Vision of the Islamic Republic of Iran Network 2*, June 15, 2009 (BBCM).
Iran TV airs footage of demonstrations by Musavi, Ahmadinezhad supporters, *Vision of the Islamic Republic of Iran Network 1*, June 17, 2009 (BBCM).
Iran unveils 12 cyber products, *Fars News Agency*, December 14, 2013 (BBCM).
Iranian blogger Derakhshan allegedly confesses to spying for Israel, *Tabnak online*, November 18, 2008 (WNC).
Iranian communications expert comments on plan to regulate blogs, *Iranian Labor News Agency*, May 31, 2006 (WNC).

Iranian culture ministry launches scheme for registration of websites, blogs, *Iranian Labor News Agency*, January 2, 2007 (WNC).
Iranian official explains scheme to regulate websites, blogs, *Voice of the Islamic Republic of Iran Radio 1*, January 3, 2007 (WNC).
Iranian TV downplays widely publicized death of young woman in Tehran unrest, *Vision of the Islamic Republic of Iran Network 1,* June 26, 2009 (BBCM)
Iranian Union of Journalists protests the closure of Iran's two biggest newspapers, Ettella'at and Kayhan by military government, *Paris AFP* in English, December 15, 1978 (FBIS).
Iraqi president congratulates Ahmadinejad on reelection, *IRNA website,* June 14, 2009 (BBCM).
IRNA chief says Iran seeking soldiers of soft war, *IRNA*, February 1, 2006 (WNC).
Jannati asks Saudis not to obstruct Iranian pilgrims, comments on satellite, TV, *Voice of the Islamic Republic of Iran Network 1*, April 22, 1995 (BBC SWB).
Jannati on West's influence, satellite dishes, *Voice of the Islamic Republic of Iran First Program Network*, July 29, 1994 (FBIS).
Karrubi discusses private TV channel, new party, *E'temad*, December 29, 2006 (WNC).
Khamene'i holds question-and-answer session with students, *Vision of the Islamic Republic of Iran Network 1*, May 15, 2003 (FBIS).
Khamene'i leads Tehran Friday prayers, *Islamic Republic of Iran News Network*, June 19, 2009 (BBCM).
Khamene'i announces changes to IRIB, *Voice of the Islamic Republic First Program Network,* February 13, 1994 (FBIS).
Khatami cited on "retrograde" influences which prompted his resignation, *Paris AFP* in English, July 18, 1992 (BBC SWB).
Khatami website, "Welcome page," December 5, 1998, www.Khatami.com via Internet Archive [September 28, 2015].
Khatami's brother's organization to help government reform programs, *IRNA in English*, February 22, 2000 (BBC SWB).
Khomeyni's 9th December Address to Radio and Television Council, *National Iran Radio* Tehran, December 9, 1979 (BBC SWB).
Kianuri, First Secretary of the Tudeh Central Committee: "the Tudeh Party of Iran has warned the government about the conspiracy of imperialism," *Bamdad*, October 9, 1979 (FBIS).
Kordestan Democratic Party radio comments on recent "suppression" by government, *Voice of Iranian Kordestan*, April 13, 1994 (BBC SWB).
Larijani comments on satellite broadcasting, *Voice of the Islamic Republic First Program Network*, April 26, 1994 (FBIS).
Launching the halal internet in Iran, *Tabnak,* April 15, 2012 (BBCM).
Leader congratulates nation on Ahmadinejad's re-election, *Vision of the Islamic Republic of Iran Network 1*, Tehran, in Persian 1135 gmt June 13, 2009.
Mahahbad judges tender resignations in protest, *Tehran Domestic Service*, November 5, 1978 (FBIS).
Majles approves all amendments requested by Guardian Council to ban satellite dishes, *Voice of the Islamic Republic of Iran Network 1*, January 25, 1995 (BBC SWB).
Majles cultural committee adopts draft bill banning satellite reception equipment, IRNA, July 27, 1994, (BBC SWB).
Majles inquiry and investigation report, *Resalat*, 03, 04, November 15, 1993 (FBIS).
Majles prepares for debate on foreign TV broadcasts, *AFP* in English, July 30, 1994 (BBC SWB).

Mashhad teachers plan strike, *Tehran Domestic Service*, November 03, 1978 (FBIS).
Media criticized for Western influenced programming, *IRNA* in English, November 03, 1993 (FBIS).
Meshkini warns against deviant culture of the West, *Jomhuri-ye Eslami*, February 24, 1990 (FBIS).
Mohammad Hashemi reinstated as broadcasting chief, *Iran,* August 24, 1989 (FBIS).
Mohammadi, Mehdi. "When America becomes angry," *Keyhan*, February 18, 2010 (BBCM).
Morteza Nabavi: The referendum issue is mentioned to continue the unrest, *Resalat*, July 27, 2009 (BBCM).
Most dailies fail to appear, journalists arrested, *Tehran Domestic Service*, November 6, 1978 (FBIS).
Muslim People's Republic Party resolution on the occasion of 17 Shahrivar, *Keyhan*, September 9, 1979 (FBIS).
National Front denounces emergence of "religious clique," *Bamdad*, September 25, 1979 (FBIS).
New Director General appointed, *IRNA* in English, February 13, 1994 (FBIS).
Nine types of spyware in the country's industrial systems, *Iran*, September 8, 2010 (BBCM).
Opposition radio reports clash in Tehran over satellite dishes, *Voice of the Mojahed*, August 17, 1994 (BBC SWB).
Outlines of satellite ban approved, *IRNA* in English, September 20, 1994 (FBIS).
Over 250 foreign journalists cover Iran election, *Press TV*, June 12, 2009 (BBCM).
Pakistani premier congratulates Iranian president on poll victory, *Associated Press of Pakistan*, June 14, 2009 (BBCM).
Pishdar, Rauf. Let's not persist in the impossible. *E'temad*, April 4, 2007 (WNC).
Plan for the prohibition of the utilization of satellite reception equipment, *Jomhuri-ye Islami,* May 12, 1994 (FBIS).
Plug pulled on moderate satellite TV, *AKI online*, December 28, 2005 (WNC).
Policy of laxness paved way for Montazeri memoirs, *Resalat*, April 11, 2001 (BBCM).
President Rafsanjani's sermon at Tehran Friday prayers, June 20, 1992 (BBC SWB).
President says Iran to utilize IT to promote Islamic culture, *IRNA*, November 13, 2005 (WNC).
President to attend regional summit in Russia, *Islamic Republic of Iran News Network*, June 15, 2009 (BBCM).
President's advisor: We have been laying the foundations of democracy for four years now, *Aftab-e Yazd*, March 15, 2010 (BBCM).
President's brother resigns post heading radio, TV, *Paris AFP,* February 12, 1994 (FBIS).
President's speech inaugurates third TV channel, *Television Third Program Network*, December 05, 1993 (FBIS).
Pressures on offices of senior clerics to prevent them from sending congratulation messages Iran website, June 15, 2009 (BBCM).
Proclamation by 170 Majles deputies congratulating the exalted Leader on the new appointment in the Voice and Vision organization, *Resalat*, April 07, 1994 (FBIS).
Protests erupt after Iran's presidential election, *Press TV* website, June 13, 2009 (BBCM).
Qamari-Vafa, Morteza. "A beginning and an end." *Iran*, February 14, 2010 (BBCM).
Radio-Television Supervisor Qotbzadeh [sic] discusses censorship, *Tehran Domestic Service*, August 5, 1979 (FBIS).

Radio-TV chief on goals of the station, *Tehran Television Third Program Network*, December 05, 1993 (FBIS).
Radio, TV chief speaks on news reporting, *Tehran Television Service*, March 10, 1990 (FBIS).
Radio, TV officials on new efforts in broadcasting, *Voice of the Islamic Republic of Iran Program*, September 19, 1994 (FBIS).
Radio, TV programs curtailed to save energy, *Tehran Domestic Service*, December 29, 1978 (FBIS).
Rafsanjani, IRIB head view media role, prospects, *Tehran Voice of the Islamic Republic of Iran First Program Network*, January 20, 1994 (FBIS).
Reformist Iranian cleric to launch TV network on 21 December, *Iranian Student News Agency* online, December 5, 2005 (WNC).
Report on absentees at president's inauguration, *Mehr News Agency*, August 5, 2009 (BBCM).
Report on Majles proceedings, *Resalat*, September 14, 1994 (FBIS).
Reports on violence, *Tehran Radio*, December 26, 1978 (FBIS).
Reza'i urges authorities to respect people, take complaints seriously, *Islamic Republic of Iran News Network*, June 18, 2009 (BBCM).
Sedition-mongers received a hard-hitting slap from people on 22 Bahman, *Iran,* February 18, 2010 (BBCM).
Shari'atmadari Hossein. "Mr. Montazeri: Such behaviour from you is not far-fetched!" Kayhan, January 16, 2001 (BBCM).
Speaker, Head of Judiciary congratulate Ahmadinejad, Vision of the Islamic Republic of Iran Network 1, June 14, 2009 (BBCM)
Statement Number Seven of Engineer Mirhoseyn Musavi about Arrest of the Editorial Board of Kalemeh-ye Sabz and Restrictions Imposed on Non-Governmental Media, Kalemeh website, June 25, 2009 (OSC).
Strikes in refineries, *Paris AFP* in English, December 27, 1978 (FBIS).
Survey reportedly shows Tehran satellite dish owners removing them "voluntarily," *IRNA*, January 12, 1995 (BBC SWB).
Tajik leader congratulates Iranian president on re-election, *Tajik Television First Channel* (June 13, 2009), (BBCM);
Tehran paper lists 41 publications earmarked for closure, *Ettella'at*, August 21, 1979 (FBIS).
Tehran relatively calm, *Tehran Domestic Service*, November 6, 1978 (FBIS).
Text of announcement by the Reza'i family, *National Iran Radio*, July 1, 1980 (BBC SWB).
Text of communique issued by Muslim People's Republic Party as Broadcast, *National Iran Radio*, Tabriz, December 08, 1979 (FBIS).
Text of Khamenei edict, *Tehran Domestic Service,* August 24, 1989 (FBIS).
Voice Vision chiefs interviewed, *Tehran Domestic Service*, March 23, 1990 (FBIS).
Voice, Vision Response to Majles Inquiry, *Jomhuri ye Eslami*, 08, 09, November 11, 1993 (FBIS).
Voting extended by one hour in Iran's presidential election, *IRNA* website in English, June 12, 2009 (BBCM).
Watchdog body closes file on Iran election, *Press TV* website, June 30, 2009 (BBCM).
Weekly political analysis, Jomhuri-ye Eslami website, June 25, 2009 (BBCM).
Week long strike of Iran Air, Paris AFP in English, November 07, 1978 (FBIS).
West using satellite transmissions to dilute other cultures, Tehran Times, April 13, 1994 (BBC SWB).

Western intelligence services, Zionists behind post-election disturbances, *IRIN,* June 19, 2009 (BBCM).
When did filtering of sites and blogs begin? *Ettella'at,* May 10, 2010 (WNC).
Yazdi on new human rights body, Eslam shahr, US prisoner, Rushdie, other issues, *IRNA*, April 18, 1995 (BBC SWB).
Zarghami's untold secrets about the management of national media during the Fitneh, *9 Dey* website, December 30, 2013 (OSC).
Zarrin, Ghalam. "And Now Satellite," *Farhang-e Ashti,* December 9, 2005 (WNC).

(V) Secondary Sources

"Afsaran-e Jang-e Narm." [Soldiers of Soft War], http://www.afsaranjnarm.ir/1394/06/18/1818 [September 18, 2015].
"Arshiv" [Archive], *Donya-e Eqtesad* (16 Esfand 1391/March 6, 2013), http://www.donya-e-eqtesad.com/archive/news//?@=350131 [March 26, 2013].
"Bashgaheh Persepolis Saheb Nekhastin Shabkeh Khosusi Iran Shod" [Persepolis Owner of Iran's First Private Network], *Jam-e Jam online*, (1 Tir 1392/June 22, 2013) http://sport.jamejamonline.ir/NewsPreview/1091505435551629085 [May 1, 2015]
"Dastgiri Gostardeh ye Fa'alan-e Siyasi Dar Iran," [The Widespread Arrests of Political Activists in Iran], *BBC Persian online,* www.bbc.co.uk/Persian/iran/2009/06/090613op_ir88_mosharekat_mojahedin_arrests.html [December 10, 2015].
"Manazere" (Debate), *IRIB online,* (June 12, 2009) http://www.iribnews.ir/News/Video/192016_413987c0.wmv [June 14, 2009].
"Edward Bernays, 'Father of Public Relations' And Leader in Opinion Making, Dies at 103." *The New York Times*, March 10, 1995, http://www.nytimes.com/books/98/08/16/specials/bernays-obit.html [December 10, 2015].
"FATA, Vahed-e Jadide Polic-e Iran Bara-ye Control-e Faza-ye Internet." [FATA, a New Iranian Police Unit for Controlling the Internet], *BBC Persian*, January 23, 2011 www.bbc.co.uk/persian/iran/2011/01/110123_l39_cyberpolice_iran_ahmadimoghadam.shtml [July 3, 2013].
"Habib Sabet Is Dead: Iranian Altruist and Industrialist, 86." *The New York Times*, February 24, 1990.
"Habibulah Sabet Pasal." *Iran Nameh,* October 14, 1389/October 6, 2010,
Eghsade Siyas Jomhuri Islami Iran Rizeh Nameh Barrasi (Political Economy of the Islamic Republic of Iran: Special Review), edition.
"Iran Opens Commercial TV," *The New York Times*, October 5, 1958, p. 82.
"Iran TV Network," *The Wall Street Journal*, January 10, 1967, p. 9.
"Iranians Say How They'll Mark Anniversary of Revolution," *BBC News,* February 9, 2009, http://news.bbc.co.uk/2/hi/middle_east/8504907.stm [October 27, 2015].
"IRNA: Iran Government Uses American Filtering Software." Stop Censoring Us website (January 24, 2005 via Internet Archive for February 6, 2005) http://stop.censoring.us/archives/013307.php [October 11, 2015].
"Live Blogging the Iranian Protests." *The New Republic,* February 10–11, 2009, http://www.newrepublic.com/article/politics/live-blogging-the-iranian-protests [December 10, 2015].

"Mo'alem, Internet, Bankha Mo'tamedtarinha-ye Jame'eh Hastand" [Teachers, Internet, Banks are Most Trustworthy Community," *Iranian Students News Agency*, September 8, 2004, www.isna.co.ir/news/NewsCont.asp?id=427457&lang=P [December 11, 2010].

"Mo'aven-e Parlemani- ye Ra'is Jomhour: Emrooz Owlaviyyat-e Keshvar Moghabeleh ba Jang-e Narm-e Doshman Ast," [President's Representative to Parliament: Today the Country's Top Priority is to Fight Against the Enemy's Soft War] *Rasa News*, October 12, 2010, http://www.rasanews.ir/TextVersion/Detail/?Id=87473&Serv=36 [December 10, 2013].

"Moruri Bar Tarikhcheh- ye Televizion-e Khosusi." [A Review of the History of Private Television], *Majaleh-ye haftegi-ye Aseman* 1, no.1 (Mehr 1390/September 2011), www.asemanweekly.com/article/64 [February 26, 2014]. Note that this magizine was closed down.

"Naghsh-e Ayatollah Shari'atmadari Dar Kudeta" [Ayatollah Shari'atmadari's Role in the Coup], (unattributed), *Teribon* (22 Tir 1391/July 12, 2012), www.teribon.ir/archives/113918 [December 9, 2015].

"Otag Fekrha-ye Jang-e Narm" [Soft War Think Tanks], Jang-e Narm, June 9, 2011, via Internet Archive https://web.archive.org/web/20110609040628/http://www.psyop.ir/?cat=48c [September 11, 2015].

"RCA (Radio Corporation of America)," Global History Network website, (u.d.), http://ieeeghn.org/wiki/index.php/RCA [November 4, 2013].

"Moqabel-e Seda va Sima" [Against Voice and Vision], *Bahar*, (13 Esfand 1381/March 4, 2003.) epah-e Pasdaran-e Enqelab-e *Markaz-e Motale'at va Tahqiqat-e Zaman-e Jang." Ruzshomar-e Jang-e Iran va Iraq*, 52. Tehran, 2003.

"Shah of Iran." Reported by Mike Wallace, *60 Minutes*, October 24, 1976, www.cbsnews.com/videos/102476-the-shah-of-iran/ [April 20, 2016].

"Shah's Cancer Spreads." *Ottawa Citizen*, April 1, 1980, p. 77.

"Slashing Red Tape on the Silver Screen." *PBS Frontline*, 2009, www.pbs.org/wgbh/pages/frontline/tehranbureau/2009/10/slashing-red-tape-on-the-silver-screen.html [April 11, 2011].

"Tarikh-e Televizion-e Iran" [History of Iranian Television], *Howzeh Riasat-e Sazman-e Seda va Sima-ye Jomhuri-ye Eslami-ye Iran*, 2010, www.hozeriasat.irib.ir/page.php?id=45 [April 5, 2014].

"Tashkil-e Gharargah-e Jang-e Narm Dar Setad-e Koll-e Niruha-ye Mosallah" [The Formation of a Soft War Headquarters in the Islamic Republic of Iran Armed Forces General Headquarters] Fars News Agency, December 1, 2012.

"The Khomeini Era Begins," *Time Magazine* 113, no. 7 (1979).

A.G. "Dishes in Iran." *Global Digital TV Magazine*, July 6, 2011, www.tele-satellite.com [February 2, 2015].

Abadi, Cameron. "Iran, Facebook and the Limits of Online Activism." *Foreign Policy*, February 12, 2010, http://foreignpolicy.com/2010/02/12/iran-facebook-and-the-limits-of-online-activism [October 15, 2015].

Abbasi, A., A. Niaraki, and B. Dehkordi, "A Review of the ICT Status and Development Strategy Plan in Iran." *International Journal of Education and Development using Information and Communication Technology* 4, no. 3 (2008), http://ijedict.dec.uwi.edu/viewarticle.php?id=506

Abrahamian, Ervand. "Ali Shari'ati: Ideologue of the Iranian Revolution." MERIP Reports 102, Islam and Politics (1982).

Abrahamian, Ervand. *Iran between Two Revolutions*. Princeton, NJ: Princeton University Press, 1982.

Abrahamian, Ervand. *Khomeinism: Essays on the Islamic Republic*. Berkeley: University of California Press, 1993.

Abrahamian, Ervand. "The Crowd in the Persian Revolution." *Iranian Studies* 2, no. 4 (1969): 128–50.
Abrahamian, Ervand. *Tortured Confessions: Prisons and Public Recantations in Modern Iran*. Berkeley: University of California Press, 1999.
Afsaruddin, Asma. "The 'Islamic State': Genealogy, Facts, and Myths." *Journal of Church and State*, n.d.
Ahmad, Al-e. Khedmat va Kheyanat-e roshanfekran (The Service and Treason of the Intellectuals).
Ahmadi, Mehdi. "Cultural Activity by Means of Chat." *Siyasat-e Ruz*, January 3, 2006 (WNC).
Akhavan, Niki. *Electronic Iran: The Cultural Politics of an Online Evolution*. New Brunswick: New Brunswick, 2013.
Alfoneh, Ali "What Do Structural Changes in the Revolutionary Guards Mean?" American Enterprise Institute for Public Policy Research, Middle Eastern Outlook 7 (S 2008).
Amant, Abbas. "The Study of History in Post Revolutionary Iran: Nostalgia, Illusion, or Historical Awareness?" *Iranian Studies* 22, no. 4 (1989): 3–18.
Amir-Ebrahimi, M. "Blogging from Qom, behind Walls and Veils." *Comparative Studies of South Asia, Africa and the Middle East* 28, no. 2 (2008): 235–49. doi:10.1215/108920 1x-2008-002.
Amiri, Morteza. "Jang-e Narm va Teheed Shenasi," [Soft War and Threat Recognition] (October 18, 2009) http://farsi.khamenei.ir/print-content?id=8239 [November 12, 2015].
Anoosheh, Ebrahim. "Islamic Republic of Iran's Strategy against Soft War."
Ansari, Ali. *Modern Iran: The Pahlavis and After*. Essex: Pearson Longman, 2007.
Ansari, Ali. *Crisis of Authority: Iran's 2009 Presidential Election*. London: Chatham House, 2010.
Ansari, Ali. *The Politics of Nationalism in Modern Iran*. Cambridge: Cambridge University Press, 2012.
Arjomandi, Gholamreza. "Direct Broadcasting Satellite (DBS) Policy in the Islamic Republic of Iran: Popular, Religious and State Discourse" (PhD dissertation: University of Leicester, 1998). https://citeseerx.ist.psu.edu/viewdoc/download?doi=10.1.1.933.170 9&rep=rep1&type=pdf [December 10, 2021].
Behdad, Sohrab. "From Populism to Economic Liberalism: The Iranian Predicament." In *The Economy of Iran: Dilemmas of an Islamic State*, ed. Parvin Alizadeh. London: Tauris, 2000.
Cooper, Andrew S. *The Oil Kings: How the US, Iran, and Saudi Arabia Changed the Balance of Power in the Middle East*. New York: Simon & Schuster, 2011.
Cooper, Jeffrey R. "Another View of the Revolution in Military Affairs." Rand Publications, 1997, 99–140.
Corman, Steven R., Angela Trethewey, and Bud Goodall. "A 21st century Model for Communication in the Global War of Ideas." Consortium for Strategic Communication, Report 701 (2007). http://csc-old.asu.edu/wp-content/uploads/pdf/114.pdf.
Cronin, Stephanie. "Writing the History of Modern Iran: A Comment on Approaches and Sources." *Iran* 36 (1998), 175–84.
CSOs Training & Research Center, "A Report on the Status of the Internet in Iran." November 8, 2005, http://www.genderit.org/upload/ad6d215b74e2a8613f0cf5416c9f38 65/A_Report_on_Internet_Access_in_Iran_2_pdf [October 3, 2015].

Dabashi, Hamid. *Iran, the Green Movement and the USA: The Fox and the Paradox*. London: Zed Books, 2010.

Dabashi, Hamid. *Shi'ism: A Religion of Protest*. Cambridge: Harvard Universary Press, 2011.

Dabashi, Hamid. *Theology of Discontent: The Ideological Foundations of the Islamic Revolution in Iran*. New York: New York University Press, 1993.

Davani, Ali. "Movazeh Ulama Dar Barabar-e Hojum Farhanghi Gharb beh Iran" [The Positions of Ulama on Western Cultural Invasion against Iran], *Ruyaruyi Farhangi-ye Iran va Gharb Dar dowreh-ye Mowaser* [The Cultural Confrontation Between Iran and the West in Modern Times]. Tehran, 1996.

Day, Wong. "Foucault Contra Habermas: Knowledge and Power." *Philosophy Today*, 2007.

Debord, Guy, and Donald Nicholson-Smith (trans.). *The Society of the Spectacle*. New York: Zone Books, 1995.

Dehghan, Ali Reza. "Media and Public Sphere in Iran." *Asian Journal of Social Science* 37, no. 2 (2009): 256–73. doi:10.1163/156853109x415372.

Deibert, R. (1998). *Parchment, Printing, and Hypermedia: Communication in World Order Transformation*. New York: Columbia University Press.

Derman, J. "Max Weber and Charisma: A Transatlantic Affair." *New German Critique* 38, no. 2 113 (2011): 51–88. doi:10.1215/0094033x-1221785.

Dinmore, Guy "Iran Internet Cafes Closed in Crackdown." *Financial Times*, May 14, 2001.

Dumm, Thomas L. "Undecidable: Legitimation Crisis and the Fork in the Road." *Theory & Event* 11, no. 4 (2008).

Ebadi, Shirin and Azadeh Moaveni. *Iran Awakening: A Memoir of Revolution and Hope*. New York: Random House, 2006.

Edelman, Murray J. *Constructing the Political Spectacle*. Chicago: University of Chicago Press, 1988.

Edelman, Murray J. "Constructing Political Reality: Language, Symbols, and Meaning in Politics." *Political Research Quarterly* 47, no. 1 (March 1994): doi:10.2307/448911.

Edgar, Andrew. *The Philosophy of Habermas*. Stocksfield: Acumen, 2005.

Elbert, Bruce R. *The Satellite Communications Applications Handbook*. Artech House, Inc: Boston, 2004.

Elwell-Sutton, L. P. "The Press in Iran Today." *Journal of the Central Asian Society* 35 (1948):

Encyclopedia Iranica, "Chronology." (u.d.) www.iranicaonline.org/pages/chronology-3 [December 10, 2015].

Eriksson, J. "The Information Revolution, Security, and International Relations: (IR) relevant Theory?" *International Political Science Review/Revue Internationale de Science Politique* 27, no. 3 (2006): 221–44. doi:10.1177/0192512106064462.

European Conference on Information Warfare and Security 35. Academic Conferences International Limited, 2012.

Fang, Irving E. *A History of Mass Communication: Six Information Revolutions*. Boston: Focal Press, 1997.

Fanon, Frantz, Jean-Paul Sartre, and Constance Farrington. *The Wretched of the Earth*. New York: Grove Press, 1965.

Farajpahlou, A Hossein. "Moruri Bar Zir Sakht Technolozi-ye Ettella'at Dar Iran," [Review of the Structure of Information Technology in Iran], *Faslnameh Ettelat* 10, no. 4 (Bahar 1373/July 1992), www.ensani.ir/storage/files/20101110081715-1.pdf [April 05, 2014].

Farhi, F. (2010). "Assembly of Experts." *Iran Primer*, US Institute of Peace. http://iranprimer.usip.org/resource/assembly-experts. Updated August 2015. Accessed June 2018.

Farhi, Farideh. "Crafting a National Identity amidst Contentious Politics in Contemporary Iran." *Iranian Studies* 38, no. 1 (2005): 7–22. doi:10.1080/0021086042000336519.

Faris, D., and B. Rahimi, eds. *Social Media in Iran: Politics and Society after 2009*. Albany: State University of New York Press, 2015.

Faza'eli, Mehdi. "The Iranian Nation Has Answered the Questions," *Jam-e Jam*, February 14, 2010 (BBCM).

Felluga, Dino. *Introductory Guide to Critical Theory*. West Lafayette: Purdue University, 2002.

Fine, Gary Alan and Kent Sandstrom. "Ideology in Action: Approach to a Contested Concept." *Sociological Theory* 11, no. 1 (March 1993): 21–38.

Fischer, Michael M. J. *Iran: From Religious Dispute to Revolution*. Cambridge, MA: Harvard University Press, 1980.

Foucault, Michel, Mauro Bertani, Alessandro Fontana, François Ewald, and David Macey (trans.). *Society Must Be Defended: Lectures at the Collège de France, 1975–76*. New York: Picador, 2003.

Foucault, Michel, Mauro Bertani, Alessandro Fontana, François Ewald, and David Macey. *The Order of Things: An Archaeology of the Human Sciences*. New York: Pantheon Books, 1971.

Friedrich, Carl J., and Zbigniew Brzezinski. *Totalitarian Dictatorship and Autocracy*. New York: Praeger, 1972.

Fry, Donald. "Continuing the Conversation Regarding Myth," *American Journal of Semioticism* 6, no. 2/3 (1989): 183–197.

Gallarotti, Giulio M. "Soft Power: What It Is, Why It's Important, and the Conditions for Its Effective Use." *Journal of Political Power* 4, no. 1 (2011): 25–47.

Ganji, Babak. "Iranian Nuclear Politics: Change of Tactics or Strategy?" Camberley, Surrey: Defence Academy of the United Kingdom, Conflict Studies Research Centre, 2005.

Geertz, Clifford. "The Integrative Revolution: Primordial Sentiments and Civil Politics in the New States." *Old Societies and New States*, (1963): 105–57.

Gieling, Saskia. "Marja'iyaya in Iran and the Nomination of Khamenei in December." *Middle Eastern Studies* 33, no. 4 (1994): 777–787.

Gieling, Saskia. "Iran-Iraq War," *Encyclopedia Iranica* 13, no. 6 (2006), pp. 572–81.

Golkar, Saeid. "Cultural Engineering under Authoritarian Regimes: Islamization of Universities in Post-Revolutionary Iran." *Digest of Middle East Studies* 21, no. 1 (2012): 1–23.

Golkar, Saeid. "The Internet, the Green Movement and the Regime in Iran." *International Journal of Emerging Technologies and Society* (2011).

Gough, Susan L. "The Evolution of Strategic Influence." DTIC Document, 2003.

Gramsci, Antonio, Quintin Hoare, and Geoffrey Nowell-Smith. *Selections from the Prison Notebooks of Antonio Gramsci*. New York: International Publishers, 1971.

Gross, Michael Joseph. "A Declaration of Cyber-War." *Vanity Fair*, March 2011. http://www.vanityfair.com/news/2011/03/stuxnet-201104 [November 12, 2015].

Grossman, Lev "Iran Protests: Twitter, the Medium of the Movement." *Time Magazine*, June 17, 2009. http://www.time.com/time/world/article/0,8599,1905125,00.htm;

Guarnieri, C., and Collin Anderson "Iran and the Soft War for Internet Dominance," *Black Hat USA*, August 2016. https://iranthreats.github.io/us-16-Guarnieri-Anderson-Iran-And-The-Soft-War-For-Internet-Dominance-paper.pdf

Habermas, Jürgen. *Legitimation Crisis*. Boston: Beacon Press, 1975.

Nader Habibi, "How Ahmadinejad Changed Iran's Economy." *The Journal of Developing Areas*, vol. 49 no. 1 (2015): 305–12. Project MUSE, doi:10.1353/jda.2015.0044 p. 307

Haghayeghi, Mehrdad. "Politics and Ideology in the Islamic Republic of Iran." *Middle Eastern Studies* 29, no. 1 (1993): 36–52.

Haji-Najari, Abbas. "Cyber Wars: Support for Soft Warfare," *Javan*, November 11, 2010 (BBCM).

Halpern, Ben "'Myth' and 'Ideology' in Modern Usage." *History and Theory* 1, no. 2 (1961). doi:10.2307/2504377.

Helmus, Todd C., Christopher Paul, and Russell W. Glenn. *Enlisting Madison Avenue: The Marketing Approach to Earning Popular Support in Theaters of Operation*. Santa Monica, CA: RAND Corporation, 2007.

Herf, Jeffery. *Nazi Propaganda to the Arab World*. New Haven: Yale University Press, 2012.

Hess, Gary. *The United States' Emergence as a Southeast Asian Power, 1940–1950*. New York: Columbia University Press, 1987.

Heydari, Ashgar. Shari'atmadari Beh Riayat-e Sanad [Shari'atmadari According to Documents], Markaz-e Asnad Engelab-e Islami [Documentation Center of the Islamic Revolution], 2010.

Hiro, Dilip. 1984. "Chronicle of the Gulf War." MERIP Reports 125/126: 3–14.

Hoffman, David. "Beyond Public Diplomacy." *Foreign Affairs* 81, no. 2 (2002): 83–95.

Howard, P., and M. Hussain *Democracy's Fourth Wave: Digital Media and the Arab Spring*. New York: Oxford University Press, 2013.

Human Rights Watch, "The Islamic Republic at 31." February 11, 2010, www.hrw.org/sites/default/files/reports/iran0210web.pdf [October 27, 2015].

Hurd, Ian "Legitimacy and Authority in International Politics." *International Organization* 53, no. 2 (1999): 379–408.

Imani, Mohammad. "Beyond the Elections." Keyhan, January 21, 2008 (WNC).

Izadi, Foad. "US International Broadcasting: The Case of Iran." *The Journal of Arts Management, Law, and Society* 39, no. 2 (2009): 132–48.

Javdani, Homa. Sal Shomar-e Tarikh-e Televizion-e Iran [Chronicles of the Iranian television]. Tehran, 1384/2005. Isc JQ1786.Z1J2

Jenkins, H. (2004). "The Cultural Logic of Media Convergence." *International Journal of Cultural Studies*, 7, no. 1: 33–43.

Johnson, James. "Habermas on Strategic and Communicative Action." *Political Theory* 19, no. 2 (1991): 181–201.

Jung, C. G, and Karl Kerényi. *Essays on a Science of Mythology; the Myth of the Divine Child and the Mysteries of Eleusis*. Princeton, NJ: Princeton University Press, 1969.

Kamdar, Nazanin. "42,000 Computers will be Isolated from the World: National Internet to Go Live Next Week." *Rooz Online*, September 13, 2012 www.roozonline.com/persian/news/newsitem/article/42000-computers-will-be-isolated-from-the-world.html [November 12, 2015].

Karpf, D. (2012). *The Move On Effect: The Unexpected Transformation of American Political Advocacy*. New York: Oxford University Press.

Kepel, Giles. *Jihad: The Trail of Political Islam*. London: Harvard University Press, 2006.

Keshavarzian, A. *Contestation without Democracy: Elite Fragmentation in Iran.* In *Authoritarianism in the Middle East: Regimes and Resistance*, ed. M. Pripstein Posusney, M. Penner Angrist, pp. 63–90. Boulder, CO: Lynne Rienne, 2005.

Khabarnameh [Bulletin], Newsletter of the National Front, Azar 22, 1357/December 13, 1978.

Khalaji, Mehdi. "Miscommunication between Iranian Society and the West on Iran's Nuclear Program." Washington Institute for Near East Policy, Policy Watch #1078. New York, 2006, www.ciaonet.org/pbei/winep/policy_2006/2006_1078/2006_1078.html [April 04, 2011].

Khatami, M. and A. Mafinezam (trans.). *Hope and Challenge: The Iranian President Speaks.* Binghamton: Institute of Global Cultural Studies, Binghamton University Press, 1997.

Khiabany, Gholam. "De-Westernizing Media Theory, or Reverse Orientalism: 'Islamic Communication' as Theorized by Hamid Mowlana." *Media, Culture & Society* 25, no. 3 (2003): 415–22. doi:10.1177/0163443703025003007.

Khiabany, Gholam. "Religion and Media in Iran: The Imperative of the Market and the Straightjacket of Islamism." *Westminster Papers in Communication and Culture* 3, no. 2 (2006).

Laclau, E., and C. Mouffe. *Hegemony and Socialist Strategy: Towards a Radical Democratic Politics.* London: Verso, 1985.

Landler, M., and B Stelter, "Washington Taps into a New Potent Force in Diplomacy," *The New York Times*, June 16, 2009, http://www.nytimes.com/2009/06/17/world/middleeast/17media.html?_r=1

Langman, Lauren. "From Virtual Public Spheres to Global Justice: A Critical Theory of Internetworked Social Movements." *Sociological Theory* 23, no. 1 (2005), pp. 42–74.

Larson, Eric V., and United States, eds. *Foundations of Effective Influence Operations: A Framework for Enhancing Army Capabilities. Rand Corporation Monograph Series.* Santa Monica, CA: Rand Arroyo Center, 2009.

Lerner, D. *The Passing of Traditional Society: Modernizing the Middle East.* New York: Free Press, 1958.

Lichtheim, George. "The Concept of Ideology." *History and Theory* 4, no. 2 (1965): 164–195.

Luca, Mori. "Consensus and Democratic Legitimacy: Political Marketing versus Political Philosophy." *Hamburg Review of Social Sciences* 5, no. 1 (2010): 62–86.

Lutfi, Manal. "Qom's Religious Leaders Intervene and Reports of 50 Messages Sent to the Guide About the Crisis," Al-Sharq al-Awsat online, June 24, 2009 (BBC Monitoring).

Mahdavi, M. "Post-Islamist Trends in Post-Revolutionary Iran." *Comparative Studies of South Asia, Africa and the Middle East* 31, no. 1 (2011): 94–109. doi:10.1215/1089201x-2010-056.

Mansell, Robin. *Inside the Communication Revolution: Evolving Patterns of Social and Technical Interaction.* Oxford; New York: Oxford University Press, 2002.

Marx, Karl, and Frederick Engels. *The German Ideology, Part One, with Selections from Parts Two and Three, together with Marx's "Introduction to a Critique of Political Economy,"* New York: International Publishers, 2001.

Marx, Karl, and Frederick Engels. Richard R. Dixon, and Friedrich Engels. *The Collected Works of Karl Marx and Friedrich Engels.* Charlottesville, VA: InteLex Corporation, 2001.

Marx, Karl, Frederick Engels, and Marx Karl. *The Eighteenth Brumaire of Louis Bonaparte.* Second and Third edition. London; Moscow: Progress Publishers, Marx/Engels Internet Archive, 1869.

Mashayekhi, Kamran. *The Shah is Iran*. The Washington Post, July 29, 1978.
Masserat, Amir-Ebrahimi. "Blogging from Qom, behind Walls and Veils." *Comparative Studies of South Asia, Africa and the Middle East* 28, no. 2 (2008): 235–49.
Mavani, H. "Khomeini's Concept of Governance of the Jurisconsult Revisited: The Aftermath of Iran's 2009 Presidential Election." *Middle East Journal* 67, no. 2 (Spring 2013): 207–28.
McChesney, Robert Waterman. *Communication Revolution: Critical Junctures and the Future of Media*. New York: New Press: Distributed by W.W. Norton & Co., 2007.
McLellan, David. *Ideology*. Minneapolis, MI: University of Minnesota Press, 1986.
McLuhan, Marshall. *Understanding Media: The Extensions of Man*. New York: Signet Books, 1964.
Metz, Helen C. *Iran: A Country Study*. Washington, DC: US Government, 1987.
Metzger, Steven Chaffee, and Miriam. "The End of Mass Communication?" *Mass Communication and Society* 4 (2001): 365–79.
Milani, Abbas. "The Green Movement." Iran Primer, US Institute of Peace, (u.d.), http://iranprimer.usip.org/resource/green-movement [December 10, 2015].
Milani, Abbas. *The Shah*. New York: Macmillan, 2011.
Milani, Abbas. *Eminent Persians: The Men and Women Who Made Modern Iran, 1941–1979*. New York: Syracuse University Press, 2008.
Mir-Hosseini, Ziba. *Islam and Gender: The Religious Debate in Contemporary Iran*. Princeton: Princeton University Press, 1999.
Modarres, Olum Mozhgan. " Iran's Government Controlled Media Still in Denial." *Rah-e Sabz online*, December 29, 2009.
Monshipouri, M., ed. *Inside the Islamic Republic: Social Change in Post-Khomeini Iran*. Oxford: Oxford University Press, 2016.
Mottaghi, Ebrahim. "The U.S. Strategy of Entangling Iran in Peripheral Conflict." *The Iranian Journal of International Affairs*, no. 2 (2008): 676–86.
Mottahedeh, Roy P. *The Mantle of the Prophet: Religion and Politics in Iran*. New York: Simon and Schuster, 1985.
Mousavi Ahmadinejad June 3 Presidential Debate Transcript, Iran Tracker, (June 9, 2009) http://www.irantracker.org/analysis/mousavi-ahmadinejad-june-3-presidential-debate-transcript [December 10, 2012].
Mowlana, Hamid. "Islamization of Iranian Television," *Intermedia*. (1989).
Munz, Peter. "History and Myth." *The Philosophical Quarterly* 6, no. 22 (1956): 1–16.
Nikazmerad, Nicholas M. "A Chronological Survey of the Iranian Revolution." *Iranian Studies* 13, no. 1–4 (1980): 327–68.
Nurizadeh, Ali "Iranian authorities said to be jamming dissident ayatollahs website," Al-Sharq al-Awsar, December 14, 2000 (BBC Monitoring).
Nye, Joseph S. *Soft Power: The Means to Success in World Politics*. New York: Public Affairs, 2004.
Ostovar, A. *Vanguard of the Imam: Religion, Politics, and Iran's Revolutionary Guards*. New York: Oxford University Press, 2016.
Owen, T. *Disruptive Power: The Crisis of the State in the Digital Age*. Oxford: Oxford University Press, 2015.
Pakulski, Jan. "Legitimacy and Mass Compliance: Reflections on Max Weber and Soviet-Type Societies." *British Journal of Political Science* 16, no. 1 (January 1986), pp. 35–56.
Jennifer Pan, "How Market Dynamics of Domestic and Foreign Social Media Firms Shape Strategies of Internet Censorship," *Problems of Post-Communism* 64, 3–4 2017. pp. 167–88.

Payanbekhesh, Iran. "Radio va Television Chegoneh beh Tasraf Engelabiyan Dar Amad?" [How did the Revolutionaries Capture Radio and Television?] Tarikh Irani, www.tarikhirani.ir/fa/files/10/listview [February 26, 2014].

Poudeh, Reza J., and M. Reza Shirvani. "Issues and Paradoxes in the Development of Iranian National Cinema: An Overview." *Iranian Studies* 41, no. 3 (June 2008): 323–41. doi:10.1080/00210860801981294.

Price, Monroe E. *Media and Sovereignty: The Global Information Revolution and Its Challenge to State Power*. Cambridge: MIT Press, 2004.

Price, Monroe E. *Free Expression, Globalism, and the New Strategic Communication*. New York: Cambridge University Press, 2015.

Quirk, P. "Iran's Twitter Revolution," *Foreign Policy In Focus* (June 17, 2009) http://www.fpif.org/fpiftxt/6199;

Rahimi, Babak. "Internet and the State: The Rise of Cyberdemocracy in Revolutionary Iran." *Working Papers on New Media & Information Technology in the Middle East*, European University Institute, Florence., 2003.

Kaveh Ehsani, "Survival Through Dispossession: Privatization of Public Goods in the Islamic Republic." *Middle East Report 250* (Spring 2009): 26–33.

Rhoads, Christopher, Farnaz Fasshi, and Andres Gonalez. "Iran Vows to Unplug Internet," *The Wall Street Journal*, (May 28, 2011).

Ricœur, Paul. *From Text to Action Essays in Hermeneutics II*. London: Continuum, 2008.

Robinson, Andrew. "The Mythology of War." *Peace Review* 17, no. 1 (2005): 33–8. doi:10.1080/14631370500292037.

Saffari, Said. "The Legitimation of the Clergy's Right to Rule in the Iranian Constitution of 1979." *British Journal of Middle Eastern Studies* 20, no. 1 (1993): 64–82.

Said, Edward W. *Orientalism*. New York: Vintage Books, 1979.

Salamini, Leonardo. "Gramsci and Marxist Sociology of Knowledge: An Analysis of Hegemony-Ideology-Knowledge," *Sociological Quarterly* 15, no. 3 (1974).

Sargent, Lyman Tower. "Ideology and Utopia: Karl Mannheim and Paul Ricoeur." *Journal of Political Ideologies* 13, no. 3 (2008): 263–73. doi:10.1080/13569310802374479.

Schayegh, Cyrus. "'Seeing Like a State': An Essay on the Historiography of Modern Iran." *International Journal of Middle East Studies* 42, no. 01 (2010): 37. doi:10.1017/s0020743809990523.

Schirazi, Asghar. *The Constitution of Iran: Politics and the State in the Islamic Republic*. London; New York: I.B. Tauris, 1997.

Seifzadeh, Hossein. "The Landscape of Factional Politics and its Future in Iran." *The Middle East Journal* 57, no. 1 (2003): 57–75.

Semati, Mehdi. *Media, Culture and Society in Iran: Living with Globalization and the Islamic State*. London: Routledge, 2008.

Shafaei, Azadeh, and Mehran Nejati, eds. *Annals of Language and Learning: Proceedings of the 2009 International Online Language Conference*. 2009.

Shari'ati, Ali. *Ravish-e Shinakht-e Eslam* [Approach to the Understanding of Islam]. Tehran, 1347/1968.

Simon, Roger D. *Gramsci's Political Thought: An Introduction*. London: Lawrence and Wishart, 1982.

Slackman, Michael. "Iran Boasts of Capacity to Make Bomb Fuel." *The New York Times*, February 11, 2010.

Sohrabi-Haghighat, M. Hadi, and Shohre Mansouri. "Where Is My Vote? ICT Politics in the Aftermath of Iran's Presidential Elections." *International Journal of Emerging Technologies and Society* 8, no. 1 (n.d.): 24–41.

Sohrabi-Haghighat, M. Hadi. "New Media and Social-Political Change in Iran." *CyberOrient* 5, no. 1 (2011). http://www.cyberorient.net/article.do?articleId=6187.

Sorel, Georges, and Jeremy Jennings. *Reflections on Violence.* United Kingdom; New York: Cambridge University Press, 1999. http://dx.doi.org/10.1017/CBO9780511815614.

Sreberny, Annabelle, and Massoumeh Torfeh, *Persian Service: The BBC and British Interests in Iran.* London: I. B. Tauris, 2014.

Sreberny, Annabelle, and Ali Mohammadi. *Small Media, Big Revolution: Communication, Culture, and the Iranian Revolution.* Minneapolis: University of Minnesota Press, 1994.

Sreberny, Annabelle. "The Analytic Challenges of Studying the Middle East and Its Evolving Media Environment." *Middle East Journal of Culture and Communication* 1, no. 1 (2008): 8–23. doi:10.1163/187398608x317388.

Staar, Richard Felix. *Foreign Policies of the Soviet Union.* Stanford: Hoover Institution Press, Stanford University, 1991.

Stillman, Peter G. "The Concept of Legitimacy." *Polity* 7, no. 1 (1974): 32. doi:10.2307/3234268.

Stecklow, Steve, Babak Dehghanpisheh, and Yeganeh Torbati, "Assets of the Ayatollah" November 11, 2013. https://www.reuters.com/investigates/iran/#article/part1 [July 10, 2018].

Stone, Brad and Noam Cohen. "Social Networks Spread Defiance Online." *The New York Times*, June 15, 2009, http://nyti.ms/1VmYl6X [December 10, 2015].

Tabaar, Mohammad A. *Religious Statecraft: The Politics of Islam in Iran.* New York: Columbia University Press, 2018.

Tager, Michael. "Myth and Politics in the Works of Sorel and Barthes." *Journal of the History of Ideas* 47, no. 4 (1986): 625–39.

Tatham, Stephen A. "Strategic Communication: A Primer." In *Defence Academy of the United Kingdom*, Advanced Research and Assessment Group Special Series 08/28. Shrivenham: Defence Academy of the United Kingdom, 2008.

Taylor, Dianna. *Michel Foucault Key Concepts.* Durham, 2011. http://dx.doi.org/10.1017/UPO9781844654734.

Tehranian, Majid. "Communication and Revolution in Iran: The Passing of a Paradigm." *Iranian Studies* 13, no. 1–4 (1980): 5–30.

Thomas, Peter. *The Gramscian Moment Philosophy, Hegemony and Marxism.* Leiden: Brill, 2009.

Thomas, Antony (dir.), "For Neda," HBO Documentary, (2010).

Thompson, John B. *Ideology and Modern Culture: Critical Social Theory in the Era of Mass Communication.* Stanford, CA: Stanford University Press, 1990.

Thompson, John B. *The Media and Modernity: A Social Theory of the Media.* Stanford: Stanford University Press, 1995.

Tschentscher, Axel. "Comparing Constitutions and International Constitutional Law: A Primer." SSRN Scholarly Paper. Rochester, NY: Social Science Research Network, February 10, 2011, http://papers.ssrn.com/abstract=1502125.

Tudor, Henry. *Political Myth.* New York: Praeger, 1972.

Ulrichsen, Kristian Coates. "Internal and External Security in the Arab Gulf States." *Middle East Policy* 16, no. 2 (2009): 39–58.

Untitled report, Fars News Agency, December 27, 2005 (BBC SWB).

Usher, Sabastian. "Iran's Leaders Harness Media Power." *BBC News*, 2006, http://news.bbc.co.uk/go/pr/fr/-/2/hi/middle_east/4804328.stm.

Vahabi, Mehrdad, and Mohajer Nasser. "Islamic Republic of Iran and Its Opposition." In *Television and Public Policy: Change and Continuity in an Era of Global Liberalization*, ed. Ward, David. New York; London: L. Erlbaum Associates., 2007

Varzi, Roxanne. *Warring Souls: Youth, Media, and Martyrdom in Post-Revolution Iran.* Durham: Duke University Press, 2009.
"Veblog-ha" [Weblogs], *Hamshahri*, (u.d.) [December 1, 2012].
Weber, Max, Talcott Parsons, and A. M Henderson. The Theory of Social and Economic Organization, 1964.
Wehrey, Frederic Jerrold D. Green, Brian Nichiporuk, Alireza Nader, Lydia Hansell, Rasool Nafisi, S. R. Bohandy. "The Rise of the Pasdaran: Assessing the Domestic Roles of Iran's Islamic Revolutionary Guards Corps." Translated by National Defense Research Institute; Office of the Secretary of Defense, 2009.
Werth, Alexander. *Russia at War 1941–1945.* New York: E.P. Dutton, 1964.
Williams, Christopher. "Iranian Hacker Claims Revenge for Stuxnet." Telegraph (March 28, 2011) www.telegraph.co.uk/technology/news/8411252/Iranian-hacker-claims-revenge-for-Stuxnet.html [November 12, 2015].
Williams, John. *After the Countercoup: Advising the Imperial Forces of Iran*, MA monograph, Fort Leavenworth Kansas: US Army Staff College, 2010.
Worth, Robert. "Opposition in Iran Meets a Crossroads on Strategy," *The New York Times*, February 14, 2010.
Zoeram, Vahid Amani. "Criticism in Public Sphere: The Press Development in Iran's Civil Society 1997–2000." *Journal of Politics and Law* 3, no. 2 (September 2010). www.ccsenet.o

INDEX

Abrahamian, Ervand 6
Abrar 75
Adib, Mohammad Hossein 110–11
Afkhami, Mahnaz 38
AFRTS. *See* Armed Forces Radio and Television Service (AFRTS)
Agha-Soltan, Neda 112–13
Ahmadi, Mehdi 100
Ahmadinejad, Mahmood 18, 90, 100, 106, 108–9, 111, 115–20, 123–4, 128, 183 n.44
AIOC. *See* Anglo-Iranian Oil Company (AIOC)
Ajax operation 24–5
Akrami, Reza 80
Alavi-Kai, Hassan 27
Al-e Ahmad, Jamal 12–13, 21
Anderson, Collin 132
Anglo-Iranian Oil Company (AIOC) 24–5
Ansari, Ali 107, 118, 159 n.37
Arab Spring 107, 123
Araki, Mohammad Ali 81
Ardalan, Ali-Gholi 27
Arjomand, Amir 7, 47–8
Armed Forces Radio and Television Service (AFRTS) 21, 30–1, 39, 151
Armed Forces Television 31–5
ARMISH-MAAG. *See* U.S. Army Mission in Iran/ Military Assistance Advisory Group (ARMISH-MAAG)
Ershad (Vezarat-e Farhang-e Ershad-e Eslami) 5, 67, 72, 78, 89–90, 103, 154, 174 n.37
Assange, Julian 129
Asymmetrical Digital Subscriber Lines (ADSL) 97
Axworthy, Michael 13
Azhari, Gholam Reza 42–3

Baha'ism 36
Bajoghli, Narges 9, 155
barefoot people 51–2, 168 n.49

Barthes, Roland 11
Basij *(Basij-e Mostaz'afin)* 5–6, 73, 104, 111, 113, 115, 128, 139, 150, 175 n.73
Baztab 103–4
BBC. *See* British Broadcasting Corporation (BBC)
BBC Persian Service 22, 43, 88, 125, 160 n.6
Beetham, David 5
Besharati, Ali Mohammad 69, 71–3
British Broadcasting Corporation (BBC) 15, 70, 77, 88, 112, 125, 150
Brzezinski, Zbigniew 10
Bush, George W. 14

Cambridge History of Iran (Avery) 23, 160 n.11
Carter, Jimmy 53, 55
Chafee, Steven H. 8
Chapin, Selden 31–2
Chavez, Hugo 116
Churchill, Winston 24
CIA operation 24–5, 54, 140
clandestine 25, 44, 48, 73, 75, 114, 166 nn. 17–18
Clausewitz, Carl Van 14
Clinton, Hillary 131
Cold War 8, 12–13, 21, 23
Compagnie de Telegraphie Sans Fil (Wireless Telegraphy Company) 37
content delivery network (CDN) 145
co-option and managed access strategy 150
Crocodile Tears (television show) 63
Cultural
  imperialism 12–13, 91, 102
  revolution 51
  transmission 175 n.1
cyberwar 129–31

Davani, Ali 91
DBS. *See* Direct Broadcast Satellite (DBS)

defacement 131–2
Democratic Party of Iranian Kurdistan (PDKI, *Hezb-e Demokrat-e Kordestan-e Iran*) 75
denial-of-service (DDoS) attacks 114
den of spies 53–5
Derakhshan, Hossein 102, 179 n.38, 180 n.40
digital revisionism 132
Direct Broadcast Satellite (DBS) 17–18, 62, 68–80, 83–5, 87, 91–2, 101, 150
Durov, Pavel 141

EARN. *See* European Academic Research Network
Eagle Claw operation 55
Edelman, Murray J. 10
Eisenhower, Dwight 24, 28–9
election crisis (2009) 18, 107–10, 115, 124
Emami-Kashani, Mohammad 59, 78
European Academic Research Network (EARN) 95

Fanon, Franz 91
Farhadi, Asghar 154
fax machine 158 n.32
FBIS. *See* Foreign Information Broadcasting Service (FBIS)
Ferdowsi, Abolqasem 149, 155
filtering software 104–5
Fixed Satellite Service (FSS) 17, 68, 70–1, 83–4, 175 n.2
forced migration 146–7
Foreign Information Broadcasting Service (FBIS) 15
Friedrich, Carl J. 10
FSS. *See* Fixed Satellite Service (FSS)

Ganji, Akbar 97
Gerdab 106, 114
Gharbzadegi. *See* westoxification
Ghotbi, Reza 38
Ghotbzadeh, Sadegh 51–3
Gieling, Saskia M. 169 n.75
Gilani, Syed Yusuf Raza 116
Goebbels, Joseph 27
Gramsci, Antonio 10, 16, 176 n.10
Green Movement 10, 109, 112–15, 119–22, 124–6, 152–3, 190 n.37

Green Revolution 107
Guarnieri, Claudio 132

hacking 128, 131–2
Hallack, Vance 34
Halliday, Fred 6
hegemonic power 2, 4–5, 10–11, 17, 35, 37, 80, 87, 118, 152
Holliday, Shabnam 6
Hosseini, Mirali 50
Huntington, Samuel 13
hypermedia 107, 181 n.4

ICA. *See* Iranian Cyber Army (ICA)
ICANN. *See* Internet Corporation for Assigned Names and Numbers
ideology 8–10
Information and Communication Network of Iran (IRANNET) 96
information-communication technology 1, 11
Information Technology Administration 135
Instagram 102, 140, 142–3, 147, 190 n.36
International Financial Tribune 135
internet
 birth of 95–7
 filtering 104–5
 growth of 97–8
 intelligence and police 106
 national 18, 132–4, 136–7, 142, 146–8, 152–4
 registration 103–4
 speed 105, 136–7
Internet Archive 15–16, 95, 169 n.69, 178 n.10
Internet Corporation for Assigned Names and Numbers (ICANN) 15, 95
Internet Exchange Points (IXPs) 137
Internet-Intranet Cohesion Model 134
Internet Service Providers (ISPs) 96–7, 105, 115, 122, 128, 137–8, 141, 145–7
intranet 134, 136, 148, 153. *See also* National Information Network (NIN)
Iranian Cyber Army (ICA) 132

Iran-Iraq war 56, 110, 120–1
IRGC. *See* Islamic Revolutionary Guard Corps
IRIB. *See* Islamic Republic of Iran Broadcasting
Islamic Consultative Assembly. *See* Majles
Islamic Republic 1–2, 4–9, 11–13, 16–17, 39, 41, 46, 50–3, 56, 59, 61–2, 72, 75–6, 78, 80–2, 87, 98–9, 101–3, 107, 109, 112, 114, 116, 118, 120, 127, 131, 141, 147, 152, 154–5
Islamic Republic Party (IRP) 52
Islamic Republic of Iran Broadcasting (IRIB) 8, 17, 52–3, 56, 59–69, 71, 73–4, 76, 78–9, 82–91, 112–13, 115, 119, 123, 152
Islamic revolution 6, 9, 13, 16, 51, 54–5, 67, 75, 79, 114
Islamic Revolutionary Guard Corps (IRGC) 5, 89, 106, 108, 111, 113, 115, 123, 128, 134, 150, 185 n.77
ISPs. *See* Internet Service Providers (ISPs)
IXPs. *See* Internet Exchange Points (IXPs)

Jahromi, Mohammad-Javad Azari 141–2, 190 n.37, 190 n.45
jang-e narm. *See* soft war
Jannati, Ayatollah Amad 76–7, 79, 91, 123
Joint Comprehensive Plan of Action (JCPOA) 130, 135, 139

Karroubi, Mehdi 89–90, 108–9, 111, 118, 125, 152–3
Kasra, Mona 120–1
Kayhan 127
Keshavarzian, Arang 3
Khamenei, Ali 1, 6, 10–12, 14, 47, 59–61, 66, 73, 75–6, 81, 84, 90, 98, 100–1, 104, 107, 109, 116–17, 126, 132–3, 139–40, 143, 146, 148, 155
Khatami, Mohammad 1, 13, 67, 97, 102, 122, 150, 159 n.45, 184 n.58
Khomeini, Ahmad 61, 133
Khomeini, Ruhollah 1–2, 6–7, 12, 25, 44–56, 59, 65, 79–80, 97–8, 161 n.21, 161 n.23, 167 n.28, 176 n.7
Khomeini, Hassan 117

Kimiachi, Bijan 165 n.78
Kraidy, Marwan 107, 181 n.4

Larijani, Ali 66, 78, 80, 89, 116–17, 174 n.51, 184 n.58
Larijani, Mohammad Javad 80, 95
legitimacy 4–7, 10, 18, 21, 41–2, 44, 82, 85, 87, 112, 117–18, 121–4, 126, 140, 150, 152–3
liberation technology 107, 110–12, 125

McLuhan, Marshall 69
Majles *(Majles-e Showra-ye Eslami)* 3, 17, 24–5, 35, 52, 61–7, 71–2, 74–5, 77–82, 85, 89–90, 102, 108, 113, 116–17, 123, 125, 145, 155, 169 n.62, 171 n.15, 173 n.21
Majles-Hashemi stand-off 60–2, 67–8
Mansuri, Hadi 111
Mardom Salari 110
Marhaba, Shapour 74
martial law 41–4
meaning machine 10
Medvedev, Dmitry 116
MEK. *See* Mojahedin-e Khalq
Meshkini, Ali 61, 69
Metzger, Miriam J. 8
Milani, Mohsen 6, 49
military and propaganda legacy 151–2
Ministry of Culture and Islamic Guidance 5, 67, 72, 78, 89–90, 103, 154, 174 n.37
mobilization 4–6, 18, 108, 139
Mohammadi, Ali 36, 51
Mojahedin-e Khalq (MEK) 49–50, 53, 141
Mokhtarpur, Ali Reza 103
monopoly 1–4, 8–10, 12, 16–17, 21, 26, 30, 39, 41–2, 46–7, 51, 56, 62, 68–9, 82, 84–5, 87–9, 92, 95–7, 115, 120–3, 132, 135, 146–7, 149, 152, 158 n.32, 175 n.2
Montazeri, Hossein Ali 97–8
Montazeri, Mohammad Ja'afar 140
Mosaddegh, Mohammad 23–6
Mousavi, Mir Hossein 108–9, 111, 117–18, 125, 152–3
Mousavi, Mohammad Mehdi 99–100
Mowlana, Hamid 119

MPRP. *See* Muslim People's Republic Party (MPRP)
Murphy, Robert 27
Muslim People's Republic Party (MPRP) 47–9
myth 5, 10–11, 14, 17, 25, 141, 153

Nasser, Gamal Abdel 27
Nategh-Nuri, Ali Akbar 74
National Front 26, 43, 45–8
National Information Network (NIN) 18, 132–8, 142, 146–8, 153–4
National Iranian Radio and Television (NIRT) 21, 29, 37–9, 42–3, 45–8, 50–2, 56, 151–2, 154, 166 n.6, 168 n.42
national television 16, 37–8, 42–3, 48, 50–1, 69–70, 76, 85, 88, 108, 113, 150, 154
NIN. *See* National Information Network (NIN)
9 Dey 119–20, 126–7, 139–40
NIRT. *See* National Iranian Radio and Television (NIRT)
Norouzian, Mohammad 139
nuclear program 129–30
Nurizadeh, Ali Reza 169 n.62
Nye, Joseph S. 13

Omid-e Iran (Hope of Iran) 169 n.62
ontological security 76, 174 n.45
Open Net Initiative (ONI) 104–5
Open Source Center (OSC) 15
Orkut 113

Pahlavi, Shah Mohammad Reza 2, 6–7, 9–11, 16, 22–4, 26–30, 37, 41–2, 44–6, 50, 53, 56, 59, 77, 151, 157 n.5, 164 n.62, 168 n.49
parliament. *See* Majles
Persepolis Television Network 90
Persian blogosphere 18, 98–101
Pishvar, Rauf 105
popular legitimacy 4–8, 18, 87, 118, 140, 150, 153
populism 6, 10
Principalist 115, 183 n.44, 185 n.77
The Prison Notebooks (Gramsci) 10

prohibition bill 72–81, 86, 88, 90–1, 149
proscription and passive tolerance strategy 149
protectionism 146–7, 154

Qom 42, 48–9, 61–2, 66, 76, 81–2, 100, 117, 139

radio
    Allied occupation 23
    CIA operation 24–5
    commercial and military television 31–4
    coup d'état 23–6
    German 22
    growth of 26–8
    Tehran 22–3, 25, 28–31, 35–7
    television and 30, 34–9, 42, 50–2, 56, 59–61, 63–4, 66, 72, 74–6, 84–5, 88, 90, 101, 109, 113, 147, 150–1, 154
    US contribution 28–30
    and war 22
Radio Corporation of America (RCA) 30
Radpur, Shahriar 43
Rafsanjani, Akbar Hashemi 59, 96
Rafsanjani, Mohammad Hashemi 53, 59–62, 65–7, 75
Rahimi, Babak 158 n.13, 178 n.10, 178 n.18, 180 n.47
Rahmon, Emomali 116
redline 154
registration 103–4
repression technology 113–16
Rezaei, Mohsen 108
Rouhani, Hassan 12, 18, 134, 136, 138, 141, 148, 190 n.34, 191 n.55
Rouyanian, Mohammad 90

Saba TV 89–90
Sabet, Farzan 4
Sabet, Iraj 33–5, 151, 164 n.60, 164 n.62
Sabet Pasal, Habibollah 30, 32–7
Safshekan, Roozbeh 4
Sane'i, Yusef 117
satellite dishes 62, 67–8, 70–82, 84–9, 91–2, 95, 99, 142, 149
satellite TV 17–18, 62, 68–83, 86–7, 89–92, 105, 110, 125, 149

SCC. *See* Supreme Cyberspace Council (SCC)
Second World War 8, 21–2
Semati, Mehdi 86–7
Sennett, Richard 41
Sepah-e Pasdaran-e Enqelab-e Eslami. *See* Islamic Revolutionary Guard Corps (IRGC)
Shahriyari, Hamid 99
Shahroudi, Mahmoud Hashemi 116
Shahshahani, Siavash 133, 188 n.5
Sharia 7
Shari'atmadari, Ayatollah Kazem 47–9
Sharif-Emami, Jafar 41–2
Sheibani, Abbas 74–5
Shiravi, Ali Reza 90
short message service (SMS) 115
Small Media 15, 143
Small Media, Big Revolution (Sreberny and Mohammadi) 14
SNSC. *See* Supreme National Security Council (SNSC)
social media 16, 102, 107, 111, 114, 132, 137–40, 142, 146, 150
soft war 6, 11–14, 18, 88, 92, 95, 102–3, 125–6, 128–31, 140–1, 153
Sohrabi-Haghighat, Mohammad Hadi 111
Sorel, George 11
Soviet Union 22, 26–7, 135
Sowt al Arab (Voice of the Arabs) 27
Sparks, Colin 12
spectacle 10–11, 45, 53–5, 119, 152–3
Sreberny, Annabelle 14, 36, 51, 164 n.61, 165 n.78, 165 n.100, 168 n.42
Star TV 70–1
state television 21, 30, 38–9, 42, 52, 65, 69, 77, 89, 111, 116, 140, 142, 149, 175 n.2
Sterns, Peter 149
Stuxnet 129–31, 133, 187 n.22, 187 n.25
Sullivan, William 41
Supreme Council of the Cultural Revolution 96, 104
Supreme Cyberspace Council (SCC) 145
Supreme National Security Council (SNSC) 128
surveillance 14, 74, 97, 109, 113–14, 126, 131–3, 137–8, 190 n.37

Tabaar, Mohammad Ayatollahi 6
Talabani, Jalal 116
Taubert, Eberhard 27
TechRasa 135, 188 n.11
Tehran 22–3, 25, 28–31, 35–7, 42–3, 45, 47–8, 50, 53, 66, 71–3, 79, 81, 83–5, 88–9, 97, 108, 115, 118–19, 128, 139, 145, 152
Telecommunication Company of Iran (TCI) 95–6, 115, 122–3, 150
Telegram 15, 18, 133, 138–48, 190 n.45
television. *See also* Armed Forces Television; national television; state television
  commercial 16, 21, 30–5
  military 31–4
  monopoly 69, 87–9, 149, 175 n.2
  satellite 17, 62, 68, 70–5, 77–81, 83, 86–7, 89–91, 105, 110, 125, 149
Televizion-e Iran (Iran Television) 21, 32–7, 39, 151
Televizion-e Melli-ye Iran (National Iran Television) 37
Third World 77
Thompson, John 8, 83, 175 n.3
Top Level Domain (TLD) 133, 188 n.5
traditional system 175 n.2
Tudeh Party 24, 46, 48
The Turban for the Crown (Arjomand) 7, 47–8
Turow, Joseph 8
22 Bahman 114, 126–7
Twitter Revolution 107, 131

The United States 8, 12, 14–15, 23–5, 28–34, 53–4, 62–3, 80, 86–7, 89, 105, 112, 130, 140
U.S. Army Mission in Iran/Military Assistance Advisory Group (ARMISH-MAAG) 29, 31–3
US Information Service (USIS) 30, 34
US-Iran hostage crisis 53

Vezarat-e Farhang-e Ershad-e Eslami. *See* Ershad
velayat-e faqih 2, 7, 47, 79, 84, 87, 97, 154–5

Venezuelan principle 24
Video Cassette Recordings (VCRs) 75
video cassettes 158 n.32
VPN 113, 138, 145–6

Wallace, Mike 165 n.99
Weber, Max 46, 158 n.14

westoxification 12–14, 51, 159 n.41
White Revolution 13, 25, 28, 42
Williams, Raymond 9

Yazdi, Ayatollah Mohammad 78

Zarghami, Ezatollah 112, 119

www.ingramcontent.com/pod-product-compliance
Lightning Source LLC
Chambersburg PA
CBHW062220300426
44115CB00012BA/2149